DANCE
AS A THEATRE ART
SOURCE READINGS IN DANCE HISTORY
FROM 1581 TO THE PRESENT

Dance as a Theatre Art

**SOURCE READINGS IN DANCE HISTORY
FROM 1581 TO THE PRESENT**

EDITED WITH COMMENTARY BY
Selma Jeanne Cohen

DANCE AS A THEATRE ART: *Source Reading
in Dance History from 1581 to the Present*

Copyright © 1974 by Harper & Row,
Publishers, Inc.

Library of Congress Catalog Card
Number: 73-15380
Standard Book Number: 06-041315-8

Fabritio Caroso's Il Ballerino *translated by Julia
Sutton. Copyright ©1974 by Julia Sutton.*

Balthasar de Beaujoyeulx's Ballet Comique de la
Reine *translated by Mary-Jean Cowell. Copyright
©1974 by Mary-Jean Cowell.*

Designed by Emily Harste

PREFACE

The idea for this anthology came from dance-book editor Nancy Reynolds, who thought to ask some teachers of dance history what kind of book they wanted for their classes. At the same time, I was struggling with the problem of making materials available for my students in survey courses at Connecticut College and the New York University School of the Arts, where my alternatives were either utter frustration or astronomical Xeroxing bills. The library might have a single copy of an important work; many of the most valuable books were out of print or had never been translated into English; wonderful articles lay hidden away in old periodicals. Despite entreaties, I did not want to produce still another one-volume overview, skimming the evolution of dance from the caveman to the present and cheating the student who had a right to learn from original texts. The answer had to be an anthology of primary sources.

Because I planned these readings to serve a single, introductory course, I limited their scope severely. And rather than presenting the student with a multitude of tidbits, I chose fewer but more substantial pieces, believing that intensive study yields greater understanding, which can then be applied to whatever other texts the reader wishes to pursue. The introductions provide continuity as well as historical background for the various periods; the bibliography suggests possibilities for further exploration.

I am particularly indebted to Miss Reynolds, who waited so patiently for me to complete this work and never ceased to believe in its importance. I am grateful to Edwin Binney 3rd, Mary-Jean Cowell, Angelika Gerbes, Leonore Loft, Patricia McAndrew, and Julia Sutton for providing heretofore unpublished English translations. I made extensive use of the Dance Collection of The New York Public Library and want to thank its curator, Genevieve Oswald, and her staff, especially Barbara Palfy, for their constant support. For help in locating materials I am grateful to Jack Anderson, Mary Clarke, George Dorris, Gladys Laskey, and John Wiley. Dorine Waszkiewicz typed the introductions from my barely legible drafts. John E. Mueller, The University of Rochester; Christena L. Schlundt, University of California, Riverside; and Shirley Wynne, the

Ohio State University, read the manuscript and made valuable suggestions for its improvement.

Most of all I want to thank those of my students who have gone on to develop their own courses in dance history, creating a constituency that did not exist when I started.

SELMA JEANNE COHEN

CONTENTS

Introduction

THE EVOLUTION
OF THEATRE DANCE

We cannot know precisely when man began to dance, but we may surmise that it was sometime in the dawn of prehistory.

In nearly all surviving tribal cultures we find dances that are not merely spontaneous outbursts of feeling—jumps of joy or stamps of anger—but patterned, rhythmical sequences, performed in a special place and designed to make a particular impression on the spectators. Most often the place is just a clearing in the grass, and the spectators are the gods whom the dancer beseeches to make the rain fall, the crops grow, the tribe increase. From these rituals, with no stage and no human audience, how did theatrical dance evolve?

We can see one instance of the development with some clarity. The most widely accepted view of the origin of the Greek theatre traces it to the Dithyramb, a song and dance performance that was part of the spring festival of Dionysus. At first the celebration was wild and improvised, but in time it began to conform to the more set structure of ritual, using composed songs and dances. In 508 B.C. a contest in the Dithyramb was inaugurated. Groups entering the competition were trained by a *choregus* (the root of our word "choreographer") and performed in the *orchestra*, the circular dancing space of the open-air theatre. Now with an audience at hand and a prize to be won, the dances became increasingly more elaborate and virtuosic. Meanwhile, a form of spoken drama was developing at the Dionysian festival; and it too had its singer-dancers, in this case forming a chorus who reacted to and commented on the action with symbolic, stylized gestures known as *cheironomia*.

The performers at the Dionysian ceremonies were amateurs, considered to be servants of the gods. But Greece also had its professional dancers, slaves who entertained at dinner parties, where they juggled with hoops and turned somersaults, but also enacted brief mimetic scenes depicting stories of the gods. Thus the professionals incorporated both the virtuosity of the later Dithyramb and the expressive gestures of the dramatic chorus.

The professional dance developed in Rome, whose pantomime entertainments are said to have originated in 22 B.C. with two great artists named Pylades and Bathyllus. Both were expert in portraying entire tragedies or myths in solo performance. Aided by appropriate music and by a variety of costumes and masks, the dancer depicted in succession all the various characters involved in the story. The mimes enhanced their mute characterizations with brilliant turns, twists, bends, and springs; but the display of physical skills was not the primary aim of the art. According to Lucian of Samosata, who wrote in the second century A.D. "it is the dancer's profession to show forth human character and passion in all their variety; to depict love and anger, frenzy and grief each in its due measure . . . there is meaning in his movements; every gesture has its significance; and therein lies his chief excellence."

Thus, nearly twenty centuries ago all the elements of standard theatre dance were present: a performer equipped with movement skills; a role to be played; a stage to play on; music, costume, and décor to enhance the spectacle; an audience to respond to it. The relative importance of these elements was subject to discussion for centuries to come. Through the ages the answers have differed, depending on a number of changing, interacting factors that have influenced the constantly evolving nature of the art.

First there is the taste of an era, its climate of ideas, the scale of values set by a particular society that incline it, in one period, to admire formal structure; in another, to care more for spontaneous expression. Tastes swerve from stylization to realism, from virtuosity to drama, from escapism to contemporary protest. Trends are incited or accelerated by social, political, economic conditions—as is true of all the other arts.

Many of these arts also influence the development of dance. The tempos and rhythms of music, the size and weight of costumes, the style of décor, the shape of the stage, the nature of lighting equipment —the state of all of these at any particular time determines a great deal of what a choreographer can and cannot do. He may find ingenious ways of coping with the limitations imposed on him by composers or designers; or he may rebel against them, instigating important reforms. Theatre dance is a collaborative art and all the participants, of necessity, affect one another.

An especially significant factor for dance is the technical skill of the performers. Unlike the actor, whose physical potential has remained virtually unchanged, the dancer has constantly extended the scope of his capacities,—striving to master movements that are higher, faster, more elaborate than any seen before. To help him, his training has been lengthened and intensified, becoming more scientific in its molding of strength, flexibility, and coordination. Each age has enriched the dance vocabulary, providing greater resources for the next generation of choreographers.

Lastly, there is the most mysterious but possibly most potent factor of all—the individual creator. Partly because of his time, partly in spite of it, the figure of genius rises suddenly to change the course of dance, lifting it into unsuspected heights of artistry.

In a single volume we cannot consider all these factors in detail. Nor can we stop to examine more than a few manifestations of the creative vitality of dance, and these limited to the theatre of the Western world since the Renaissance. Regretfully, we are omitting not only the theatre dance of the East, but also such forms as folk dance, mime, musical comedy, and film—not because they lack significance but because their inclusion would have eliminated the possibility of any in-depth study.

From the sixteenth century, when this anthology begins, we can trace the development of theatrical dancing, virtually without a break, down to the present. While contemporary forms began to evolve well before our starting point of 1581, the publication of a considerable body of accessible materials, enabling us to study the interaction of technical accomplishments and choreographic ideas, stems from this date. Of the many documents that might have been chosen, we have made selections from only three categories: technical manuals; statements of theory; librettos or discussions of particular productions. The bibliographies will lead the student to some of the other vast resources that await his perusal.

History shows the dancer his heritage, his place in a line of distinguished, artistic ancestors. It is a legacy to instill a sense of pride—and responsibility. For those of us who love to watch dance, a study of history broadens our perspective by enlarging our range of experience. Our personal knowledge of dancing is largely limited by the time and place in which we live, and we tend to attach value to what we know, to what is comfortable because it is easily understood. The vicarious experience obtained from a knowledge of history shows us that different forms are not invalid simply because they are unlike our own. Such knowledge increases our tolerance by expanding our capacities to perceive values in the unfamiliar. At the same time, history makes us discriminating: we learn to recognize forces of outworn convention and deterioration, to distinguish the fashionable novelty from the genuine innovation. History teaches us not only tolerance but a critical attitude.

Within the past forty years theatrical dancing has attained an unprecedented popularity. Within this time, the United States has witnessed a great renaissance in classical ballet and the establishment of an idiom called "modern dance." We have seen a surge of interest in dance as drama followed by a swing back to concern with dance as pure movement, succeeded by a counterswing toward symbolic action. We have seen brilliant developments in stage design and have seen dance move away from stages into museums and city streets. We have seen dance adjust to the use of slide projections, films, and tape recorders. Now, with changes occurring so rapidly, may be the time to refresh ourselves with a knowledge of the past in preparation for a fresh evaluation of the present.

Section One

THE COURT BALLET

The pantomime theatre, popular throughout the Roman Empire in the early years of the Christian era, was thoroughly disliked by the Church fathers, who told their congregations that since devils had stage plays in hell that was reason enough not to have them on earth. Players, however, apparently continued to perform extensively at least through the fifth century, when the religious diatribes against them finally lessened. We have evidence too of traveling entertainers, including dancers, who amused the gentry of the manor houses throughout the Middle Ages.

Quite apart from the professionals, the people continued to dance. Much as the Church authorities wanted to stop pagan rituals, they found the traditions almost impossible to uproot, though they did succeed in stripping them of their original magical significance. In accordance with a pattern that we will see recurring, the pastimes of the folk were taken up by the nobility, dignified and elaborated however to serve the social functions of courtly life.

The fertility rites of the pagan spring were usually accompanied by mimetic enactments of death and rebirth by costumed and often masked performers who believed themselves possessed by the spirits they were made to resemble. Deprived of their mystical purpose, such rituals became social diversions. In fifteenth-century England, noble maskers paraded through the streets, entering houses to play a game of dice in silence. In Italy, bands of maskers roamed through towns on May Day, New Year, and Carnival, singing and dancing and playing practical jokes on the bystanders.

Meanwhile, specifically Christian spectacles were developing. Italian *edifizi* (pagents) bore masked performers through the streets, where they enacted Biblical episodes in dumb show. From *nuvole* (clouds), their wooden frames and wires hidden by cloth sprinkled with stars, the actors descended to the playing platform to tell their story.

As the Renaissance brought renewed interest in classical antiquity, the devices of both the secular masquerade and the religious processional were used to portray mythological subjects. In the lavish *trionfi* (triumphant parades) of Lorenzo de' Medici maskers were carried on elaborately designed floats, while verses were circulated among the onlookers to explain the symbolic significance of the characters represented. As the procession filed past the throne of state, each float in turn would pause as the maskers descended to declaim verses, sing, and dance. At the end, performers from all the floats joined in a grand dance.

As individual Italian dukedoms began to vie with one another for power and prestige, similar lavish entertainments were provided at court banquets. One of the most elaborate was given by the Duke of Milan in 1489, when the serving of roast lamb was heralded by a portrayal of the legend of Jason and the Golden Fleece; the course of wild boar was introduced by Atalanta, while the fruits were accompanied by the appearance of Pomona. Attendants to the main characters danced appropriate measures during each of the episodes.

In the early sixteenth century these dances are first referred to as *balletti*, meaning simply a figured dance, a composition characterized by the arrangement of the performers in sequences of changing floor patterns. Though each dance had a theme, it was related to the others only by the mythological nature of its content. No more cohesion than this was attempted.

Basically the *balletti* were staged, or semistaged, versions of the social dances of the day, some of them originating in the protocol of court etiquette, others stemming from the rough and hearty pleasures of the peasants but refined by contact with the prevailing, decorous restraint of the style of the nobility. Some treatises concerning these dances have come down to us from the mid-fifteenth century, though they are not as clear and precise as one might wish them to be. From those by Guglielmo Ebreo, Antonio Cornazano, and Giovanni Ambrosio we learn that the dances were divided into two major groups: the *bassa danza*, considered the queen of them all, was slow, solemn, and dignified, the feet being kept always close to the floor; the *ballo* was a livelier type in which the feet were raised. The basic movements, which included stately walking but also gracious swayings of the body and gentle turns, were combined in a variety of sequences to form individual dances, each being given some fanciful title by the master who composed it. The directions stipulate how many performers are involved and whether they are arranged in couples or in a line.

By the late sixteenth and early seventeenth centuries the texts have become much more precise. From Italy we have two by Fabritio Caroso and one by Cesare Negri; but the most accessible is *Orchésographie* by the French canon Jehan Tabourot, writing under the pseudonym of Thoinot Arbeau. Published in 1589, *Orchésographie* provides the first specific definitions of the proper placing of the dancer's feet at the beginning of steps, the basis of what have become the five positions of classical ballet. Only three are named, however, and they are not identified by numbers but by descriptive names: *pieds joints, pieds largis, pieds obliques*. Illustrations show the feet pointing outward away from the body—not so much as to require any special flexibility but enough to give an impression of elegance. Here is the beginning of the balletic turnout. The rudiments of many steps are here also, though often under different names: Arbeau's *entretaille* is like our *coupé*; his *capriole* is like our *entrechat*.

While all these manuals were intended as guides for social dancing, their directions are relevant to the history of theatre dance, for at this time "ballets" were not performed by professionals but by members of the court, for the entertainment of their peers. Although the choreographers were professionals, they were employed primarily to teach ballroom dancing to the nobility and were well aware of the limited capacities of their student-performers. Therefore, when a performance was required, they obliged by arranging simple steps in intricate patterns that made them interesting to observe. Encumbered by heavy, fashionable apparel and trained only to the extent of proper social proficiency, the dancers hardly provided inspiring material for technically exciting choreography. Besides, the ballets were performed, not on raised stages, but in the central space of large halls with the audience seated above the floor in galleries that extended around three sides of the dancing area. The wise masters reasoned out that the way to dazzle was not with steps, which the performers could not do expertly and the audience could not see well, but with floor patterns—complex geometrical shapes that formed, dissolved, and reformed to display a tantalizing variety of designs. Precision and memory, lightness and grace, an elegant ease of execution, were admired. Arbeau urged his pupil to observe virtue and decorum, to keep his head and body erect, to have his hose well secured and his shoes clean.

As folk customs had been refined into courtly diversions, so now it was time for the social dances of the Renaissance to nourish the burgeoning form that was to become the dance of the theatre. Artistic innovation was not the motivating force, however. When Catherine de' Medici of France commissioned her musicians and designers in 1573 to produce a lavish entertainment of song and dance, her purpose was political. It was a matter of diplomacy—a gesture to impress the Polish ambassadors who had arrived to negotiate a royal marriage—which brought about the event of the *Ballet des Polonais*, an elaborate figured dance performed by sixteen ladies of the court representing the sixteen provinces of France. The invited audience commended the dancers for their "interlacings and confusings, encounters and arrests, in which not one lady ever failed to turn in her place nor in her rank, so well that every one was amazed by such confusion and such disorder never ceasing from a superior order."

France's next major dance venture, also politically motivated, came in 1581. This is commonly called the "first ballet," though the accuracy of the designation depends largely on the definitions used. Although Balthasar de Beaujoyeulx, the choreographer of the *Ballet Comique*, claimed the idea of combining dancing, music, and poetry, the concept had been formulated some time before when Jean Antoine de Baïf had founded an academy to attempt the revival of the chorus of Greek tragedy with its synthesis of theatrical elements. Baïf, however, did not carry out his ideas in any actual productions; Beaujoyeulx did. Further, breaking with the tradition of combining unrelated interludes of music and dance, he used recitation, song, and movement to convey a single story line, the triumph of virtue, represented by Jupiter, over evil, personified by the goddess Circe. This dramatic coherence marks the historic significance of the *Ballet Comique*, but it was the lavishness of its production that made it famous throughout Europe. Here the *edifizi* and *nuvole* of the Italian *trionfi*, the rich costumes, the complex figures of the dance combined to stir the emulation of all who saw them. The dramatic line that we find of such significance was of lesser moment to the audience of the *Ballet Comique*.

Beaujoyeulx's work was a tremendous success, but nothing like it was produced again; it was just too expensive. In place of the patiently skilled interweaving of plot, music, and dance, succeeding choreographers resorted to a simpler form, one more easily contrived and less costly to execute. The following years saw the creation of a genre that became known as *ballets mascarades*—sequences of episodes loosely connected by a thread of plot. Replacing the grand mythological subjects were slighter scenes built on topics and characters drawn from everyday life, more amusing than ennobling. Generally each episode was introduced by a spoken verse or song which was followed by a dance, called an *entrée*. Then for a time there was a return to narrative, but this was soon dropped for the *ballet à entrées*, a series of thematically related dances, serious and comic, concluding with a grand figured dance in which all the characters appeared together. It is this form that is described by M. de Saint-Hubert.

Elsewhere in Europe French models were eagerly copied and often staged by French ballet masters. Some of the most lavish were presented in Sweden, where the philosopher Descartes wrote a libretto for one at the request of Queen Christina. Holland and Italy also had their share of elaborate productions. The Italians were especially intrigued with a form derived from the elaborate floor patterns of the ballet combined with the ideas of courtly tournaments. Using classical plots, songs, and décors, choreographers staged spectacles for riders on horseback. The steeds were trained to execute elaborate figures, all in strict time to the accompanying music.

England evolved its own form of the *ballet de cour*, the masque, a unique form merging elements borrowed from the masquerade of the Italians and the figured dances of the French. The masque was a production involving dialogue, song, music, and dance, terminating in "revels" in which the masked performers invited the audience to join them in social dancing. All these components were present also in the *Ballet Comique*, but in the hands of poet Ben Jonson and architect Inigo Jones the emphasis was altered; the masque had more elements of drama than of dance. It was in France that classical ballet really developed.

The most famous dancer of the mid-seventeenth century was Louis XIV; garbed as Apollo, the Sun-King, he dominated the ballet of France, which dominated the ballet of Europe. Though the general public was now sometimes admitted to performances and occasional professionals appeared in some of the *entrées*, the ballet was primarily a vehicle for the nobility. Louis chose the finest talent to compose for him: Isaac de Benserade wrote verses for his ballets; Jean-Baptiste Lully composed their music; in 1661, Molière contributed the first of his brilliant comedies, with dance interludes cleverly linked to the text. That same year, a group of dancing masters obtained permission from the king to establish the Académie Royale de Danse. Though most of their meetings were held at a local tavern and consisted of little more than theoretical discussions, they had formed a professional organization. When Louis stopped dancing in 1670, possibly because of his increasing corpulence, ballet was on its way to becoming a professional art.

Fabritio Caroso (c. 1530–1605)
RULES AND DIRECTIONS FOR DANCING THE "PASSO E MEZO"

Translated from the Italian and edited with notes by Julia Sutton

Caroso was a prominent Italian dancing master. His published work provides us with an extensive vocabulary of contemporary steps and with instructions for performing more than 100 dances.

Caroso's manual was intended for ballroom dancing, but evidence indicates that the staged dances of the time followed much the same rules, though giving more attention to the showier steps. In both cases, the performers were members of the court. While the author provides directions for a substantial number of slow group dances, his descriptions also include a variety of livelier dances, such as the Passo e Mezo; *and though he obviously advocates grace and elegance of execution, his frequent urgings to the dancer to "show off" indicate the potential of this social style for evolving into theatrical forms.*

Of the Reverences [*Riverenze*], and First of the Grave[1] Reverence
Rule II

The grave reverence is made by keeping the body and legs quite straight, with half the left foot ahead of the right, and four inches away from it, noting that the toes of both feet have to be quite straight. Now because in most of the *Balletti*[2] there are eight perfect beats of music, which equal sixteen ordinary beats, one must know that in the first four beats one begins and ends the entire reverence; and in the last

SOURCE: From *Il Ballarino* (Venice, 1581).

[1] Grave simply means slow; its precise metric value is defined for each rule. Other terms referring to metric length are:
Beat (*battuta*): semibreve, or one half note.
Ordinary beat (*battuta ordinaria*): minim, or one quarter note.
Perfect beat (*battuta perfetta*): normally, a beat with a triple subdivision, but Caroso is not entirely clear on this point. Most frequently he equates this with a semibreve, regardless of how it is subdivided. The music is usually marked off with a bar line for every semibreve.
[2] A *Balletto* is a generic dance type of the sixteenth century, consisting of choreography for one couple, though the term is applied to other groupings as well. Most commonly there is a series of dance variations to two sections of music in contrasting meter (usually a slow duple followed by a more rapid triple meter), each section being repeated as often as necessary. Usually the basic musical material of all sections is the same.

four, the two continences, as will be described in the appropriate place. In the first beat, one stands facing [the lady] with the left foot forward, as I have said, and with one's face turned toward that of the lady (and not as others do, who continue to face toward the surrounding onlookers; for if they do this, they seem to despise the lady with whom they are dancing); for she must ever be revered and honored with all [due] affection.

During the second [beat] one has to pull the left foot back in a straight line, so that its toe is level with the right heel, keeping it [the left] flat on the ground, and without raising the heel at all. In pulling the foot back, be sure to bend the head and body somewhat, accompanying this action with all the grace one possesses, and keeping both knees quite straight. During the third one must bend the legs together with the body, gracefully separating the knees a little. During the fourth and last one must raise oneself, returning the left foot to the right, at the same time raising the body and the head.

I had you begin the reverence with the left foot because one shows reverence to someone close to one's heart; and also because the strength and stability of one's body is in the right foot, which must not be moved first when making a reverence or when dancing. Note also that every action or movement at the beginning of the dance must always be done with the left foot. . . .

Of the Two Continences [*Continenze*], the Grave and the Minim
Rule V

The first continence [which is called] grave, must be begun in this way: having completed the grave reverence, which is begun and ended during four perfect beats of music, and with the left foot, the man must move toward the left four inches, joining the right foot to the left; or else he can do it more gracefully by drawing the heel of the right foot toward the arch of the left. And in moving this way he must lower his body a little, raising it then as gracefully as he can, as I said in the rule for the grave reverence. And one must strut[3] a little toward that side on which one is doing [the continence]; this effect is usually achieved by raising the hip a little toward that side on which one is completing the continence. And do not do as others do, who neglect to show off and to bend and raise themselves, standing still with feet together, a way which is very awkward and dry, even though it is done in time and accurately; therefore it should be avoided.

[3] Italian *pavoneggiandosi*; literally, "peacocking oneself."

The second continence, which is called minim, must be divided into half the time of that above, and done in two beats for each continence; and it must be done with all the actions and movements I explained above.[4]

Of the Grave Pointed [*Puntate Grave*]
Rule VI

The grave pointed [step] is . . . done in two beats. Move the left foot during the first, thrusting it so far forward as to pass the toe of the [right] foot a little, and having it four or five inches laterally apart from the same foot, strutting all the time; then stop a little, as if to pause. Then, in the middle of the second beat, one moves the right foot, joining it to the left, bending the body a little and raising it gracefully. . . .

Of How to Learn to do the Grave Steps [*Passi Gravi*] in *Balletti*
Rule VII

The grave steps in *Balletti* are all done in one beat, moving the left foot and thrusting it forward, as I just said of the grave pointed step; then moving the right foot past [the left], one will do the same as he has done with the left. And all [movements must be done] with grace and beauty, accompanying them a little with the body and strutting. Be sure to keep the toes of the feet straight and the knees quite straight.

Of the Quick Steps [*Passi Presti*] in *Cascardas*[5]
Rule VIII

The quick steps in *Cascardas* are done as above, except that while those are done in one beat of music, these [are done] in half [a beat] and quickly.

Of the Ordinary Sequence [*Seguito Ordinario*]
Rule XII

The ordinary sequence is done . . . in three steps, and in four ordinary beats, though to tell the truth, during the last beat one holds his body still the entire time. And it is done in this way: one begins on the first beat with the left foot, thrusting it on the toe so far forward that its heel is level with the toe of the right and about two inches away from it. Then, raising the right on the second beat, it also must be thrust forward on the toe and as far away from the left as the left

---

[4] This continence equals two minims, or one semibreve.
[5] A rapid couple dance in triple meter.

was before. Then, during the third beat, the left is thrust forward in the same way, but ending with both feet flat on the ground, precisely as one should stand when facing [one's partner] in the reverence. Now this is the way one must hold oneself, as has been said, during the time of the fourth beat. Then, at the beginning of the fifth beat, one has to continue on, thrusting the right foot forward according to the rule given for the left. Note that in each sequence one must strut a little with one's body.

Of the Half-Double Sequence [*Seguito Semidoppio*]
Rule XIII

One does this sequence in the time of four ordinary beats, beginning with the left foot. In the first two beats one takes two steps [see Rule VIII] and in the other two beats [one does] a broken sequence [see Rule XVI], beginning also with the left foot, and accompanying each step and sequence with that grace and beauty which these movements deserve.

Of the Broken Sequence [*Seguito Spezzato*]
Rule XVI

One does this broken sequence in two ordinary beats in this way. First (standing with feet together), on the first beat one must thrust the left foot half a palm[6] forward and two inches away from the right, keeping [i.e., placing] it quite flat on the ground. Then, at the beginning of the second beat, one must move the right foot, first raising the heel, and one must place its toe near the heel of the left foot. Now at the same time, as one touches the ground with the toe of the right, one must raise both heels a little, simultaneously with the body; then, at the end of the beat, one must lower the heel of the left simultaneously with the body. After this, at the beginning of the third beat, one must move forward with the right in the same way as was done with the left. And this sequence is called broken because one does two of the aforesaid in the time of an ordinary sequence by breaking it.

Of the Way to do the Grave Leaning Jump [*Trabuchetto Grave*]
Rule XXIIII

The grave leaning jump is done this way: standing with feet together, one must spread the left foot to the side by means of a small jump, about one palm away from the right; and at the moment that the left touches the ground, one must raise the right, bringing it within about

6 A palm is a unit of measurement based on the breadth of the hand.

two inches of the left (which is lightly on its toe), keeping both legs quite straight, but not touching the ground with the right foot. Then, returning the right foot to its original place, one must repeat with the left what was done with the right. Note that one must strut a little with each leaning jump and do it with bodily agility and dexterity. . . . The time of each of these leaning jumps is one perfect beat of music.

Of the Way to do the Ordinary Flourish [*Fioretto Ordinario*]
Rule XXVI

The ordinary flourish must be done by raising the left foot and thrusting it so far ahead of the right that the left heel is two inches from the toe of the right, but one inch to the side and raised two inches, with the knees quite straight. At the same time elevate the body somewhat by doing a little jump [see Rule XLIII], placing the right on its toe so far forward that the end of the heel is near the toe of the left and about two inches away from it. Then, raising the left foot, one must put it [down] in place of the right, which must be raised as was the left at the beginning of this flourish; and one must follow the same order as with the left. Others, when they finish the ordinary flourish (raising the left foot and putting it in place of the right after raising that foot forward a little, as I have said), bring it together [flat] with the right, ending it this way. Now even though this procedure seems good, I like the first much better. For the body is rendered more graceful by stepping nimbly on the toes than by placing the feet flat on the ground. The time of each of these flourishes is one minim beat.

About the Five Steps [*Cinque Passi*] of the Galliard[7]
Rule XXX

. . . . First one does a limping hop [see Rule XXXIX] with the right foot on the ground, raising the left forward. Then, dropping [the left], one raises the right backward; and placing its toe to the heel of the left, one immediately lifts the left, which will [then] be put down in the place where it was before [while] again lifting the right foot forward. Then dropping it [the right] and drawing it back, one does the cadence [see Rule LIII], adding grace to it by separating the knees a little, and ending with the right behind. . . . Note that the legs must always be kept quite straight, with the toes down and the arms down, but showing

[7] The Galliard was the showy, vigorous dance of the sixteenth century. Its basic step pattern was known everywhere: in France as the *cinq pas*, in Italy as the *cinque passi*, in England as the *five steps* or *sinkapace*. Caroso's version is a simple one. Innumerable variations exist in the manuals of the period, many of them involving double *tours en l'air*, *entrechats*, and *pirouettes*.

off occasionally with the right [arm] because it would look ugly if it were always held straight. Do not move the fingers, and carry your body erect and your head high.

Of the Limping Hop [*Zoppetto*]
Rule XXXIX

The limping hop is done (beginning with feet together, or otherwise, according to the circumstances which can occur in the Galliard), by raising both feet [at once], the first a little above the ground and the other passing forward. One does as many of them as will be required by the variations and they will be done this way, keeping one of the feet raised forward or keeping it similarly raised to the side. These movements have taken the name of limping hop because one keeps one foot forward, raising the other by hopping, exactly as if one were to limp.

Of the Foot Under [*Sottopiede*]
Rule XLI

One does the foot under always to the side in this way: first one does one leaning jump to the left with the left foot. Then, in putting the left down, one lifts the right back, putting it down in the place where the left was and raising the left in the air. And with it [the left] one goes on to do more of them. Thus the name foot under is derived from this movement of placing one foot where the other was.

Of the Little Jumps with Feet Together [*Balzetti à Piedi Pari*]
Rule XLIII

These little jumps are done by standing with feet together (one inch apart), lifting both feet above the ground about two inches, and landing with them at the same time a little distance away from where they were, keeping them together in the same way. One jumps this way with little jumps, now to the left, now to the right, according to circumstances, and one does as many as the variations require. . . .

Of the Knot [*Groppo*]
Rule XLIIII

This is done by beginning with the body and feet in the same position as when one prepares to do the reverence. First, one does a leaning jump to the left with the left foot. Then, at the same time as one lands on the left, one crosses the right behind. With this one does another

From *Il Ballarino*

To help his readers understand the starting position of the *Passo e Mezo*, Caroso wisely provided an illustration. At this point the gentleman has removed his hat according to the rules that insure his making this action graceful and attractive, and he is shown performing the third beat of the reverence. The disparity of the costumes clearly shows that the man could enjoy far more freedom of movement than could his lady.

leaning jump to the right, crossing the left behind the right. Then one does another leaning jump to the left with the left, crossing the right behind it. With this [right] foot one does a foot under (putting it in place of the left, which must be raised), keeping the left foot raised forward a little. And drawing back that [foot] and thrusting the right forward, one does the cadence, and thus one ends this knot. Now from this crossing over of the feet in a knotlike way, this name has been derived.

Of the Toe and Heel [*Punta e Calcagno*]
Rule L

This is done by taking one limping hop on the ground with the right and at the same time putting the toe of the left on the ground four inches from the right. Then do another limping hop again with the right, putting the heel of the left on the ground and holding its toe up four or five inches from the ground. Finally, putting the left down flat as in the limping hop, one begins [again] doing the toe and heel in the same order with the right. . . .

Of the Cadence [*Cadenza*] in the Galliard
Rule LIII

First one raises the left foot forward; and pulling oneself backward, and simultaneously lifting oneself up a little, one lands with both feet on the ground; that is, with the left in back and the right in front. And from this way of landing with both feet at the same time, this movement has taken the name of cadence.

Step and a Half [*Passo e Mezo*][8]
Author Unknown
With Variations and a New Promenade by the Author of this Book
In Honor of the Most Illustrious and Excellent Signora, The Duchess of Monte Lione

This *Passo e Mezo* is begun with the couple facing each other without holding hands, as appears in the illustration, doing the grave reverence and two continences facing each other. Then, promenading together in a circle to the left, they will do two grave steps and an ordinary sequence, beginning with the left. They will continue by doing one grave step with the right and two quick steps, one with the left and the other with the right, and one grave leaning jump with the left.

[8] The *Passo e Mezo* may be related to the Pavane, the slow processional dance of the period. With Caroso it is an extremely sophisticated and showy dance whose introduction alone shows traces of the basic Pavane. Musically, the *Passo e Mezo* is based on either of two repeated bass patterns (*bassi ostinati*), known as the *passamezzo antico* and *passomezzo moderno*; and many sets of virtuosic variations for instruments on these basses were written at this time. Caroso's choreography is equally virtuosic; the original gives six variations for each partner, plus two variations for the couple. We have chosen one variation for each. This dance is in duple meter.

Dropping the right foot (which will have been raised), they will do a little jump with feet together to the right. Having finished this promenade, they will repeat it once again.

The Gentleman's First Variation
and the Lady's Promenade

When they have finished doing these first two promenades together, the gentleman will begin his first variation by raising his left foot a little in the air, and making a quick reverence[9] with it. Then, with the same foot, he will do a limping hop in the air, and one step with the right as in the Galliard, and a cadence with the same foot behind, immediately [following this] with a knot to the left and two quick reverences with the left. Then he will continue with a leaning jump to the left, one foot under to the right, [then] a toe and heel, first with the right and then with the left, with one leaning jump, one foot under to the left, a quick reverence, [and] a Galliard cadence with the left behind. Then he will do one limping hop with the left in the air, a step of the Galliard with the right forward, and conclude in time with the music with a cadence with feet together.

At the same time as the gentleman is doing his first variation, the lady will promenade, doing two grave steps and one ordinary sequence to the left, beginning them with the left foot. Then, turning to the right, she will do one grave step with the right and two quick steps, one with the left and the other with the right, followed by one grave leaning jump to the left. Then, putting the right foot down (which will have been raised), she will gracefully do one little jump with feet together to the right.

The Lady's First Variation
and the Gentleman's Promenade

The lady will begin her first variation by doing two broken sequences sideways forward, plus three grave leaning jumps, beginning with the left foot. She will then repeat the same once more in the opposite direction, being careful to do the last leaning jump with feet together. At the same time as the lady is doing her variation, the gentleman will do two grave steps and a half-double sequence, beginning with the left foot; then, turning to the right, he will do one quick step with the right and three flourishes turning to the left, with a Galliard cadence with the right foot behind. Then he will do two steps of the Galliard and a cadence with feet together. . . .

[9] The quick reverence is not described in the rules.

Balthasar de Beaujoyeulx
BALLET COMIQUE DE LA REINE
Translated from the French by Mary-Jean Cowell

Baltazarini di Belgiojoso, wise to the ways of political promotion, took a French name when he left Italy for Paris around 1555 as a member of a band of violinists. He became court valet to Catherine de' Medici and as such was responsible for the royal entertainments.

In the "first ballet," dancing was only one of several important elements: instrumental music, songs, spoken verses, costumes, and scenic effects all received attention. In fact, the author of this libretto devotes far more space to the texts of the speeches and songs and to descriptions of the decorations than he does to the dances. After all, most of his readers knew the steps from their own experience in court ballrooms, where rules like Caroso's prevailed. The Ballet Comique *was first of all a grand spectacle designed to enhance the glory of France. Since the audience consisted exclusively of invited dignitaries, the publication of the libretto provided a means of extending recognition of the national image.*

To the Reader

In as much, dear Reader, as the title of this book is unprecedented, the word "Comic" having never been applied to a Ballet, nor has any Ballet been published previous to this one, I ask you not to find my usage peculiar.

As for the Ballet, it is a modern invention or is, at least, a revival from such distant antiquity that it may be called modern; being, in truth, no more than the geometrical groupings of people dancing together, accompanied by the varied harmony of several instruments. I confess to you that, merely presented in print, the recitation of a simple Comedy would have had much novelty but little beauty; nor would such an offering be distinguished or worthy of so noble a Queen who desired to present something magnificent and splendid.

Therefore, I bethought myself that to combine the two would be in no way improper: to diversify the music with poetry; to interlace the poetry with music; and most often to intermingle the two, even as the ancients never recited poetry without music and Orpheus played only with verse.

SOURCE: From *Balet Comique de la Royne* (Paris, 1582).

I have, nevertheless, given the first title and honor to the dance, and the second to the story, which I designated "Comic" more for its beautiful, tranquil, and happy conclusion than for the nature of its characters, who are almost all gods and goddesses or other heroic personages.

Thus I enlivened the ballet and made it speak, and made the Comedy sing and play; and, adding some unusual and elaborate décor and embellishments, I may say that I satisfied the eye, the ear, and the intellect with one well-proportioned creation.

I entreat you not to judge this work harshly because of its title or novelty; for my invention, being principally composed of two elements, could not be designated a Ballet without slighting the Comedy clearly evident in the scenes and acts; nor could it be called a Comedy without prejudice to the Ballet which ornaments, enlivens, and completes with harmonious movements the beautiful meaning of the comedy.

Having amply explained my intentions, I ask your indulgence of my title and hope you will find the work pleasing, since I, for my part, wished to satisfy you.

[The libretto begins with an explanation of the author's commission to create the ballet: the Queen Louise had requested him to contribute to the festivities planned for the marriage of her sister, Mlle. de Vaudemont, to the Duke of Joyeuse. The queen approved the design Beaujoyeulx brought her, bidding him to execute it promptly. Since he felt he could not take the responsibility for all the parts of the work, the queen assigned the poetry to Lord de la Chesnaye, the music to Lord de Beaulieu, and the painting to Master Jacques Patin.

Beaujoyeulx then describes the arrangements he directed to be made in the Bourbon hall. At one end he had constructed a low dais to serve for the seating of the king, the queen, the princes and princesses. On each side of the dais were places for the ambassadors and for ladies of the court. Others sat on the two galleries that stood around the walls of the hall. To the King's right was a grove for Pan and the dryad nymphs. Directly opposite was a gilded vault, called the "golden," where the music was performed. On the ceiling between the grove and the vault was an immense cloud from which Mercury and Jupiter would descend.

In the center of the hall at the end opposite the king was Circe's garden and behind it, the wall of a castle. On either side of the garden was an arched trellis with imitation leaves and grapes, and through these trellises passed the interlude musicians and the mobile sets that presented themselves to the king. Circe, played by Mlle. de Sainte-Même, was to sit at the portal of the castle, dressed in a golden

From the *Ballet Comique*

The reader looks over the shoulder of the King as the Fugitive Gentleman delivers his complaint against Circe. Also to be seen are Pan's grove (right), the golden vault (left), and Circe's castle and garden (background center). The highest ranking members of the court are seated by the King; other invited guests fill the galleries along the side walls.

robe with many jewels and holding a golden rod. One hundred white wax candles shed their radiance on the garden, while further light shone from the "infinite" number of torches at the top of and all around the hall.

On Sunday, the fifteenth of October, some 900 renowned and notable persons took their places in the hall.]

At the tenth hour of the evening, silence being imposed, the sound of hautboys, cornetts, sackbuts, and other soft instruments issued from behind the castle. This music having ended, lord de la Roche (a gentleman in the service of the Queen mother, handsomely attired in silver cloth, his garments covered with jewels and pearls of great value) ran out of Circe's garden to the middle of the room where he stopped short and looked back, terrified, at the garden to see if the enchantress Circe were pursuing him. And having seen that no one was running after him, he drew from his pocket a gold-trimmed handkerchief with which he wiped his brow, as if he perspired from fatigue or fear. Then, being somewhat reassured and having caught his breath, he walked slowly toward the King. And after a deep bow to his Majesty, he began in a confident manner and in language expressing sage eloquence, to speak as follows.

THE FUGITIVE GENTLEMAN'S SPEECH TO THE KING

Always some fatal evil intervenes
In that which gracious Heaven is disposed
To send to mortals, and the man too much
Desirous of good, by hope deceives himself.
    I wished first to announce the tidings that
The season of iron, cruel and inhumane,
Was changing to a better age, and the Gods
Holding, with Saturn, the world in their grasp,
Came to live as intimates of men in France,
Forever gracing her with peace and wealth.
But whom did I encounter on the way?
Oh, Gods, turn evil back upon its wicked chief!
    This was not a woman: none who breathes
Has so much beauty or such great wrath . . .
No sooner had I seen her, e'en as soon,
My life and liberty were well nigh ravaged.
She, for her pleasure having some concern,
Came toward me, speaking to me thus:
    ["]Halt, Cavalier, fear nothing and approach,
And if your heart is neither wood nor stone,

Yield without struggle, yield to the laws
Of this winged archer, God of all-pervasive power,
To whom (perhaps) you would make vain resistance.
Because he holds Gods subject to his power,
I feel now the sharp touch of his darts,
And, vanquished by your eyes, surrender to you.
I would not, with my wand, form you as beast,
You have some destiny which makes me love you,
Come, possess my riches, use my wealth,
And like myself, be served by these goddesses.["]
    I followed, for there is no stronger bond
Than the conception of pleasure and of wealth,
Dwelling there I was happy (if he who yields
To pleasure's rule may so be called)
When an evil Destiny, a Fate severe,
Poisoned with hate and jealousy the heart
Of Circe, who in a moment bewitched me,
Struck me on the chest with her golden wand
Transformed my body into that of a Lion,
And shut me in a park among her herds.
But some occasion softened the sorceress,
Who made me regain my earlier form.
Wary of the jurisdiction of her
Cruel laws (who dares trust spells too often?)
I made my escape while she, agitated
By suspicion, which makes her distrust
Her arts, mounted to the top of a tower
Where she goes to spy on the nymphs from afar,
In order to charm them with cunning magic
And keep them from seeing this King who calls them
To a temple in France, with the other Gods
The golden age brings back from the skies.
    More than a cruel Serpent, one whose spine
The fleeing shepherd breaks with a staff,
Her eye is inflamed, and fear which combats
Her dubious hope beats in her breast.
    To this King, who has assumed the Gods' defense,
I come swiftly to disclose the action,
And to entreat his aid against this Circe.
    Will you not, great King, help so many Gods?
You will, Henry, more valiant than Hercules
Or he who killed the murderous Chimera,
And for so many mortals and Gods held fast

In the Fairy's bonds, you will be divine,
And posterity, which will build you temples,
Will crown your temples with verdant laurel.

His speech completed, he knelt on one knee near the King, as if placing himself under his protection. Then Circe came out of her garden, holding her golden wand raised high; she rushed to the center of the room turning her gaze to all sides to spy out the gentleman who had escaped from her prison. And failing to detect him, having lifted her eyes to the cloud suspended above, she began with a sorrowful voice and a grace few damsels could imitate and none surpass, to lament in the following manner.

CIRCE'S LAMENT, HAVING LOST A GENTLEMAN

I pursue in vain, with no hope
Of ever seeing him again in my power.
Ah, Circe, what have you done?
You should never re-form as human
One you once deprived of reason.
Alas, Circe, little cunning and sly,
Who comes to be wary through her error!
This fugitive, fearless, will go his way,
Everywhere spreading your shame, to your detriment.
Vain, the spells you cast upon your captives,
Vain, your magic murmurs which transform,
For you are mutable, and cruelty
And pity each have a half of you.
Foolish, thrice foolish Circe, senseless and
Believing one restored to native form
Would love you still, and be deceived by pleasures
When he could exercise his reason.
Expel this mercy which renders you fickle.
Kindness becomes ill deed when detrimental.
Follow your natural self: your ways are wrath
And cruelty; leave good to another.
Come, come, cast off such feeble courage
And arm your heart with serpents and with ire
That none struck by your wand may later vaunt
Himself that he escaped your bondage.

As soon as Circe had vented her anger in this complaint, she returned to her garden with the countenance of a most irritated woman. She sallied from the hall, leaving the spectators astonished by the two acts they had seen, as much by the fugitive gentleman as by the furious Circe.

But when silence was established, there came from one of the trellises three Mermaids and a Triton with their tails, fashioned of burnished gold and silver scales, with barbels and fins of burnished gold, tucked up in their arms. Their bodies and locks were entwined with golden threads, hanging down to the waist; and all carried golden mirrors in their hands. Thus attired, they entered the hall singing the following song, each stanza of which was answered by an ensemble in the golden vault, singing unaccompanied.

THE MERMAIDS' SONG

MERMAIDS: Hoary father ocean,
      Father of the Gods,
      Shall we leave the waves
      At the summons of this Triton?

GOLDEN VAULT: Go, daughters of Achelaus,
      Follow Triton, who calls you,
      Blend your voices with his horn
      In endless praise of a noble king.

MERMAIDS: The goddess Thetis
      Emerges from the sea,
      With the attendance of
      The chorus of Nereid sisters.

GOLDEN VAULT: Go, daughters of Achelaus, etc.

MERMAIDS: Jupiter is not alone above,
      The sea lodges a thousand Gods,
      But one king only reigns in France,
      Henry, great King of the French. . . .

Having made a full circuit of the hall, these marine creatures retired near the trellis, where they encountered a fountain which one could truly say was the most beautiful in superb design and artifice and the most magnificent in embellishment that had ever been seen. . . .

[Beaujoyeulx then describes the fountain, which contained three basins adorned with sculptures of dolphins, mermaids, and tritons made of burnished gold and silver. Scented water flowed from the topmost basin into the third and largest basin, which had twelve golden pulpits on its rim. In these sat the queen and eleven other royal ladies representing naiads, dressed in silver cloth and wearing many precious

From the *Ballet Comique*

Beaujoyeulx' fountain, lighted by one hundred white wax candles, had its highest basin supported by the burnished tails of three dolphins. From spouts at the top of the pyramid, water fell down to the feet of twelve Naiads seated on the lowest basin. The choreographer says nothing of the Naiads' dancing, but is eager to note that their attire was esteemed the richest and most stately ever seen in a masquerade.

stones. The mermaids joined this company. Then, to music and singing, the fountain moved toward the king, made a turn in front of
him, and slowly withdrew, leaving the hall empty.]

Once behind the castle, the Naiads climbed down from their fountain,
and immediately ten violinists entered the hall through the two trellises,
five from one side and as many from the other, dressed in white satin
trimmed with gold tinsel, beplumed and adorned with egret feathers;
and in this apparel they began to play the first entry of the Ballet.
Following these violinists, the twelve pages entered the room through
the same trellises, six from one side and six from the other; and the
pages being in place, the twelve nymphs quickly appeared after them,
also entering six by one trellis and six by the other; who were no sooner
spied by the violinists than they changed their tune in order to commence
the second part of the entry of the Ballet, in which these nymphs came
dancing up to their majesties the King and the Queen his mother, in
this fashion. During the first passage of the entry, there were six, all
in a line across the room, and three in front in a quite large triangle,
the Queen being its foremost point, and three behind in like manner.
Then, in accord with variations in the music, they also revolved, winding
backwards around each other, sometimes in one fashion, sometimes
in another, and then returned to their original position. Having arrived
close to the King, they went on continuously with the part of this Ballet
composed of twelve Geometric figures, all different the one from the
other; and at the last passage, the violins played a very lively tune
called "The Little Bell."

Circe, still hidden in her garden by the closing of the curtain, had
no sooner heard the sound of the little bell than she emerged in a
rage, holding in her right hand her golden wand raised high. She came
the full length of the hall to the nymphs (arranged in the form of a
crescent facing their majesties), touching them one after another with
her golden wand, which light touch suddenly rendered them immobile
like statues. She did likewise to the violinists, who could no longer
sing nor play, thus remaining without any movement whatsoever. And
afterward, she returned to her garden, with a bold and gleeful countenance like that of a Captain who has won a glorious victory in some
perilous and difficult enterprise of his own. Thus she could rightly vaunt
herself, having brought low such an intrepid grandeur of courage as
that of the nymphs.

When Circe, therefore, had retired to her garden in such glory, from
the top of the ceiling of the room and above the cloud, one heard a
great clap of thunder which rumbled and murmured for some time;
which having ceased, the cloud described above suddenly began to

descend little by little, wherein was borne and enveloped Mercury, messenger of the God Jupiter, by whom he was sent to earth to break the spells of the fairy Circe and to deliver the Naiads from her enchantment with the juice of the Moly root. Mercury was attired just as the poets describe him: in Spanish carnation satin, laboriously laced with gold, with gilded boots having wings at his heels to signify the fleetness of his course; his head also covered with a small cap winged on both sides and gilded all over; his mantle being of violet gold cloth; and bearing in his hand the caduceus with which of old in the service of Jupiter he lulled Argus to sleep. This God while descending sang the verses inserted below most pleasingly, being represented by lord du Pont, an attendant of the King having many honorable accomplishments.

MERCURY'S SONG

I, common messenger of all the gods,
Winged of heel, flitting, nimble, swift. . . .
Bear the Moly root of excellence
To cure the mind disarmed of reason, which,
Forsaking virtue, was beguiled by pleasure. . . .
  This Circe has eyes shameless in desire,
Mistrusted at first glance by everyone,
And the lure of Cupid is no more swift.
But pleasure past is odious to her,
The men she renders self-oblivious,
Losing their reason with their human form.
  She knows how to subdue nymphs with her art,
But she cannot transform them into beasts,
For of their nature, Gods are immutable.
Yet by the Gods she makes herself revered,
Striking them with her wand, making them
Stay, charmed of foot, more stable than a rock.
  I wish the art to disclose her fantasies,
I have distilled in water the Moly root,
And would undo her craft with my stronger art.
I know how much power and strength she has,
But great peril pleases the victor, after
Honored by the name of a powerful foe.

While Mercury was still in the air some two feet above the nymphs, having ended his song, he scattered the Moly root potion, which he had in a golden vial, over the heads of the nymphs, and cast it with such industry that it also splashed on the violinists, who were no sooner sprinkled by this water than they suddenly began to play again, the nymphs also beginning to dance and to continue their Ballet as before their enchantment. However Circe, thinking that Mercury did her great wrong and injury by usurping her art, resolved to make him feel what she knew how to do and what power she had over him and even over the strength of his caduceus.

For this purpose she again came out of her garden and, almost in a frenzy, rushed to the center of the room. Passing through the lovely troop of dancers, as she had done before, she touched them a second time, likewise the violinists, returning them to the state from which Mercury had delivered them; and retiring four steps backward, she began to speak as follows:

CIRCE

Man is never content with his lot, but yearns
Continually for greater happiness. . . .

All human action proceeds from appetite,
Where one is incited or led by pleasure.
Of rest and labor, pleasure is the guide,
Presiding o'er the movements of the will:
The action pleasing and commonly practiced
Serves as rule of life and law for everyone. . . .

I will imprison this foolish Mercury
Who comes presumptuously with craft and courage
To aid the nymphs, also promising himself
To have some power against my golden wand,
And to dissolve my spells with a root which one day
Served Ulysses as a medicine against
My poisons; but it was Pallas guarding
Ulysses, not he, who hindered my success.
Of the gods this Minerva alone I fear,
Only she preserves mankind from my arts.

Having completed her speech, Circe drew near to Mercury, who was still enveloped by the cloud, and raising her golden wand, struck him: who no sooner had felt the blow than, abandoning his caduceus, he stood enchanted, and thus the cloud bore him immobile to earth. Then taking him by the hand, Circe led him to her garden, the nymphs following prettily in line two by two, with no other movement than that which seemed to be given them by the power of Circe's spell. Once inside her garden, the nymphs disappeared instantly, so that no one was able to perceive what had become of them. Immediately the curtain which covered Circe's garden dropped, clearly revealing the beauty of this delightful garden, which sparkled with a thousand kinds of flames and lights. Moreover, one saw Circe in front of her castle door, seated in majesty with the evidence of her victory: at her feet Mercury lay on his back, unable to move in any way without the permission of the enchantress. After the opening of the curtain, a large stag emerged from the garden and passed in front of Circe, followed by a dog, and the dog by an elephant, the elephant by a lion, the lion by a tiger, the tiger by a hog, and the hog by other beasts—men thus transformed by her sorcery and the power of her enchantments.

The preceding act being finished, the second interlude began to enter from the other trellis. . . .

[After further songs and discourse, Pallas entered in a car drawn by a serpent. She called on Jupiter, who descended on a cloud. As all the divinities assaulted Circe's palace, Jupiter struck the enchantress with a thunderbolt and led her captive before the King.]

Then the violinists began to play the entrance of the grand Ballet, composed of fifteen passages, arranged in such a manner that at the end of each passage all faced toward the King; having arrived before his majesty, they danced the grand Ballet of forty passages or Geometric figures. These were exact and considered in their diameter, sometimes square, now round, and with many and diverse forms, and as often triangular, accompanied by some square and other small figures. Which figures being no sooner traced out by the twelve Naiads, dressed in white (as was said) than the four Dryads dressed in green came to break them; so that the one ending, the other immediately began. In the middle of this Ballet a chain was formed, composed of four interlacings different from each other, such that to see them one would have said this was a battle array, so well was the order kept, and so dexterously each endeavored to observe her rank and cadence; so that everyone believed that Archimedes could not have better understood Geometric proportions than these princesses and ladies employing them in this Ballet. And in order that one might recognize how many different airs it was necessary to use, some austere, others gay, some in triple time, others for a step smooth and slow, I wished to show them also, as you see below, so as to have nothing lacking and imperfect in the relation of all that took place.

[Ballet Music]

This Ballet completed, the Naiads and Dryads made a deep reverence to his majesty; and the Queen, approaching the King her lord, took him by the hand and made him a present of a large gold medallion, having thereon a Dolphin swimming in the sea, which all took for a certain omen of he [the heir] that God will give to them for the prosperity of this kingdom.

Following the Queen's example, all the princesses, dames, and ladies, according to their rank and degree, took the princes, lords, and gentlemen who pleased them; and to each one, they made their golden present, with their emblems, all nautical things, in as much as they represented the nymphs of the seas, as you see below. . . .

[Beaujoyeulx then enumerates the gifts bestowed by each lady.]

In this order and rank, they led out the princes to dance the grand Ball; and this ended, they began branles and other dances customary at great feasts and celebrations. These being finished, their majesties the King and Queens withdrew, the night being already well advanced; seeing that this Comedy Ballet lasted from ten o'clock in the evening until three hours and a half after midnight, without such length boring or displeasing the spectators, each one being so greatly satisfied; seeing most especially such a noble, excellent, dignified, and sovereign lady so much honoring her subjects as to humble herself to take part in the pastimes created to delight her, and to present herself in public; so that all recognized that our Kings and Queens, since they reign over a liberal people, also treat them liberally, and with all kindliness, freedom, candor, and courtesy.

Saint–Hubert
HOW TO COMPOSE SUCCESSFUL BALLETS
Translated from the French by Andrée Bergens

Unfortunately we know nothing of the life of M. de Saint-Hubert beyond what he tells us in this little book.

Marie-Françoise Christout has remarked on Saint-Hubert's "common sense and clarity of mind." Indeed, he packs a great deal of sound instruction into this very brief treatise (only the last section, concerned with the role of the stage manager, is omitted here), telling us a great deal about the structure and values of the ballet à entrées. *He makes no claim to particular originality and, from what we know of contemporary librettos, rather reflects the taste*

SOURCE: From *La Manière de composer et faire réussir les ballets* (Paris, 1641).

of his time. An interesting advance over the previous century is revealed, however, in Saint-Hubert's remark that he likes to see people dance according to the characters they represent, even though he later admits that the dancers should be given only such steps as they can perform with what they have to carry, since the audience identifies them by their properties. The next century will carry the concept of expressive movement much further.

I did not intend to have this little discourse published for I was afraid of wronging my profession, and if one of my friends had not tried to make me believe (which is true) that dancing is one of the three activities of nobility, it would never have appeared. Everyone knows that, for a young nobleman to be polished, he must learn how to ride, to fence, and to dance. The first skill increases his dexterity, the second his courage, the last his grace and disposition. Each of these exercises being useful at an appropriate time, one can say that they are of equal value, since Mars is no less the god of war when resting on Venus' bosom than when thundering in the midst of battles.

And even kings, princes, and noblemen enjoy this divertissement; it must be praiseworthy and, this being so, I decided to express my opinion, which will be shared by those who approve of it; as to the others, who do things which are not worthwhile, they will do as they like. I will accordingly say that there are two kinds of ballets, the serious and the grotesque which, when well made, can be equally successful.

A great ballet, which we call a royal ballet usually includes thirty *entrées*.

A fine ballet contains at least twenty *entrées*. And a small ballet, from ten to twelve. Not that it is necessary to comply with this rule but rather with the subject that requires the number to be either increased or decreased.

Since *mascarades* do not usually tell a story, no rule can be applied. The *mascarade* is improvised by people who disguise themselves with no specific purpose in mind and just follow their fancy. It is just a pretext for wearing imaginative costumes, and the participants sing tunes and dance steps of their own choice, most frequently ordinary dances but with the ladies who are present.

In order to produce a fine ballet, six things are necessary: subject, airs, dancing, costumes, machines, and organization, concerning all of which I shall give my opinion.

Of Subjects

I shall start with the subject, upon which all the rest depends and to which everything must be subordinated. The most important requirement for making a successful ballet is finding a good subject, which is the most difficult thing.

I find many perfect musicians for the airs, excellent dancers for the *entrées*, good designers for the costumes, extremely skillful craftsmen for the machines, but very few people are able to deal with a good subject and follow its necessary progression.

To be fine, it must be new and it also must be well developed so that none of the *entrées* will be irrelevant; each must be pertinent. If there is a mixture of the serious and the grotesque, two grotesque *entrées* should not appear in succession; if they can be harmoniously mixed in with the serious, they will be much more diverting, and the audience will be more inclined to admire the former and laugh at the latter.

When I say that it is necessary to make a ballet that has not yet been seen, I mean only the main part of the subject, for, as far as the *entrées* are concerned, it is impossible to make more than a few that have not been seen. For example, if during the development of the story there is a need for noblemen, Turks, or young ladies, one should not hesitate to use such characters simply because they already have appeared in several ballets. They are no longer the ones belonging to those previous subjects but integral parts of yours, which is completely different from the others, and you use them because they belong here and not because you saw them before.

If you can find *entrées* and costumes that have not yet been seen, this will enrich your ballet and make your inventiveness more admirable. So look for a fine new subject of your own devising, since it is the trend nowadays. And may Ovid's *Metamorphoses* no longer be danced as in former times.

This reminds me of a gentleman I know who once asked my opinion concerning an idea he had of presenting Homer's *Iliad* in ballet form. I told him frankly that it would be a play rather than a ballet, that the ceilings of the halls were too low for the masts of the Greek vessels, that the horses of Hector's chariot, if frightened, might injure people, and that the burning of Troy would scare the ladies.

Entrées should be organized in such a way that the number of dancers appearing in each will be different; that two using the same number will not be too close together; and that *entrées* with just one or two protagonists will be kept at a minimum. Those with three, four, five, six, seven, and eight dancers are the most attractive and make possible the most beautiful figures; it is true that those with seven and eight are rarely used because they would require too many dancers except for a finale or in great ballets which require brilliance, or when they are necessary to indicate the conclusion of a ballet. I strongly advocate writing out the story of the ballet, either in prose or in verse, so that it can be passed out to the audience before the performance to let them enjoy it more by knowing what it is about.

Of Airs

It would be well for the airs not to be written before the subject is perfectly set and the *entrées* carefully planned so that they will be appropriate and will follow what the dancers are to do and represent, and the musician will be much more successful in this way than by composing many airs which can only with difficulty be adjusted to the *entrées* and the subject afterwards.

Of Dancing

One must fit the dancing and the steps to the airs and the *entrées* so that a vine-grower or a water-carrier will not dance as a knight or a magician. I would like to see people dance according to the characters they represent and sometimes there are *entrées* where perfect dancing is not necessary. I remember that in the first ballet in which I had the honor of performing in the presence of His Majesty, I impersonated a student and I constantly danced out of step and against the beat. Everyone believed I was doing it on purpose and my *entrée* was very much appreciated. It is possible to have many types of individuals dance in ballets, even lame persons, who in certain things can be as successful as others. It is not that good dancers would not be even more successful, but there are some *entrées* where it is a waste to use them; they should be kept for fine dancing and the best steps, for the beauty of a ballet requires that there be some good dancers and *entrées* perfectly danced.

I cannot stand short steps and capers against the beat so commonly used by men who take ladies' or other women's parts. Instead of modest dancing, they do two or three serious steps, then start skipping about in a wild and crazy way. I have seen others representing limping or maimed people who, after coming on stage with crutches, dance a little, then throw away their canes and crutches, and caper about as if ballet could miraculously cure the halt and lame.

It is necessary that *entrées* conclude as they began, since what is shown at the end is what was shown at the beginning (unless it is a metamorphosis). I think it is not right for people to arrive in one way and leave in another as most of our dancers customarily do when they impersonate soldiers, villagers, or porters. The soldiers arrive with swords and shields, the villagers with baskets, and the porters with hooks. This is fine, but as soon as they have danced one figure in this attire, they throw swords, baskets, and hooks into the hall in order

The characters in the court ballet were identified more clearly by what they wore than by what they danced. For *Ballet des Fêtes de Bacchus*, performed in 1651, here are designs for the Marquis de Pify-Genlis as Autumn, with headdress of sheaves of wheat and overflowing cornucopia (left), and the Marquis de Villequier as the River of Forgetfulness, strewn with poppies (right).

to be more at ease in their dancing, and one can no longer recognize what they were, which is very bad. They should have signs on their backs to identify them, like those used by painters who, when they have made a poor picture, write the name of an animal so badly represented that it could not be recognized if they had not done so.

Ballet being a silent play, costumes and actions must enable the spectators to recognize what is represented, and the choreographer must create steps and figures that permit the dancers to perform with what they have to carry; everything will be much better thus. He also must be sure to have an uneven number of figures instead of an even one, and he will keep in mind that comical *entrées* with grotesque costumes ought to be short, for sometimes what seems excellent at first because it is ridiculous becomes boring before long, like good tales that make the wise laugh only once.

As to the serious *entrées*, well danced and with handsome costumes, they must be made to last even longer; if they include five or six figures, airs and steps must be varied to avoid boredom.

It is also very important to take time to study steps and *entrées*. Improvised things are never successful; two weeks are not too much for a great ballet, one week for a small one; and for every three or four *entrées* there must be a dancing master to create the steps and rehearse with singing accompaniment when they will later be accompanied by violins. There is always something that has to be redone; I know very well that those who are used to dancing ballets can learn a step or an *entrée* in a day, but if they dance it well with two days' practice, they will dance even better with four and much better still with eight. Time allows people to see their faults and to correct them, both in dancing and other necessary things. This is not possible when things are done in a hurry.

Of Costumes

Ballet costumes can never be too handsome provided they are made according to the subject. To this end, they must be carefully designed since tailors and headdress-makers follow very exactly the sketches they are given. It is very important that the dancers be dressed in accordance with the characters they represent. One may object that if a cook were to be clothed according to his trade, he would have to be given a greasy outfit and towels, which would nauseate the company; but I would answer by saying that he can be dressed in a more embellished way and one can give him, instead of a greasy towel, one of white taffeta or gauze. It would be ridiculous to see a vine-grower wearing embroidered clothes and a nobleman coarse cotton. One should seek not so much lavishness as fitness, since a buckram or a frieze costume, well related to the subject, will be finer and better than an inappropriate silk one. It is not by spending more but by carefully observing a ballet's organization that one will make it more pleasant.

I have created ballets in which gold-and-silver-bedecked costumes cost no more than a crown apiece, and this is easy to believe since for five pennies I would bespangle it in such a way as to make it appear as impressive by candlelight as a richer one. This device is perfectly satisfactory for those whom I want to delight at little expense. Everything I have said about costumes applies to headdresses, especially the importance of having the costumes of those who represent the same thing look alike, without any difference.

Of Machines

As to machines, they bring a great embellishment to ballets and add to their brilliance when they are beautiful, skillfully maneuvered, and made to fit appropriately into the story. One can give an idea of how to build them only when the subject is perfect and one knows what they are to represent. It is up to the author of the subject or to the organizer to look for good craftsmen to build them and to put them in the hands of people who know how to move them at the right time.

Section Two

DANCE FOR THE EYE
AND THE HEART:
THE EIGHTEENTH CENTURY

In 1682 Claude Ménestrier published a treatise titled *des Ballets anciens et modernes*. Looking back to the standard format of the *ballet de cour*, he agreed with Saint-Hubert that a good subject was most important and also agreed that a dancer's character was established by means of costumes, symbols, and masks as well as by appropriate movements. But going further than his predecessor, Ménestrier asserted that the motions of the body were capable of depicting inner feelings that could be made known in no other way. He distinguished "*danse simple*," which merely observed musical cadences, from "ballet," which was an imitation, in Aristotle's sense, of the actions and passions of man. Alas, he sighed, dancers would rather do pretty steps than represent something—thus setting the problem for the coming century.

When he retired from performing in 1670, Louis XIV had established a school for the training of dancers and therefore the following year, when the Paris Opéra opened, its directors knew where to turn for a corps de ballet. At first all the dancers were men, but as early as 1681 a Mlle. Lafontaine appeared on the Opéra stage. Her ballet master was Charles-Louis Beauchamps who, we are told, got ideas for choreographic patterns by watching pigeons as they scurried after the corn he threw them. He was succeeded by Louis Pécour, and soon other dancers are being mentioned—Marie-Thérèse Subligny, Jean Balon, Louis Dupré.

In 1700 Raoul Feuillet published his *Chorégraphie*, describing a system of dance notation that conveniently tells us a good deal about the technique of the time. All five positions are now properly numbered. Many of the steps notated by Feuillet sound familiar to us—*coupé, pirouette, entrechat, sissonne*. In most instances their execution was somewhat different from ours, but the basic shape of the movement was sufficiently similar that we can recognize the foundation of our present forms.

Most important was the increasing emphasis on the turnout, which now had the feet placed to form a right angle. Since the introduction of the proscenium arch in the mid-seventeenth century, dancers had been performing on a stage with an audience seated in front of them. The floor patterns which had been so dazzling to spectators placed above and around three sides of a ballroom were no longer visible. Very visible, however, were the designs made by the individual dancer. Light jumps became more frequent and were ornamented with small beats; varieties of *pirouettes* appeared. By increasing his turnout, the dancer found such movements easier to perform; his legs moved more freely in the hip sockets and his base of support was more stable.

There was still comparatively little distinction between the steps of the ballroom and those of the stage, both aiming for the qualities admired in the most typical of eighteenth-century dances, the minuet. Nobility, precision, grace, and lightness were the attributes of the accomplished dancer. Rameau's *The Dancing Master* (1725) illustrates the five turned-out positions, but they are demonstrated by a gentleman in full courtly regalia, ready to embark on a minuet.

As dancing masters perfected their teaching methods and professional dancers acquired greater skills, the gulf between social and theatre dance widened. Decorum remained the standard, but for the stage the norm was somewhat relaxed. Soame Jenyns marked the distinction in his *The Art of Dancing* (1729):

'Tis not a nimble Bound or Caper high
That can pretend to please a curious Eye;
Good judges no such Tumblers Tricks regard,
Or think them beautiful because they're hard;
Yet in Stage-dancing, if performed with Skill
Such active Feats our Eyes with Wonder fill. . . .

Soon after the Restoration (1660) French dancers began appearing in England, most often in dances inserted between the acts of a play or in afterpieces to a dramatic offering. Their formal, elegant manoeuvres were brightened by dazzling bits of virtuosity that made them the delight of London. Native dancers often appeared on the same bills, but usually in what we would now call character dances, with titles like "The High-land Lilt" and "The Dutch Skipper." Nevertheless, it was the Englishman Josias Priest who choreographed the distinguished ballets in the operas of Henry Purcell, beginning with *Dido and Aeneas* (c. 1689).

Another choreographer, John Weaver, commended Priest for his ability to represent "all manner of passions," but he derided the visiting Balon for showing nothing more than "modulated motion." In his *Essay Towards an History of Dancing* (1712) Weaver asserted that with a genuine performer

the Spectator will not only be pleas'd and diverted with the Beauty of the Performance and Symmetry of the Movements; but will also be instructed by the Positions, Steps *and* Attitudes, *so as to be able to judge of the* Design *of the Performer. And without the help of an Interpreter, a Spectator shall at a distance, by the lively Representation of a just Character, be capable of understanding the* Subject *of the Story represented, and able to distinguish the several* Passions, Manners, *or* Actions, *as of* Love, Anger, *or the Like.*

This sounds like Ménestrier, with the important difference that Weaver makes no mention of the aids to characterization afforded by costumes, masks, and verses. Indeed, he felt them unnecessary, believing that bodily movement by itself was sufficient to make the dramatic points. Significantly Weaver's favorite ballerina—the first produced by England—was the lovely Hester Santlow, who later became a distinguished actress.

Unfortunately, the few pantomimes that Weaver produced in accordance, he believed, with the principles of the ancient Greeks, were not nearly so successful with the public as the virtuosity of the inexpressive French dancers or the rollicking Harlequinades of his rival John Rich, who diverted his audiences by being hatched from an egg and turning into a flower.

Across the channel, the vogue for virtuosity accelerated. Probably a number of women wanted to emulate the jumps of the men, but they were weighted down with farthingales or panniers. Marie Camargo, who made her Paris Opéra debut in 1726, is credited with shortening the ballerina's skirt by several inches to gain freedom and visibility for her *entrechat quatre*. Since she was the first woman on the Parisian stage to manage this jump, enhanced by a quick beating together of the feet, she had reason to want her ankles to show. She may also have been the first to dance in heelless slippers, another innovation explainable by the desire for elevation, which is facilitated when the starting position is a solid *plié* with the heels firmly planted on the floor.

While Camargo was famous for her brilliant style, her rival Marie Sallé was known as a dancer-actress. Sallé was not happy in Paris and danced frequently in London, which appreciated her dramatic abilities. Her costume reforms were even more extreme than Camargo's, but she made them for purposes of characterization rather than display. In *Pygmalion*, which she danced in 1734, she discarded not only the conventional skirt but even her corset, wearing a simple muslin robe draped like that of a Greek statue. Sallé was the first woman choreographer of note, and *Pygmalion* was her own composition. A contemporary critic, Louis de Cahusac, remarked that one could read in Sallé's movements a whole range of emotions.

But among dancers Sallé was an exception, and she had no immediate followers. Succeeding ballerinas, like Anna Heinel, the first woman to do double *pirouettes*, concentrated on virtuosity. In this area the ballerinas had strong competition, for in the second half of the eighteenth century the male dancers were supreme. Outstanding among them were Gaetan and Auguste Vestris, the father and son who dominated the Paris Opéra. Both were vain, Auguste claiming that there were only three great men in Europe—Voltaire, the King of Prussia, and himself; Gaetan admitted Auguste's superiority, but attributed it to the advantage of his having so great a father.

Fortunately, they were not rivals for roles, since the Opéra maintained strict categories. Gaetan was a *danseur noble*, tall and stately in bearing, suited to the serious and heroic ballets. Of medium height, Auguste played lighter roles in the *demi-caractère* class. The third rank was that of *danseur comique*, who played humorous roles exclusively; there was no crossing of the lines. Rigidly, the Opéra designated which steps were to be allotted to which category. Whether the characters were courtiers or gods, they danced in the same majestic manner; when they were Turks or American Indians, as in *Les Indes Gallants* of 1735, the costumes rather than the movement style remained their chief mode of identification.

Outside of Paris, however, some choreographers were working to promote the cause of the *ballet d'action*. In Vienna Franz Hilverding staged mimed versions of the great tragedies; his student, Gasparo Angiolini, was especially concerned with dramatic gestures that were closely related to musical rhythms and phrases, and he numbered Gluck among his collaborators.

The best known of the dramatic choreographers was Jean Georges Noverre, who not only created many ballets but also wrote about his artistic convictions with proselytizing zeal. While his contemporaries at the Paris Opéra were devising nothing but pretty combinations of steps to exhibit the fancy new *pirouettes* and *entrechats*, Noverre insisted that ballet should represent action, character, and feeling. He was more vehement than Weaver in his proclamations. The art, he complained, in his *Letters* of 1760, "has remained in its infancy only because its effects have been limited, like those of fireworks designed simply to gratify the eyes; although this art shares with the best plays the advantage of inspiring, moving, and captivating the spectator by the charm of its interest and illusion. No one has suspected its power of speaking to the heart." Noverre's ballets, with their finely wrought dramatic structure and well-developed characterizations, won him the admiration of the great English actor David Garrick. The nymphs and gods of Noverre, unlike those of Beaujoyeulx, who conceived them as symbols of good or evil, were individuals; even when composing for the corps de ballet, Noverre wanted expressive movement to replace the formal symmetry that then dominated the stage of the Opéra.

Still, Noverre was a man of his time. When he said that dance should be an imitation of nature, he was quick to qualify that he meant "beautiful" nature. His characters were nymphs and shepherds, goddesses and epic heroes; the plots were filled with noble passions and sentiments of grandeur. His pupil, Jean Dauberval, shared his master's beliefs but felt the influence of the ideas that were rapidly changing European society. He was the first ballet choreographer to treat peasants as real people, and though *La Fille Mal Gardée* hardly presented a realistic view of folk life, its ambitious mother, willful daughter, rich fiancé, and simple suitor were likeable and believable.

Dauberval's student Salvatore Viganò, whom Stendhal compared to Shakespeare, carried the idea of dramatic movement still further. Though his early works provided opportunities for set dances, his later ballets made fewer concessions. In 1819 his last production, *The Titans*, told its epic story of greed and violence in unrelieved stretches of rhythmic pantomime.

Ménestrier had remarked that dancers would rather do pretty steps than represent something. Now that their technical skills were approaching new heights, it was unlikely that they would consent for long to appear in ballets that offered no occasions for them to display their virtuosity. A solution was at hand—but it arrived with another era.

Gottfried Taubert (c.1673–17?)
THE MINUET

Translated from the German by Angelika Gerbes

Born around 1673, Taubert lived in Saxony, spending eleven years at the University of Leipzig. In 1702 he moved to Danzig, where he had an apparent monopoly on the teaching of dance and decorum. He returned to Leipzig in 1714.

Taubert's description of the minuet, agreeing in many respects with the French manuals, is clearer than most contemporary accounts and is especially interesting for the extent of the embellishments it specifies. The details he gives should be viewed in the context of the period style, which is so well described by Shirley Wynne in "Complaisance, An Eighteenth-Century Cool" (Dance Scope *[Fall, 1970]):*

SOURCE: From *Der Rechtschaffener Tantzmeister* (Leipzig, 1717).

To move impulsively, explosively, or exuberantly was a breach of etiquette. . . . Ball dances and ballets, the lines of separation between them being still very indistinct in the earlier period, conformed entirely to these social codes. The chief action features of these dances can be described as vertical (no elevation implied), narrow, and slender, with a general gathering in toward the vertical axis; the torso remained still, with a firm upright tension, while the head tilted and turned, and the shoulders shifted slightly in an épaulement limited in ladies during the turn of the century by the shoulder bands of the corset. The forearms, wrists and fingers, the lower legs and feet were highly decorative. They performed fluttering embroideries on the periphery of a controlled and tranquil center.

Dance—*Révérence*, social—gentleman

1. Both knees bend gently and not very far. In rising, one steps a little back with the right leg (that is: with the right leg *coupiret*[1] to the back). Others, not without reason, pull the right foot up against the left one during the knee bend either in front, to the side, or also in back as it is customary in the *coupé*. Others, before the bend, beat several times with the extended right leg against the front of the extended left leg. Still others beat in front and back, and only then *coupiren* with it to the back or side and brush back with the left. . . . In straightening up [after the bow[2]] the right foot, with the heel released from the ground, is at the same time pulled high onto the half-toe and held there quietly for a moment.

(This is the first cadence or dance measure. . . .)

Then 2. Both knees bend again. In rising, the right foot high on point is brushed forward toward the left side. Then with bent knees step on the heel, and balance the body over the right leg. In rising, the left one is placed against the right one. On the toes of the right foot make a quarter turn to the right to come to rest facing the partner, who has swung to her left. (During the turn for purposes of grace one can beat with the left foot several times in back, or also once in front and back. This is the other cadence.)

Finally, 3. Once again both knees bend. In rising one steps with the left one away upwards [up the hall] on a straight side line, so that one can see heel next to heel but with the space of a foot between them. Then, in the third cadence, the other back-*révérence*, which is performed toward the lady, is brushed back with the right foot. . . .

---

[1] *Coupiret*, also *coupiren* or *coupire* depending on the usage, consists of the French *coupé* with a German ending. The term describes the cutting action of the leg as it is brought from fourth position back through first position to fourth position front.

[2] Of the bow, Taubert says, "the body gently and slowly bends deeper and deeper from the hips . . . letting the arms hang naturally in front."

Dance—*Révérence*, social—lady

Like the gentleman, the lady makes a double *révérence* both before and after the dance. In both instances she performs the ordinary back *révérence*. . . . [3] One *révérence* is toward the spectators and the other one toward her partner. With the exception of the *battement* of the feet all that her partner does on the right leg the lady performs on her left and vice versa. . . .

Pas ordinaire or common step in dancing

The *pas ordinaire* or ordinary straight steps which in dancing are executed without bending have their name from the ordinary steps in walking. They are performed as in walking, except that instead of occurring on the whole foot they are executed on the toes.

Each of these steps be it forward, backward, or sideward can be divided into two parts. The first part contains three considerations. While standing firmly and straight on one leg:

1. the heel of the other foot is lifted off the ground with a slightly bent knee.
2. The whole foot is raised, and
3. is brought bent and close over the ground up to the heel of the other foot.

The second part has four considerations. Namely: the foot which was brought to the side of the other one

1. from there is extended close to the ground a good shoe's length (according to the person's stature) either to the front, back, or side (depending into which direction one is dancing).
2. There, well turned-out and neatly closed, it is set down on the toes.
3. The body is brought onto it firmly and in good balance.
4. The other foot, as has already been mentioned in the first part, is made to follow bent, and is firmly pulled close either in front, back, or to the side (depending upon the direction in which one has made the stiff step). . . .

Demi-coupé

Part I

1. The left leg having been set forward and with the body resting on it, one bends both knees well out to both sides, but not too deeply.
2. During the bending the right foot advances close to the ground up to and next to the heel of the left. (The point may thereby not rise

---

[3] Her bow is like the man's but she replaces the forward bend of the torso with a bending of the knees.

up. The body must remain steadily in a perpendicular line.) And that is the *plié*.

Part II

1. One rises and extends both knees again, and
2. during the extending, places the right foot forward without brushing. And this is the *pas élevé*.

In short: a half *coupé* is when one bends with both knees at the same time, and in rising places the back foot down in front. . . .

Coupé

Part I

After having placed the body weight over the left leg, which is located not too far in front of the right leg, and at the same time having lifted the heel of the right foot (which is in back) off the ground,

1. one bends both knees at the same time, and
2. while the bending continues, advances the right leg forward until it is next to the left one. (This is the *plié*.)

Part II

1. One *coupiret* and finishes by bringing the right leg off the ground and bent to the front.
2. Then one rises somewhat more strongly than in the *demi-coupé*. (This is the *pas élevé*.)

Part III

1. In rising one brings the left foot to the heel of the right one, and
2. from there brushes it forward on the point. (This is the *pas glissé*.)
   Here it is to be noted that like the *demi-coupé* the whole *coupé*
1. can be performed on the left as well as the right leg as well as
2. forward, backward, and sideward to the left and right,
3. that the other step is not always a brush but very frequently can be a *pas ordinaire*. . . .

Tems de Courante or Pas grave—forward

Part I

1. Resting on the left leg, both knees are bent and well turned out.
2. In bending, the ankle bone of the right foot is brought close up against the back of the left one. (Some bring the right heel next to the left heel during the bending. And this is the *plié*.)

Part II

1. During the rising the right foot goes side right. Then with the heel

it is brought around the left heel to the front of the ankle [of the left]. This is the *élevé*.

2. From there it is brushed stiffly and high on the point straight forward. This is the *pas glissé*. . . .

Port de Bras of the Pas de Menuet

1. In the upbeat or last quarter note of the previous cadence while resting on the left leg but both knees bending, the arms are brought at the same time from both sides (or only one if one is leading the lady by the hand)
2. slightly bent and with cupped hands and finger ends more inward toward each other and [facing] behind one instead of away from each other sideward or forward,
3. gently fall together in front, but not all too exactly.
4. One carries them like this in the cadence (i.e., during the downbeat) and rising of the first *coupé*
5. for the duration of three quarter notes during the first two steps with the right and left leg, of which either both or only the right one is bent, and the other one executed straight.
6. With the elbows still slightly bent and the hands related,
7. very slowly and gradually they move apart from each other directly to both sides, but not all too far from the body.
8. One extends and rotates them during the extending, which coincides with the second ¾ measure, for the duration of two quarter notes stiffly under the shoulders so that the cupped hands for the most part face forward.
9. Once again they are prepared for the lowering in front which occurs on the fourth step and last quarter [note] of the measure.

And all this must be considered not only for each main *pas* in the Minuet, but also in all low chamber dances which consist of *pas de Menuet*, no matter what their names or figures.

High Port de Bras

1. Whenever the first foot [right] executes a *pas*, then (from the shoulders to the elbows both arms held nearly at the same height) at the same time the left arm, attractively bent at the hand and elbow, is carried upward to a point where the fingers are level with the ear or at least with the shoulder. The right arm is gently extended and lowered a little.
2. When the left foot performs a *pas* or movement unit, then the right arm must follow along in the above described manner, and the left arm is extended and lowered.

Pas de Menuet à deux mouvements—forward

1. If the left foot is in front not far from the right, one bends both knees gently outward (whereby the right one lifts slightly off the ground and goes to the side of the left one, so that the left supports the weight). One rises, and during the rise lifts the right foot forward. (The left one follows close to the ground to the side of the right, so that both legs close with straight knees. Consequently the weight is supported by the right leg, because the left foot which was brought up against the right may not make contact with the floor with the ball of the foot. Instead it must be well turned out and extended downward.)
2. One places the left foot (from the side) stiff and well stretched forward on the point;
3. also the right one, and brings the body weight unnoticed onto it.
4. With the weight on the right, one bends both legs. (During the bending one draws the ankle of the left foot up against the back of the right ankle, or also to the side with the heel against the right heel.) Then one rises and during this rise places the left foot (well stretched outward . . .) forward on the point and brings the body weight perpendicularly onto it.

In continuing the dancing one bends again on the left leg right away. During the bending the right heel is brought next to the left one. Thereby the next *pas* has started with this *plié*, with which some persons always conclude the Minuet *pas* for the sake of the connection [continuity]. . . .

[Like all the other basic steps, the *pas de menuet* was also done backwards and to either side. Taubert describes the execution of the step in each direction in detail.]

[Taubert here begins to describe the sequence of the performance of the Minuet.]

. . . After completing two *révérences*, as they have been described in the discussion of the dance *révérences*, one takes the lady by her left hand with the right hand and leads her through a side *pas* and a forward *pas* straight up the hall, and with two side *pas* around one half to the left coming to rest in the center of the floor facing each other, he facing down and she facing up the hall. Letting go of hands, both dance directly back and away from each other with a *pas en fleuret*. . . . Then both perform the main figure "Z" with two side *pas* to the left, two forward *pas* for the diagonal, and two side *pas* to the right. . . . The hat, which until now has been carried in the left hand, is replaced after the gentleman has passed the lady once.

From P. Rameau, *Le Maître à danser*

In the eighteenth century the King's grand ball was conducted with the strictest social decorum. The correct order of procedure stipulated that the King and Queen dance the first minuet. When His Majesty had returned to his throne (as shown in the illustration), the Queen could lead out a gentleman of her choice or could let the prince next in rank select a lady. Only one couple danced at a time.

Further, after having danced the main figure two, three, or at the most four times, they take right hands and execute one side *pas* to the left, a *contretems* straight forward, two forward *pas* in a circle, and two *pas fleuret* directly behind themselves. . . .

Immediately thereafter they take left hands and both execute a side *pas* to the right, a *contretems* forward, two forward *pas* in a circle, a *fleuret* to the right, and two *pas de Bourrée* to the left and right. . . .

Then they either dance the main figure again once or twice and then take both hands, or take hands immediately after the presentation of the left hand. This happens with a side *pas* to the left, a *contretems* straight forward (for the lady, instead of the *contretems*, we have always prescribed two *pas graves*), and three forward *pas* to the right in a circle. (Here it is to be noted that the gentleman coming downward from up the hall must describe one and one half circles in three main *pas* and therefore in the last main *pas* must turn one quarter with each of the last three steps. The lady, however, moving up from down the hall, describes only one complete circle.) Together they move to their starting place, he with a back *pas* and she with a forward *pas*, and having arrived there finish as they began with a double *révérence*. . . .

[Variations used in the Minuet]

Chassé battu or *de Gigue en tournant*—whole circle

. . . After having made the *plié* in the upbeat, the right foot chases the left foot from its place with a gentle leap, so that it comes to be in the air over the buckle of the right. In this position one makes a complete turn to the left, steps forward with the crossed over left foot, and also with the chasing right, but well outward a little to side right. In the upbeat one takes the preparation for the other *chassé*, which is executed in the same way to the right on the left foot, during the other ¾ measure.

If one wishes to precede this with a half *pirouette* with the right foot behind the left, then the left chases the right around the other half of the circle to the right. . . . But if one wishes to turn the half *pirouette* with the right in front over the left, then the *chassé battu* is completed around to the left by the right foot. . . .

It is even more pleasing if one makes a complete *pirouette* with the right over the left foot as follows: At first, having made a *plié* during the upbeat, during the first two quarter notes the right foot is thrown over the front of the left foot, and a complete turn is made on the toes with both knees straight while rising up. Then, in the third quarter while turning [the body] a little toward the left, the left foot is placed down well outward and the preparation for the *gigue chassé* is taken on it. This *pirouette* and *chassé* together take up the same amount of time as a main *pas de Menuet*, and they can be repeated.

One can also make this whole *pirouette* twice in a row to the left. And after that one can also perform the *chassé* with a complete turn twice in a row, the first one to the left and the other to the right. If there is occasion to frolic a little longer, one can also add a *pas de sissonne* with the right and left leg springing around to the right. . . .

Pas de sissonne

. . . In short: One springs either forward or backward [landing with the legs] bent and crossed so that the feet are well turned out and close together and the knees are well bent outward. The legs are closed so that the calves touch each other. In this elevation one can occasionally turn one quarter or one half. Then one springs again into the air on one leg [going from two supports to one] and at the same time again extends one foot sideward.

This crossed air step can occur on the left or right leg, as well as in front or in back of the other leg. Also, after the crossed springing sometimes the stepping foot and sometimes the other foot is lifted to the side. . . .

Straight *capriole*—from one leg onto the other

A very attractive *capriole*, used in the Minuet either in moving forward or backward across the dance floor or while standing still, is one in which one springs from one leg to the other several times in a row. Each time one makes in the air either quick little beats with both legs extended next to each other while suspended, landing with the springing foot earlier than the other one, or one beats two or three times from the side with the leg on which one lands. In that case the calves are not brought in contact with each other. One can also spring from one leg to the other so that in the air the back foot always beats over the front one.

This springing from one leg onto the other can be repeated four or eight times in the Minuet, that is, repeated four times in each dance measure. As in the main *pas de Menuet*, each time the first elevation requires two quarter notes and the second one only one quarter, the third again two, and the fourth only one quarter note of the measure. . . .

The best place for variations is at the end of the main figure in turning about. Not only has one room to turn here, especially if one prepares for it in time, but one also has the lady in line of vision and can therefore see exactly when she turns so that at all times one can continue forth with her and not confuse her with prolonged variations. . . .

In short: a well-prepared dancer must not tie himself down in the Minuet. Instead, he should mingle in this place and that place these steps, and another time those steps, but always attractively and fitting correctly into the cadence.

John Weaver (1673–1760)
THE LOVES OF MARS AND VENUS

Born in Shrewsbury, Weaver probably taught there before coming to London in 1702. We have only a few records of him as a performer, but he left us three librettos of his "dramatick entertainments of dancing" along with several major historical and theoretical works on the art. Though he apparently attracted a small, loyal following, there is no evidence that his innovations caused any great theatrical excitement; perhaps he lacked the aggressiveness of Noverre, who later proposed similar reforms, or perhaps the time was not yet ripe. Sometime after 1733 Weaver returned, contentedly it would seem, to teaching in Shrewsbury, where he was remembered as "a little dapper cheerful man."

The libretto for The Loves of Mars and Venus *shows that the verses and songs of the* Ballet Comique *have vanished and that the dancers no longer need to carry badges of identification. Now the choreographer could create individual portraits in movement—if he so wished. At this time John Weaver was practically unique in wishing to do so.*

Preface

I know it will be expected that I should give the Reader some Account of the Nature of this kind of Entertainment in Dancing, which I have here attempted to revive from the Ancients, in Imitation of their Pantomimes: I call it an Attempt, or Essay, because this is the first Trial of this Nature that has been made since the Reign of Trajan, as far as I have been able to trace it; Pliny, in his Panegyrick to that Emperor, being the last Author of the Ancients that takes any Notice of 'em:

SOURCE: *The Loves of Mars and Venus; A Dramatick Entertainment of Dancing, Attempted in Imitation of the Pantomimes of the Ancient Greeks and Romans* (London, 1717).

Therefore I am in hopes the Town will judge favourably of this Performance; and I have the more reason to depend upon their Candour on this Account, because that I have not been able to get all my Dancers equal to the Design; not but that I must acknowledge my Obligations to all the Performers for their obliging Willingness, and being ready to perform, as far as they were capable of entring into a Design so entirely novel and foreign to their present Manner of Dancing.

It will be necessary that I let my Reader know, that these Mimes and Pantomimes were Dancers that represented a Story or Fable in Motion and Measure: They were Imitators of all things, as the Name of Pantomime imports, and perform'd all by Gesture and the Action of the Hands, Fingers, Legs and Feet, without making use of the Tongue. The Face or Countenance had a large Share in this Performance, and they imitated the Manners, Passions, and Affections, by the numerous Variety of Gesticulations. And it is evident from the Writers of those Times, that they pursued the Rules of the Drama in their mute Performances, by confining each Representation to a certain Action, with a just Observation of the Manners and Passions, which that Action naturally produced. No Body can deny, but that their Performances were surprizing, and that the Difficulty of doing it appear'd almost beyond Conception; yet the Testimonies of those who saw these Things done, are too strong to suffer us to doubt of the Matter of Fact. Indeed the Force and Beauty of graceful Motion, and handsome Gesture, were so little understood amongst us some few Years ago, that it seem'd still more incredible: And I am satisfied, that the agreeable Appearance some of our best Players make upon the Stage at this Time, is as much owing to the Justness of their Action, as any other Qualification whatsoever.

In short, this is an Art or Science imitative and demonstrative, and not to be attain'd without Difficulty and Application: And a Master who would manage this Art skilfully, ought to be endued with a good Fancy, and sound Judgment, actively apt and industrious in observing Mens Natures, and assimilating their Manners, and imitating all things with Gesture; for Nature assign'd each Motion of the Mind its proper Gesticulation and Countenance, as well as Tone; whereby it is significantly and decently express'd: And indeed Decency of Expression doth so depend on this Art, that the Grammarians observe, Decency is properly spoken of Gesture.

Tho' I have endeavour'd to enter into the Characters, I represent, and describe their Manners and Passions by proper Actions and Gesture suitable to the Fable: Yet I must confess it may be objected, that I have in this Entertainment too much inclin'd to the Modern Dancing; but when the Spectator shall consider the Greatness of such a Design, and could he be apprized of the Difficulties attending such an Undertaking, with the Necessity of having both Dancers and Spectators instructed by degrees, with the Rules and Expressions of Gesticulation, I hope they will readily excuse my not sticking so very close to the Pantomime, especially since this Performance was design'd only as an Attempt to encourage others more capable of bringing it to its ancient Perfection.

Those who would know more of the Pantomimes, may look into the Essay towards the History of Dancing.

Drama

MARS,—The God of War, the Son of Juno. The Ancient Latins gave him the Title of Salisubsubus, from Dancing and Leaping; he intrigued with Venus, was discover'd in his Amour by Vulcan, and taken by him in a Net. Danc'd by Mr. Dupré, Senior.

VULCAN,—Son of Jupiter and Juno; for his Deformity Jupiter threw him down from Heaven; he fell on the Isle of Lemmos, and broke his Leg in the Fall; he kept a Forge there, and work'd for the Gods; he was Husband to Venus. Danc'd by Mr. Weaver.

VENUS,—The Goddess of Love and Beauty, was Daughter of Jupiter and Dione; she was Wife to Vulcan, and Mistress to Mars. Danc'd by Mrs. Santlow.

AGLAIA, THALIA, EUPHROSYNE, were the 3 Graces, constant Attendants on Venus/ Mrs. Bicknall, Mrs. Younger, Mrs. Willis.

THE FOUR FOLLOWERS OF MARS/ Danc'd by Mr. Prince, Mr. Bovall, Mr. Wade, Mr. Birkhead.

FOUR CYCLOPS. They were Workmen to Vulcan.

THREE MORE CYCLOPS.

GALLUS, Attendant on Mars.

ONE OF THE HOURS attending on Venus.

CUPID.

JUPITER, JUNO, APOLLO, DIANA, NEPTUNE, THETIS/ Gods and Goddesses.

SCENE I. A CAMP

The Entertainment opens with a Martial Overture; at the Conclusion of which four Followers, or Attendants of Mars, arm'd with Sword, and Target, enter and Dance a Pyrrhic to a March; then follows a Warlike Prelude which introduces Mars attended by Gallus carrying his Sword and Buckler; he performs his Entry, and then joyns in Pyrrhic Mood with his Followers; wherein he appears engaged sometimes with two at a time, and sometimes with all four: At last he clears the Stage; which finishes the Entry, and first Scene. . . .

The manner of the Performance of the Pyrrhic Dance seems to have consisted chiefly in the nimble turning of the Body, the shifting, and avoiding the Stroke of the Enemy; and therefore, this was one of the Exercises in which young Soldiers were train'd; and was in such Esteem in Thessaly that they stil'd their Princes, and Generals, Leaders of the Dance. The Nature then of this Dance being warlike; and as we have shewn, made use of by the Ancients for the Discipline and Marshalling their Soldiers, I thought it the most proper for the introducing the Character of Mars. . . .

SCENE II

After a Simphony of Flutes, etc., the Scene opens and discovers Venus in her Dressing-Room at her Toilet, attended by the Graces, who are employ'd in dressing her. Cupid lies at her Feet, and one of the Hours waits by. Venus rises, and dances a Passacaile: The Graces joyn her in the same Movement, as does also the Hour. The Dance being ended, the Tune changes to a wild rough Air. Venus, Graces, etc., seem in Surprize; and at the Approach of Vulcan, the Graces, and Cupid run off.

Enter to Venus, Vulcan: They perform a Dance together; in which Vulcan expresses his Admiration; Jealousie; Anger; and Despite; And Venus shows Neglect; Coquetry; Contempt; and Disdain.

This last Dance being altogether of the Pantomimic kind; it is necessary that the Spectator should know some of the most particular Gestures made use of therein; and what Passions, or Affections, they discover; represent; or express.

Admiration. Admiration is discover'd by the raising up of the right Hand, the Palm turn'd upwards, the Fingers clos'd; and in one Motion the Wrist turn'd round and Fingers spread; the Body reclining, and Eyes fix'd on the Object; but when it rises to

Astonishment. Both hands are thrown up towards the Skies; the Eyes also lifted up, and the Body cast backwards.

Jealousy. Jealousy will appear by the Arms suspended, or a particular pointing the middle Finger to the Eye; by an irresolute movement throughout the Scene, and a Thoughtfulness of Countenance.

Upbraiding. The Arms thrown forwards; the Palm of the Hands turn'd outward; the Fingers open, and the Elbows turn'd inward to the Breast; shew Upbraiding and Despite.

Anger. The left Hand struck suddenly with the right; and sometimes against the Breast; denotes Anger.

Threats. Threatening is express'd by raising the Hand, and shaking the bended Fist; knitting the Brow; biting the Nails, and catching back the Breath.

Power. The Arm, with impetuous Agitation, directed forwards to the Person, with an awful Look, implies Authority.

Impatience. Impatience is seen by the smiting of the Thigh, or Breast with the Hand.

Indignation. When it rises to Anguish, and Indignation, it is express'd by applying the Hand passionately to the Forehead; or by stepping back the right foot, leaning the Body quite backward, the Arms extended, Palms clos'd, and Hands thrown quite back; the Head cast back, and Eyes fix'd upwards.

These are some of the Actions made use of by Vulcan; those by Venus are as follows:—

Coquetry. Coquetry will be seen in the affected Airs, given her self throughout the whole Dance.

Neglect. Neglect will appear in the scornful turning the Neck; the flirting outward the back of the right hand, with a Turn of the Wrist.

Contempt. Contempt is express'd by scornful Smiles; forbidding Looks; tossing of the Head; filliping of the Fingers; and avoiding the Object.

Distaste. The left Hand thrust forth with the Palm turn'd backward; the left Shoulder rais'd, and the Head bearing towards the Right, denotes an Abhorrence, and Distaste.

Detestation. When both the turn'd-out Palms are so bent to the left Side, and the Head still more projected from the Object; it becomes a more passionate Form of Detestation, as being a redoubled Action.

SCENE III

With this last Action Venus quits the Stage in order to meet Mars;
  Vulcan remains, and moving up the Stage strikes at the Scene which
  opens to Vulcan's Shop, where the Cyclops are discover'd at Work;
  some at the Forge; some at the Anvil; some Hammering; and some
  Fileing; while Cupid is pointing his Arrows at the Grindlestone.
  Jupiter's Thunder; Mars's Armour; Neptune's Trident; Pallas's Spear,
  etc., are all laid on the Floor. A rough Consort of Musick is heard
  while they are at Work, adapted to the particular Sounds of the Shop;
  after which four of the Cyclops advance, and perform their Entry;
  with whom Vulcan joyns; and in the Dance, delivers Wire to the
  Cyclops to form a Net; and turns them in, to their Work, and the
  Scene shuts.

To exalt, or lift up the stretch'd-out Hand, expresses some notable Exploit in Hand.

SCENE IV—A GARDEN

A Prelude of Trumpets, Hautbois, Violins and Flutes alternate; to which
Mars with his Followers enter on one Side; and Venus, with Graces,
etc., on the other. Mars and Venus meet and embrace; Gallantry,
Respect; Ardent Love; and Adoration; appear in the Actions of Mars:
An affected Bashfulness; reciprocal Love; and wishing Looks, in Venus;
they sit on a Couch, while the four Followers of Mars begin the Entry;
to whom the Graces joyn; and Afterwards Mars and Venus: At which
time Cupid steals away the Arms of Mars and his Followers.

This Performance is alternate, as representing Love and War: It is
somewhat in Imitation of a Dancing among the Ancients, in which
the Lacedemonian Youth delighted much, as being equally inclin'd to
Love, and Arms; one singular Beauty in this sort of Dance, is; that
Strength, and Softness, reciprocally, and alternately are seen in their
full Power: when in the same Representation; and at the same time;
the Fire; Robustness; and Strength of the Warrior is seen, mixt with
the Softness, and Delicacy of Love; Boldness, and Vigour, in one, and
a coy, and complying Reluctance, in the other.

As to the Gestures made use of in this Scene; they are so obvious,
relating only to Gallantry, and Love; that they need no Explanation.

The Dance concludes, with every Man carrying off his Woman.

SCENE V

Vulcan is discover'd leaning in a thoughtful Posture on his Anvil; the
Cyclops appear working the Net; they joyn it together; Vulcan dances.
The Cyclops having finish'd, bring it forward, and shew it Vulcan,
he approves of it, and they carry it off, etc.

Pleas'd at some Contrivance. To rub the Palms of the Hands together,
after the manner as those who take Pains to heat their Hands; is an
Expression of being pleas'd at some Thought of Deceit.

SCENE VI

A soft Symphony of Flutes, to which the Scene draws and discovers
Mars and Venus sitting on a Couch; Gallus sleeping; and Cupid play-
ing; etc. Mars and Venus express by their Gesticulations, equal Love,
and Satisfaction; and a pleas'd Tenderness which supposes past
Embraces. Vulcan and Cyclops enter; the Net falls over Mars, and
Venus, who seem slumbering, and being catch'd, appear in the utmost
Confusion. An insulting Performance by Vulcan and the Cyclops.
After which enter Jupiter, Apollo, Neptune, Juno, Diana and Thetis.
Vulcan shows them his Prisoners. Shame; Confusion; Grief; and Sub-

mission, are discover'd in the Actions of Venus; Audacity, Vexation; Restlessness; and a kind of unwilling Resignation; in those of Mars. The Actions of Vulcan are of Rejoicing; Insulting; and Derision. Neptune intercedes with Vulcan for them. Vulcan at length condescends; and forgives them; and they are releas'd. Mars, with the rest of the Gods, and Goddesses, dance a Grand Dance, which concludes the Entertainment.

Triumphing. To shake the Hand open, rais'd above our Head, is an exulting Expression of Triumph, Etc.

Entreaty. The stretching out the Hands downward toward the Knees, is an Action of Entreaty, and suing for Mercy.

Grief. Grief is express'd by hanging down the Head; wringing the Hands; and striking the Breast.

Resignation. To hold out both the Hands joyn'd together, is a natural Expression of Submission and Resignation.

Forgiveness. To extend and offer out the Right Hand, is a Gesture of Pitty, and Intention of Forgiveness.

Shame. The covering the Face with the Hand, is a Sign of Shame.

Reconciliation. To shake the given Hand, or embrace the Body, is an Expression of Friendship, Reconciliation, and the like.

FINIS

Jean Georges Noverre (1727–1810)
TWO LETTERS ON DANCING
Translated by Cyril W. Beaumont

Trained at the Paris Opéra, Noverre longed to be ballet master there, a goal he achieved in 1776 only to leave a few years later, embittered by jealousies and intrigues. Previously he had served the courts of Stuttgart and Vienna, where he taught the young Marie Antoinette. Noverre's first visit to London was nearly disastrous due to the outbreak of hostilities between England and France, but his later engagements there met with great success. Acclaimed by many of his contemporaries as a genius whose works were unsurpassed for taste and imagination, Noverre excited less enthusiasm for his backstage behavior, being

SOURCE: II and IV from *Letters on Dancing and Ballets* (London: Beaumont, 1951)

recalled as "a passionate little fellow" who "swore and tore behind the scenes."

The temperament is amply evident in the famous **Lettres sur la danse et les ballets,** *which was first published in Stuttgart in 1760 and went through several editions in the author's lifetime. Here he inveighs against prevailing customs of costume design; the use of masks that hid the potentially expressive features of the dancers; the composition of dances to suit the personality and skills of the performer rather than the dramatic needs of the role. Unlike Weaver, Noverre attracted disciples, who carried on his concepts of the* ballet d'action *in spite of the cool indifference of the Paris Opéra.*

Letter II

I cannot refrain, Sir, from expressing my disapproval of those *maîtres de ballet* who have the ridiculous obstinacy to insist that the members of the *corps de ballet* shall take them as a model and regulate their movements, gestures and attitudes accordingly. May not such a singular claim prevent the development of the executants' natural graces and stifle their innate powers of expression?

This principle appears to me the more dangerous in that it is rare to meet with *maîtres de ballet* capable of real feeling; so few of them are excellent actors competent to depict in gesture the thoughts they wish to express. It is so difficult, I say, to meet with a modern Bathyllus or Pylades, that I cannot avoid condemning all those who, from self-conceit, have the pretension to imitate them. If their powers of emotion be weak, their powers of expression will be likewise; their gestures will be feeble, their features characterless, and their attitudes devoid of passion. Surely, to induce the *figurants* to copy so mediocre a model is to lead them astray? Is not a production marred when it is awkwardly executed? Moreover, is it possible to lay down fixed rules for pantomimic action? Are not gestures the offspring of feeling and the faithful interpreters of every mood?

In these circumstances, a careful *maître de ballet* should act like the majority of poets who, having neither the talent nor the natural gifts necessary to declamation, have their works recited and rely entirely on the intelligence of the actors for their interpretation. They are present, you will say, at the rehearsals. I agree, but less to lay down precepts than to offer advice. "This scene appears to me feeble; in another, your delivery is weak; this incident is not acted with sufficient fire, and the picture which results from that situation leaves something to be desired": that is how the poet speaks. The *maître de ballet*, for his part, must continually rehearse a mimed scene until the performers have arrived

JASON ET MEDEE.   BALLET TRAGIQUE.

In a scene from Noverre's *Jason and Medea*, as performed in London in 1781, the dancers are (left to right) Giovanna Baccelli, Gaëtan Vestris, and Madame Simonet. Noverre based many of his ballets on the plots of such classical Greek tragedies. The histrionic gestures, which seem exaggerated to us, are similar to those depicted in contemporary prints of actors and probably show the influence of the style of David Garrick.

at that moment of expression innate in mankind, a precious moment which is revealed with both strength and truth when it is the outcome of feeling.

A well-composed ballet is a living picture of the passions, manners, customs, ceremonies and customs of all nations of the globe, consequently, it must be expressive in all its details and speak to the soul through the eyes; if it be devoid of expression, of striking pictures, of strong situations, it becomes a cold and dreary spectacle. This form of art will not admit of mediocrity; like the art of painting, it exacts a perfection the more difficult to acquire in that it is dependent on the faithful imitation of nature, and it is by no means easy, if not almost impossible, to seize on that kind of seductive truth which, masking illusion from the spectator, transports him in a moment to the spot where the action has taken place and fills him with the same thoughts that he would experience were he to witness in reality the incident which art has presented to him in counterfeit. What accuracy is required to avoid passing above, or falling below, the model it is desired to copy! To over-refine a model is as dangerous as to disfigure it: these two faults are equally opposed to truth; the one transcends nature, the other degrades it.

Ballets, being representations, should unite the various parts of the drama. Themes expressed in dancing are, for the most part, devoid of sense, and offer a confused medley of scenes as ill-connected as they are ill-ordered; however, in general, it is imperative to submit to certain principles. The subject of every ballet must have its introduction, plot and climax. The success of this type of entertainment depends partly on the careful choice of subjects and their arrangement. . . .

Diana and Acteon, Diana and Endymion, Apollo and Daphne, Tito and Aurora, Acis and Galatea, as well as all other themes of this nature, cannot provide the plot for a *ballet d'action* without the inspiration of truly poetic genius. Telemachus, in the Isle of Calypso, offers a wider field and would provide the theme for a very fine ballet, always presuming the composer had the skill to omit everything of no value to a painter, to introduce Mentor at the right moment, and to remove him the instant his presence became superfluous.

If the licence that is taken daily in theatrical productions cannot be stretched so far as to make Mentor dance in the ballet of Telemachus, then it is a more than sufficient reason that the composer should not employ this character save with the greatest caution. If he do not dance he is foreign to the ballet, besides, his powers of expression, being deprived of the graces which dancing affords to gestures and attitudes, would make him appear less animated, less passionate, and consequently of less interest. A genius may break ordinary rules and advance by new paths when they lead to the perfection of his art. . . .

Mentor, in a ballet, can and ought to dance. This will offend against neither truth nor probability, provided that the composer has the skill to devise for him a manner of dancing and expression consonant with his character, age and employment. I believe, Sir, that I would hazard the adventure, and that I should avoid the greater of two evils, that sense of tedium which should never be experienced by the spectator. . . .

Undoubtedly, one of the essential points in a ballet is variety; the incidents and pictures which result from it should succeed each other with rapidity; if the action do not move quickly, if the scenes drag, if enthusiasm be not communicated everywhere equally; indeed, if the ballet do not constantly increase in interest and attraction in proportion to the development of the theme; the plan is ill-conceived, ill-ordered; it sins against the laws of the theatre, and the representation has no other effect on the spectator than that of the boredom induced by it. . . .

Every complicated and long-drawn-out ballet which does not explain to me, simply and clearly, the action which it represents, the plot of which I cannot follow without constant reference to the programme—every ballet of which I do not understand the plan, which does not afford me an introduction, plot and climax—will be no more, in my opinion, than a simple entertainment based on dancing, more or less well executed. It will move me but little, since it will be expressionless and devoid of action and interest.

But the dancing of our time is beautiful, it will be said, able to captivate and please, even when it does not possess the feeling and wit with which you wish it to be embellished. I will admit that the mechanical execution of that art has been brought to a degree of perfection which leaves nothing to be desired; I will even add that it often has grace and nobility; but these represent only a portion of the qualities which it should possess.

Steps, the ease and brilliancy of their combination, equilibrium, stability, speed, lightness, precision, the opposition of the arms with the legs—these form what I term the mechanism of the dance. When all these movements are not directed by genius, and when feeling and expression do not contribute their powers sufficiently to affect and interest me, I admire the skill of the human machine, I render justice to its strength and ease of movement, but it leaves me unmoved, it does not affect me or cause me any more sensation than this arrangement of the following words: *Fait . . . pas . . . le . . . la . . . honte . . . non . . . crime . . . et . . . l'échafaud.* But when these words are ordered by a poet they compose this beautiful line spoken by the Comte d'Essex:—

Le crime fait la honte, et non pas l'échafaud. [1]

It may be concluded from this comparison that dancing is possessed of all the advantages of a beautiful language, yet it is not sufficient to know the alphabet alone. But when a man of genius arranges the letters to form words and connects the words to form sentences, it will cease to be dumb; it will speak with both strength and energy; and then ballets will share with the best plays the merit of affecting and moving, and of making tears flow, and, in their less serious styles, of being able to amuse, captivate and please. And dancing, embellished

---

[1] The crime causes the shame and not the scaffold. A celebrated passage from Act 4, Scene 3 of the *Comte d'Essex* (1678) by the playwright Thomas Corneille (1625–1709). The phrase is imitated from Tertullian—*martyrem fecit causa, non poena.*

with feeling and guided by talent, will at last receive that praise and applause which all Europe accords to poetry and painting, and the glorious rewards with which they are honoured.

Letter IV

. . . Painting and dancing have this advantage over the other arts, that they are of every country, of all nations; that their language is universally understood, and that they achieve the same impression everywhere.

If our art, imperfect as it is, seduce and captivate the spectator: if dancing stripped of the charm of expression sometimes occasion us trouble and emotion, and throw our thoughts into a pleasing disorder; what power and domination might it not achieve over us if its movements were directed by brains and its pictures painted with feeling? There is no doubt that ballets will rival painting in attraction when the executants display less of the automaton and the composers are better trained.

A fine picture is but the image of nature; a finished ballet is nature herself, embellished with every ornament of the art. If a painted canvas convey to me a sense of illusion, if I am carried away by the skill of the delineator, if I am moved by the sight of a picture, if my captivated thoughts are affected in a lively manner by this enchantment, if the colours and brush of the skilful artist react on my senses so as to reveal to me nature, to endow her with speech so that I fancy I hear and answer her, how shall my feelings be wrought upon, what shall I become, and what will be my sensations, at the sight of a representation still more veracious and rendered by the histrionic abilities of my fellow-creatures? What dominion will not living and varied pictures possess over my imagination? Nothing interests man so much as humanity itself. Yes, Sir, it is shameful that dancing should renounce the empire it might assert over the mind and only endeavour to please the sight. A beautiful ballet is, up to the present, a thing seen only in the imagination; like the Phoenix it is never found.

It is a vain hope to re-model the dance, so long as we continue to be slaves to the old methods and ancient traditions of the *Opéra*. At our theatres we see only feeble copies of the copies that have preceded them; let us not practise steps only, let us study the passions. In training ourselves to feel them, the difficulty of expressing them will vanish, then the features will receive their impressions from the sentiments within, they will give force to exterior movements and paint in lines of fire the disorder of the senses and the tumult which reigns in the breast.

Dancing needs only a fine model, a man of genius, and ballets will change their character. Let this restorer of the true dance appear, this reformer of bad taste and of the vicious customs that have impoverished the art; but he must appear in the capital. If he would persuade, let him open the eyes of our young dancers and say to them:—"Children of Terpsichore, renounce *cabrioles, entrechats* and over-complicated steps; abandon grimaces to study sentiments, artless graces and expression; study how to make your gestures noble, never forget that it is the life-blood of dancing; put judgment and sense into your *pas de deux*; let will-power order their course and good taste preside over all situations; away with those lifeless masks but feeble copies of nature; they hide your features, they stifle, so to speak, your emotions and thus deprive you of your most important means of expression; take off those enormous wigs and those gigantic head-dresses which destroy the true proportions of the head with the body; discard the use of those stiff and cumbersome hoops which detract from the beauties of execution, which disfigure the elegance of your attitudes and mar the beauties of contour which the bust should exhibit in its different positions.

"Renounce that slavish routine which keeps your art in its infancy; examine everything relative to the development of your talents; be original; form a style for yourselves based on your private studies; if you must copy, imitate nature, it is a noble model and never misleads those who follow it.

"As for you young men who aspire to be *maîtres de ballet* and think that to achieve success it is sufficient to have danced a couple of years under a man of talent, you must begin by acquiring some of this quality yourselves. Devoid of enthusiasm, wit, imagination, taste and knowledge, would you dare set up as painters? You wish for an historical theme and know nothing of history! You fly to poets and are unacquainted with their works! Apply yourselves to the study of them so that your ballets will be complete poems. Learn the difficult art of selection. Never undertake great enterprises without first making a careful plan; commit your thoughts to paper; read them a hundred times over; divide your drama into scenes; let each one be interesting and lead in proper sequence, without hindrance or superfluities, to a well-planned climax; carefully eschew all tedious incidents, they hold up the action and spoil its effect. Remember that *tableaux* and groups provide the most delightful moments in a ballet.

"Make your *corps de ballet* dance, but, when it does so, let each member of it express an emotion or contribute to form a picture; let them mime while dancing so that the sentiments with which they are imbued may cause their appearance to be changed at every moment. If their gestures and features be constantly in harmony with their feelings, they will be expressive accordingly and give life to the representation. Never go to a rehearsal with a head stuffed with new figures and devoid of sense. Acquire all the knowledge you can of the matter you have in hand. Your imagination, filled with the picture you wish to represent, will provide you with the proper figures, steps and gestures. Then your compositions will glow with fire and strength, they cannot but be true to nature if you are full of your subject. Bring love as well as enthusiasm to your art. To be successful in theatrical representations, the heart must be touched, the soul moved and the imagination inflamed.

Section Three

THE INVASION OF THE AIR: THE ROMANTIC ERA

The era of the romantic ballet was one of the greatest that theatrical dance has ever known. It resulted from a marvelous simultaneity of developments: of ideas, technical progress, mechanical inventions, and—inevitably—the appearance of persons of genius who could mold the disparate elements into a single artistic entity.

In the last years of the eighteenth century the Paris Opéra, under the despotic direction of Pierre Gardel, stubbornly perpetuated ballets based on the old Greek myths that no longer had much appeal for the general audience. In spite of a few ventures into patriotic propaganda just after the French Revolution, choreography remained dignified, calculated, cold. The popularity of Jean Dauberval's *La Fille Mal Gardée* should have warned Gardel that tastes were changing. So should the success in London of Charles Didelot's *Flore et Zéphire* in 1796. Though still of classical derivation, the plot of this ballet was treated much like a pretty romance whose protagonists merely happened to be gods. Most important in the ballet was Didelot's use of flying, the dancers' aerial travels made possible by invisible wires attached to their waists. Audiences were equally enchanted by other Didelot ballets that employed picturesque settings—Scotland was used in one, Poland in another—for here was a new kind of subject matter for ballet. But Didelot did not combine the themes of ethereal creatures and exotic lands. That was yet to come.

In Paris, while the Opéra remained stuffy, the popular stages did not. The boulevard theatres, as they were known, catered to a less elite audience—the rising middle class—which liked exciting action, a bit of mystery, and a touch of bourgeois sentiment. From these boulevard houses came melodramas of Jocko, a Brazilian ape; of the Incas of Peru; of Captain Cook in Tahiti—all later made into successful ballets. The noble savage—untutored, spontaneous in action, motivated by feeling rather than decorum—was replacing the classical hero.

At the 1830 premiere of Victor Hugo's *Hernani*, which extolled the image of the passionate social outlaw, Théophile Gautier appeared wearing flowing hair to his shoulders and a brilliant rose-colored waistcoat. He became a symbol of the romantic revolution.

The new themes demanded a new style of dancing—freer, lighter, more versatile. And at this very time the dancer's technique had advanced to a point where such a style was possible. In Carlo Blasis' *Code of Terpsichore* (1820) we see the legs rotated to a full 180 degree turnout. The ballet class had become codified into a progressive set of exercises, starting with simple, controlled movements, then building up to the most complex and vigorous leaps and turns. Such scientific training stimulated the rapid progress of technical mastery. New strength produced a new style, *ballonée*, as opposed to the earlier *terre à terre* manner.

Women were discovering their special technical innovation. Probably it evolved gradually, for we have no record of anyone suddenly exclaiming, "Look, she's dancing on the tips of her toes!" But she was. At first it was very likely a momentary pose, then a few fleeting steps, and then a few more. In time the ballerina learned to reinforce the tips of her slippers with darning to provide a touch of support (the blocked toe shoe came much later), and her new-found strength provoked fresh experiments. There was the fascination of a protracted balance in *arabesque*, the back leg extended waist high; there was the *bourrée*, rapid little running steps on the *pointes*. But more than the creation of individual steps, the technique eventually engendered a wholly new way of moving.

Our first evidence of *pointe* work comes from engravings that date before 1820 and that show women hovering somewhat awkwardly on their narrow supports. But it took another decade for the technique to find its true function. Then Marie Taglioni—painfully thin, round-shouldered, with arms too long for her body—nurtured her capacities for speed and lightness so that the audience had no time to notice her defects. In 1831 her teacher and father, Filippo, presented her in Paris in the opera *Robert le Diable*, in which she led a group of dead nuns in an eerie scene of supernatural spirits. But the success of this work was only the harbinger of her first really great triumph, which came the following year in *La Sylphide*.

In this ballet the themes of romanticism—the ethereal and the exotic—were combined and enhanced by the technical innovations of the past decade. The sylphide is the ideal but unattainable woman who lures the Scotsman James away from his peasant sweetheart and off into the misty highlands, where he seeks in vain to tame her evasive flights. The essence of a dream, the sylphide skims over the stage on her delicate *pointes*; unlike earthly creatures she seems unconstrained by the laws of gravity. In *La Sylphide* a technical achievement had acquired a dramatic motivation.

Helping the illusion considerably were the varied effects of illumination now possible because of the introduction of gas lighting. Even more recent was the practice of lowering the curtain between the acts of a play or ballet so that the audience did not see the mechanics of scene changing. Now too the lights in the auditorium were lowered while the spectacle was on, and new rules banished boisterous members of the audience from sitting on the stage to watch the performance. Music had become less formal, more descriptive and evocative. And there was the novel costume devised for the ballerina—a fitted bodice topping a buoyant skirt of white gauze. The sylphide indeed seemed to float on waves of mist and moonlight, an apparition of loveliness, untouchable and all the more desirable for being unreal.

Parisian women dressed their hair "à la Sylphide" and "taglioniser" became a verb. Later London and St. Petersburg were equally enchanted with this and other ballets that Filippo Taglioni created for his daughter. A Russian critic wrote that "it is impossible to describe the suggestion she conveyed of aerial flight, the fluttering of wings, the soaring in the air, alighting on flowers and gliding over the mirror-like surface of a river. . . ."

But it was Paris that set the fashions. At the Opéra, Director Louis Véron inaugurated the star system and, in 1834 when his success with Taglioni had been generally acknowledged, he cleverly turned his attention to promoting a rival, arousing even greater interest—and box-office receipts—by stirring up a popular controversy. Gautier characterized Taglioni as a Christian dancer, Fanny Elssler as a pagan; and he found the virginal grace of the former less to his taste than the sensuous passion of the latter. Though Elssler was also admired for her elegance, grace, and lightness, the Viennese ballerina excelled in those earthy dances of other lands that had become so popular as a foil to the flights of the sylphide. In particular, Gautier delighted in Elssler's Cachucha:

Now she darts forward; the castanets begin their sonorous chatter. With her hand she seems to shake down great clusters of rhythm. How she twists, how she bends! What fire! What voluptuousness! What precision! Her swooning arms toss about her drooping head, her body curves backwards, her white shoulders almost graze the ground.

No wonder that when she danced in Washington Congress had to adjourn for lack of a quorum! In Transcendental Boston, Margaret Fuller exclaimed, "This is poetry." But Ralph Waldo Emerson replied, "No, it is religion."

The romantic ballet that is still most widely performed today was inspired by a ballerina who combined the ethereal qualities of Taglioni with the dramatic powers of Elssler. Gautier conceived the scenario of *Giselle* (1841) as a vehicle for Carlotta Grisi. Early in the ballet she was an innocent peasant girl; later, having died for the love of a count in rustic disguise, she reappeared as a spirit, forgiving but elusive. In the first part she was said to be "nature and artlessness personified"; in the second she exhibited "lightness . . . a chaste and refined seductiveness." Adolphe Adam's music, with its extensive use of leitmotifs associated with dramatic episodes, set a high standard. Though the choreography was officially credited to the Paris Opéra ballet master Jean Coralli, it was generally known that Grisi's husband, Jules Perrot, had composed most of her dances. Having started his career in the boulevard theatres, Perrot was adept at inventing expressive movement, as he was to prove in later works that acknowledged his authorship.

Perrot was almost unique in this period for being recognized as a great male performer. On the whole, this was a time of eclipse for the male dancer. With the development of *pointe* work and the emergence of the sylphide character, attention was focused on the ballerina. Innovations in theme, in technique, costume, all centered on her. The concept was epitomized in 1845 when Benjamin Lumley, director of Her Majesty's Theatre in London, gathered together four outstanding ballerinas to perform a *pas de quatre* especially choreographed for them by Perrot. Joining Taglioni and Grisi were the fleet-footed Italian Fanny Cerrito and the poetic Dane Lucile Grahn.

It was Grahn who created the title role in the Danish version of *La Sylphide* (1836), choreographed by August Bournonville. Apart from this one production, Bournonville generally domesticated the romantic themes of the period into cozy romances, ending with happy village weddings that were celebrated with brilliantly theatricalized folk dances. The majority of his ballets were simple love stories, full of the *joie de vivre* that critic Svend Kragh-Jacobsen has noted as the special distinction of the Danish style. Bournonville's choreography reflected the qualities he attributed to himself: "I danced with virility, my spirit and my energy have created the same impression in every theatre. I brought joy to the audience, and before they admired me they had to like me."

At this same time Italy was turning to melodrama: kidnapped princesses, swashbuckling outlaws, chaste heroines, valiant lovers, and cruel villains were rampant on stages from Milan to Naples. Since the plots were extraordinarily complicated, a distinctive system of double casting was employed: *ballerini per le parte* mimed the action with stylized, rhythmical gestures; *ballerini* performed the dances that were inserted wherever the plot could be made to justify an entertainment or a celebration. The arrangement, similar to the recitative-aria division of opera, seemed to satisfy both the adherents of the *ballet d'action* and the devotees of virtuosity; actually, it obliterated the touchstone of expressive movement that marked the peak of the romantic ballet.

Meanwhile, the romantic style had found its way to America. In the United States, ballet had gotten off to a slow start. Prior to the War of Independence, Puritan morality had inhibited the development of any kind of theatre, for playhouses were referred to as "schools of seduction" and "resorts of the licentious"; even in 1784 entertainments were cautiously advertised as "lectures." The first native American dancer was John Durang, whose specialty was the hornpipe. Largely self-taught, he was soon outshone by foreign, classically trained performers who began to arrive in the early 1790's as refugees from the French Revolution. Most prominent among them was the notable rope-dancer, acrobat, actor, singer, and choreographer Alexandre Placide. For some time Durang appeared with the Placide company, whose repertory included "heroic pantomimes" on historical themes as well as "dancing ballets" of pastoral romances. While some patriotic spectacles commemorated the 4th of July and the birthday of George Washington, the basis of the repertory consisted of adaptations of ballets that the new Americans remembered from their European performances.

In 1837, as the romantic ballet was flourishing abroad, two young girls made a joint debut in Philadelphia. Mary Ann Lee was to enjoy a brief but important career. After a period of study in Paris, where she learned several of the currently popular ballets, she returned to the United States, becoming the first American to dance *Giselle*. When she performed the famous role a Boston critic reported the "loud and continued plaudits at the grace and agility of the beautiful heroine," and added that "her salient qualifications evinced a truthfulness of action that conveyed as plainly almost as in language the feelings and passions of the character." The other debutante, Augusta Maywood, left the United States in 1839, never to return. In the course of a brilliant career, Maywood danced throughout Europe, enjoying particular success in the course of twelve years spent in Italy, where she was called "the queen of the air." Rather ironically, one of her triumphs was in a ballet based on an American novel; *I Bianchi ed i Negri* was Giuseppe Rota's version of *Uncle Tom's Cabin*.

From 1840 to 1842 Elssler toured America. Since ballets with large casts obliged her to assemble additional performers in each city where she appeared, a number of Americans had the opportunity of dancing with her. Probably the most important of these was George Washington Smith. In the remarkable years that followed his tours with Elssler, Smith supported a number of other visiting European ballerinas, partnered Mary Ann Lee in *Giselle*, choreographed for companies of Spanish dancers, and staged a number of ballets from the romantic repertory. He was the first outstanding male classical dancer of American origin.

By around 1850 the romantic ballet had run its course in both Europe and America. The fashion for sylphs had faded, leaving ballerinas with *pointe* work and male dancers with nothing much to do. Men's roles were commonly assumed by women, a matter that seemed satisfactory enough to the audience, for one critic remarked of a *travesti* performer that she "dances as much like a man as can be desired"—meaning not too much.

Tastes turned to spectacle. *The Black Crook,* premiered in New York in 1866, established a vogue for extravaganzas. The Italian ballerinas Marie Bonfanti and Rita Sangalli were deemed "exceedingly graceful"; but observers were most impressed by the production's "startling transformations," "elegant scenes," "brilliant effects," "lavish richness," and "barbaric splendor." Fairies floated on silver couches; chariots descended from clouds. With constant revivals, *The Black Crook* ran for some forty years.

European ballet moved in similar directions. A single work has survived from this time: *Coppélia*, choreographed in 1870 in Paris by Arthur Saint-Léon. The hero was danced in *travesti*, but the mischievous heroine delighted audiences by pretending to be a doll come to life, and Delibes' music enhanced the entire work. In the period since the demise of the romantic ballet, only two potential ballerinas had appeared: Emma Livry, a protégée of the aging Taglioni, and Giuseppina Bozzachi, who created the leading role in *Coppélia* at the age of seventeen. Both died tragically young. Ballet in Western Europe went into a state of decline. Now it was Russia's turn.

G. Léopold Adice
AN ACCOUNT OF THE PRINCIPLES OF OUR TRADITIONS
Translated from the French by Leonore Loft

After more than a decade of performing at the Paris Opéra, Adice taught the male dancers there from 1848 to 1863. He was then the instructor for the elementary boys' class until his retirement in 1867.

We have no records prior to the nineteenth century of the structure of a ballet class, but the lesson described by Blasis in Code of Terpsichore *(1820) was probably the culmination of a form that had been evolving for some time. The development of intensive training was certainly accelerated by the needs of the romantic choreographers, who required dancers with strength and control to realize their characterizations. The class described by Adice is aimed at nurturing energy and endurance; the emphasis is on sustained movement, what Blasis called* grands temps *and we now call* adagio. *The dancers acquired precision by the daily execution of set exercises. Blasis says they should be done "with the hand resting on something firm"; Adice names the support—it is a* barre. *Writing in a period of decadence, he urges a return to the high standards of the romantic ballet. If this is the class that Filippo Taglioni gave to his daughter Marie, we can appreciate the story that she fainted when it was over.*

After I have extolled traditional dance and disapproved of the new methods with such vigor, both young students and advanced dancers, always desirous of improvement, would without doubt like to know exactly what these traditions are . . . A description given by Blasis of the daily exercises used in his time . . . provides details on the first dance exercises the students had to execute in their classes. . . .

"The student first practices *pliés* in all positions, then both *grands* and *petits battements*, *ronds de jambe sur terre*, and *en l'air*, followed by *petits battements sur le cou-de-pied*. He must then go on to *temps de courante simples* and *composés* [with any kind of elaboration], *coupés* in first position, then in second position, and then *composés*. He will then do *attitudes*, *grands ronds de jambe*, and *temps de chaconne*, and finally *grands fouettés de face* [*flic-flac*] and *en tournant*, *quarts de tour*, *pas de bourrée*, and several combinations using various kinds of *pirouettes*.

SOURCE: From *Théorie de la gymnastique de la danse théâtrale* (Paris, 1859).

"These exercises serve to form a good dancer and to give him the means to succeed."

Let us remember these final words, for we shall need to cite them frequently as we continue.

"The lesson ends with *pirouettes, temps terre à terre*, and *temps de vigueur*."

Such was the lesson that we executed each morning without fail, and often, in order to hasten our progress, we would repeat parts of it alone during the day when we had returned home.

Now we are going to complete what M. Blasis has given us. We shall describe this lesson in detail. . . .

"The student first practices *pliés*. . . .

What is indicated here is all our basic elementary exercises at the *barre*, for in those days, whatever the level or strength of the dancer, he never allowed himself to begin work in the center without having first spent a half hour at the *barre*. This was not done as it is today, by simply extending the legs in some isolated exercise, which may have

From Carlo Blasis, *Code of Terpsichore*

Here Blasis illustrates the correct manner of standing in third and fourth positions as well as the proper height and form of a *grand battement* in second position and in fourth (facing page). Although third position is seldom used any more and contemporary choreographers expect extensions considerably higher than the hip level shown here, the degree of turnout and the placement of the body demanded by Blasis would be perfectly satisfactory in today's ballet classroom.

some use though it is done without care and as if it were of little consequence, but rather by making an integral sequence of all the exercises that we are about to describe, still in keeping with the text of M. Blasis.

"Practice *pliés* in all positions." The five principal positions. In first, in second, in third with the right leg in front, repeat placing the same leg in back; in fourth with the right leg in front and once again placing the same leg in back; in fifth with the right leg in front and then with the same leg in back. Six *pliés* in each position, three slow and three sharp, or accelerated. There are forty-eight *pliés* altogether.

One then went on to the *grands battements*. These were done in the following manner: *grand battement* in fourth position front with the right leg; repeat with the left leg. *Grand battement* in second [closing in] front with the right leg; repeat with the left. *Grand battement* in fourth position back with the right leg; repeat with the left leg. *Grand battement* in second [closing in] back with the right leg; the same with the left. Sixteen for each leg [in each position]; in all, there are one hundred and twenty-eight.

Then follow the *petits battements*, which are *petits battements glissés par terre* from the third position *élémentaire* [with the whole foot on the floor] to the second position *dérivée* [*pointe tendue*]. Thus: *petits battements glissés* in front with the right leg; repeat with the left leg. *Petits battements glissés* in back with the right leg; repeat with the left leg. Twenty-four for each leg [in each direction]; ninety-six in total.

Then *ronds de jambe sur terre*. These include *petits ronds de jambe arrondis par terre* without leaving the floor, passing through first position *élémentaire* each time. Thus, *petits ronds de jambe arrondis par terre en dehors* with the right leg; repeat with the left leg. *Petits ronds de jambe arrondis par terre en dedans* with the right leg; the same with the left. Thirty-two for each leg [in each direction]; in all, one hundred and twenty-eight.

And *en l'air*. These are the same *petits ronds de jambe* that are done in demi-second position [extended only halfway to the side], always with the lower part of the leg curved and the knee firmly turned out. Thus, *petits ronds de jambe* in demi-second position *en dehors* with the right leg; repeat with the left. *Petits ronds de jambe* in demi-second position *en dedans* with the right leg; repeat with the left. In all, one hundred and twenty-eight.

After this, *petits battements sur le cou-de-pied*, etc. Here Blasis has once again failed to indicate slow and rapid steps. Let us first describe the slow ones. These slow *petits battements sur le cou-de-pied* are those that all students know and execute by placing the leg in demi-second position while simultaneously bringing [the lower part of] the same leg in and extending it in a straight line, bringing the foot to the inner [front or back] ankle once and once to the outer [side] ankle, without changing the position of the knee. Thus, slow *petits battements sur le cou-de-pied* with the right leg; repeat with the left leg; thirty-two for each leg; sixty-four altogether. Rapid *petits battements sur le cou-de-pied* with the right leg; repeat with the left leg. Sixty for each leg; in all, one hundred and twenty. A total of six hundred and forty-eight gymnastic movements before going on to the lesson in the center!!. . . .

Now all this difficult work, which frightens you, was merely a preliminary exercise. After the work at the *barre*, the dancers moved to the center of the floor to repeat exactly the same exercises without holding on before proceeding to the *aplombs* [exercises of balance]; and this, as has already been said, was done every day and even twice a day. M. Blasis can testify to this.

Now we come to the lesson done in the center of the floor. Once again we shall take the text of M. Blasis while adding commentaries as we go along. The *temps de courant*, *simples* and *composés*. This is an exercise now given only to young beginners to practice; artists have rejected it, feeling that it has little importance to their training and improvement. There are even those who are literally ignorant of the sequence, which is composed of *pliés* in third and in second *élémentaire*, with rounded movements of the arms *en dehors* and *en dedans*; first simple, which means with only one movement of the arm, and then *composé*, which indicates a doubling of this same movement with both arms moving in opposite directions. This was done four times *en descendant* [downstage; that is, forwards] and four times *en montant* [upstage, backwards] simple, and the same thing *composé*, so that this same sequence was repeated sixteen times, with thirty-two *pliés*, serving as a prelude to the lesson in the center—after the exercises described above, of course. These sequences were meant to prepare the arms, the body, and above all the hips, the knees, and the insteps, for the *temps d'aplomb* that were to follow. . . .

Then they did *demi-coupés* in first, in second, and *composés*. This study is at present completely ignored in all classes. It is done with preparation in third position *élémentaire, dégagé* to second *dérivée*, return and *coupé* right to first *élémentaire*. While in *demi-plié, coupé* right in front to fourth *dérivée*, placing the heel *par terre* in line for *coupé* and *dégagé* with the other leg in *grande seconde,* lowering it and placing it in second *dérivée*, and begin the sequence once again in order to work out the opposite leg. The same thing is done *en montant*; however, after having completed *coupé* from second *dérivée* to first *élémentaire* and *demi-plié*, one continues with *dégagé* to fourth *dérivée* in back, placing the heel in line for *coupé* and *dégagé* with the other leg in *grande seconde*, lowering it once again to second *dérivée*. One then begins the sequence once again from the opposite side. The word *"composé"* merely indicates that when the same sequence is done again it is done in double time, and when the leg is in *grande seconde* one is slowly turning on *demi-pointe* in a *tour d'aplomb en dehors*. Similarly, *en montant*, this is done with a *demi-tour, grand rond de jambe*, and *tour d'aplomb en dedans*. Then beginning once again and immediately afterwards, doubling the same sequence *en descendant* and *en montant*, with a *grand rond de jambe* and *double tour d'aplomb en dehors* and *en dedans*. Four times *en descendant* and four times *en montant*. In all, there are thirty-two *coupés*.

Then came the *attitudes*. These were not done, as they are now, with simple poses and easy transitions of short duration, but rather as in the preceding sequence, with a long, integrated series involving a preparation of *demi-coupés* in third, one of *relevés* in fourth, and *jetée allongée*. Four *en descendant* and four *en montant en face*, with the preparation of *demi-coupé*. The same number is done *en descendant* and *en montant*, with the preparation of *relevé* in fourth and *jetée allongée*; repeat *en tournant*; one turn, again with two turns. In all, there are thirty-two *attitudes*.

Then follow the *grands fouettés de face* and *en tournant*, not in ornamental poses, as students say now, or in detached steps, but once again by an extended sequence of twelve *en face* and the same number *en tournant*, beginning with one for each leg, two and then three *en face*, and similarly with one, two and three turns after having done them *en face*. In sum, there are twenty-four *fouettés*.

Then the class continued with *temps de chaconne*, or *fouettés ballottés*; not two *en face* and two *en tournant*, as children do, but by connecting twenty-four *posés*, beginning very slowly and accelerating progressively into the *enchaînement sauté*, all in one breath and without interruption. In all, forty *fouettés ballottés*.

Then they proceeded to the quarter turns, not interrupted by resting after each half-sequence, but done all together; first *en face* and then *en tournant*, both *en dehors* and *en dedans*, eight *en face*, eight turns *en dehors* by quarter turns, four by half turns and two with one turn. Exactly the same number is done *en tournant en dedans*. There are thirty-six in total.

Several combinations using various different kinds of *pirouettes* followed. These combinations were preparations for *pirouettes* in *grande seconde en face*, beginning with one, two, and three for each leg. This has been eliminated from modern teaching, as have preparations for *pirouettes en face d'attitude*, done in a similar way, with one, two, and three for each leg. Finally they did preparations for *pirouettes sur le cou-de-pied*, not in an isolated and interrupted manner as they are done today, when by chance—once or twice a month—someone really wants to practice them; but each day, on a regular basis and without fail, in studies of sequences of one, two, and three for each leg *en face* and *d'aplomb en tournant*. Altogether, there were forty-eight preparations for *pirouettes en face* before going on to the prolonged execution *en tournant*. . . .

There are other studies in *pirouettes*, which Blasis has forgotten. . . . These were *pirouettes* in *grande seconde* and *pirouettes serrées sur le cou-de-pied*, in *grande seconde serrée en attitude*, in *grande seconde liée* with *arabesque*, and *pirouettes, renversées, simples,* and *composés*, each in a series of three, six, or even more, depending upon the inclinations of the dancer. And to finish off the session, the class attacked the *temps terre à terre* and the *temps de vigueur*. The latter were sequences of *entrechats sous le corps* [without traveling], of *ronds de jambe, brisés,* of *entrechats à cinq,* of *fouettés sautés,* of *sissonnes*. These were designated by the name of *entrée de ronds de jambe, entrée de fouettés,* etc., and from them each dancer chose the one that seemed fitting to his inclinations. He gave particular attention to the task of perfecting it in order thus to create for himself a kind of dance and execution of it that were uniquely his. Unfortunately, there is not even a question of such a thing occurring today when all trained dancers, both men and women, resemble one another in their imperfection and the monotony of their execution.

Such was the lesson of the past—this is what is called tradition. In keeping with it, we fulfilled these exercises religiously each day, without change or variation.

In this description we have advisedly itemized the *adages*, which make up the part that has been most neglected by modern teaching, even though it is the most useful in furthering the progress of young students and in perfecting dancers. . . .

As for exhaustion, we admit it was enormous; but as a result it produced talent, which is never the fruit of today's lessons, which have been made more gentle and are aimed at the level of the lazy among our coquettes and pusillanimous women.

August Bournonville (1805–1879)
LA SYLPHIDE.
A ROMANTIC BALLET
IN TWO ACTS
Translated from the Danish by Patricia N. McAndrew

Born in Copenhagen to a French father and a Swedish mother, Bournonville was a loyal Dane all of his life. He studied under Auguste Vestris in Paris and could have won fame throughout Europe as a performer, but chose instead to develop the artistry of the Royal Danish Ballet, which he served almost without interruption for forty-seven years.

Bournonville had seen Taglioni's Sylphide *in Paris. Taking the original libretto of Charles Nourrit, he commissioned a new score from Herman Løvenskjold and created his own choreography. Though the Sylphide was his protégée Lucile Grahn, he considerably strengthened the role of James, making him more important than he had been in the French version, for thanks to Bournonville's remarkable teaching methods, Danish male dancers maintained their status even during the romantic period. The Danish* Sylphide *was an immediate success and has been kept consistently in the repertory, the roles being passed down from one generation to the next; this is the version most often seen today. Erik Bruhn, the great contemporary interpreter of James,*

SOURCE: Libretto (Copenhagen, 1836). Theatre History Museum, Copenhagen.

has aptly characterized the lasting validity of the role; "All he wants to catch is a dream which exists only in his head and which nobody else can see. He is a true escapist. . . . He believes only in this dream and it is sad that he could never grasp reality."

The Characters

THE SYLPHIDE.
ANNA, a tenant farmer's widow.
JAMES, her son.
EFFY, her niece, James's bride.
GURN, a peasant lad.
MADGE, a fortune-teller.
Scottish Peasant Folk. Sylphides and Witches.

The scene is laid in Scotland.

Act One

A spacious room in a farmhouse. In the background, a door and a staircase leading to the sleeping chamber. To the right, a window. To the left, a high fireplace. Dawn.

James is asleep in a large armchair. A feminine being in airy raiment and with transparent wings is kneeling at his feet. Her arm is resting on the seat of the chair. With her hand beneath her chin, she fixes her loving gaze on the sleeping youth. She expresses the joy she feels in being near the one she loves. She hovers round him and flutters her wings in order to cool the air he breathes.

James slumbers restlessly. In his dreams he follows every one of the airy creature's movements and when, carried away with tenderness, she approaches him and lightly kisses his brow, he suddenly wakens, reaches out to grasp the lovely image and pursues it about the room as far as the fireplace, into which the Sylphide vanishes.

Beside himself at the sight of this vision, which has already enchanted him several times in dreams but now stood alive before his eyes, James awakens and questions the farmhands, who are sleeping in the same room. Confused and sleepy, they do not know what he is saying and do not understand his questions. He rushes out the door in order to see whether the Sylphide might still be outside; but he does not notice that in his haste he has run into Gurn, who has already been out hunting. Gurn and the farmhands regard one another with astonishment, but when James immediately returns to overwhelm them with questions about the airy figure who knelt by his couch, kissed his brow, fluttered about the room, and flew up through the chimney, their wonder dis-

Photo, Fred Fehl

La Sylphide was the first ballet to crystallize the concept of romanticism by setting a supernatural heroine among earthly peasants and by dooming the mortal who tries to possess her ethereal perfection. Constant surveillance by the Royal Danish Ballet has preserved much of Bournonville's choreography. Here Carla Fracci attends the dreaming Erik Bruhn in the American Ballet Theatre production of 1968.

solves into laughter and they strive to convince James that the whole thing has been a dream.

James comes to himself again and remembers that this very day he is to be betrothed to his cousin, the amiable Effy. Vexed, Gurn leaves him, bemoaning the injustice he must suffer because of the superiority that Effy bestows upon this daydreamer.

James sends the farmhands away to prepare everything for the celebration and quickly finishes dressing in order to please his lovely bride. But as he draws closer to the fireplace, he falls ever deeper in thought. Effy is brought in by her aunt. Her first glance is directed at James, who takes no notice of her. Gurn, on the other hand, is immediately at her service. He begs her not to reject the spoils of the hunt and gives her a bouquet of fresh wild flowers. Effy rather absent-mindedly accepts his compliment and goes over to the thoughtful James in order to ask him what he is brooding about, whether he is distressed, and why. He begs her to forgive him for being so distracted and assures her that he is really very happy, especially today, when he shall be united to the one he loves and will live for eternally. Tender and happy, Effy gives him her hand to kiss. Gurn also tries to take one of her hands, but she quickly withdraws it. James threateningly steps between her and Gurn, who, ashamed and distraught, goes away in order to hide the tears he can no longer hold back. His sorrow is further augmented by seeing Anna unite the young couple who, kneeling, receive her blessing.

Some young girls, friends of Effy, come to congratulate the loving

Theatre Museum, Copenhagen

The original costume design for Bournonville, in a water color by Christian Bruun, shows James confident and oblivious of Madge, who crouches by the fireplace, plotting his destruction. The virile Bournonville established a tradition of strong male dancing in Denmark where it was preserved long after the ballerinas reigned supreme on the other stages of western Europe.

couple. They bring presents for the bride; a plaid, a scarf, a wreath, a veil, a bouquet; in short, everything that can delight her. Gurn begs them to put in a good word for him but they make fun of him and offer him their love amid laughter and teasing. Weeping, he tears himself loose and goes over to sit down in a corner.

Effy thanks and embraces her childhood playmates while James once more becomes lost in thought. He approaches the fireplace—but what does he see! A loathsome figure! Old Madge, the fortune-teller, who has stolen in among the young girls. "What are you doing here?" "I am warming myself by the fire!" "Get away from here, witch! Your presence is an evil omen." James is about to drive her away but the girls plead for her. Gurn bids her be seated and offers her a glass of spirits, which she greedily swallows.

Madge knows hidden things and the girls cannot resist their desire to know what lies in store for them. They surround the witch and hold out their hands in order to have her predict their fortunes. To one she promises happiness in marriage, while she tells the other she will never be wed. This one is but a child and gets no prediction at all, but another has her fate whispered in her ear, and walks away blushing. Finally, Effy asks if she will be happy in marriage? "Yes!" is the answer. "Does my bridegroom love me sincerely?" "No!" James begs her not to believe this hateful old woman. Gurn also gets the desire to question Madge. "AH!" she says, "this man loves you with his heart and you will soon come to regret the fact that you have spurned his love." James now becomes furious, seizes the fortune-teller, and hurls her to the door. Gurn quotes her statement and makes yet another effort to hinder the wedding he detests so much, but everyone laughs him to scorn and calms James by reassuring him that they do not believe at all in the prophecy.

Anna and the young girls follow Effy to her room to array her in festive dress. Gurn goes sadly away, looking back at Effy all the while. James wishes to accompany his beloved but the girls hold him back and Effy blows him a parting kiss. James is delighted with this amiable bride but the memory of the Sylphide soon returns to his soul. He cannot account for the nature of this being. Perhaps she is his good angel, a powerful fairy who watches over his destiny! With this, as if by a gust of wind, the casement opens. The Sylphide is seated in the corner, melancholy and hiding her face in her hands.

James bids her approach, and she glides down from the wall. He asks the cause of her grief, but she refuses to answer. When he continues to demand her confidence she finally confesses that his union with Effy constitutes her misfortune; from the first moment she saw him her fate was joined to his and this hearth is her favorite place of refuge.

She hovers about him, visibly and invisibly, night and day, follows him on the hunt, among the wild mountains, watches over his sleep, wards off the evil spirits from his bed, and sends him gentle dreams. James has listened to her with mounting agitation. He is touched by the Sylphide's love, but does not dare to return it. Effy has received his vow: his heart belongs to her alone. The Sylphide rushes desperately away. She has nothing to hope for, only death to desire. James calls her back. He cannot hide his confusion; he does not understand what magic is controlling him; but despite his love for Effy he is enraptured by the Sylphide.

She expresses the liveliest joy, regains her airy lilt, and hovers about the youth as she flutters her transparent wings. She tries to use his agitated state of mind in order to lure him away with her, but he shudders at the thought of deserting Effy, tears himself loose from the Sylphide, and spurns her. But the Sylphide has wrapped herself in Effy's plaid, and when he turns around he finds her at his feet, reminding him of the beloved object. James is intoxicated at this sight. He raises the Sylphide, presses her to his heart, and enthusiastically kisses her.

Gurn, who has witnessed part of the foregoing scene, hastens to acquaint Effy with everything that has happened, but when James hears a noise he hides the Sylphide in the armchair and covers her with the plaid. Gurn has summoned Effy and her friends in order to take the unfaithful bridegroom by surprise. At first, they see nothing at all. However suspicion soon falls on the covered armchair. James is bewildered; Effy turns pale with jealousy and, together with Gurn, lifts the plaid aside. The Sylphide has vanished. The girls laugh. Effy becomes angry at Gurn, who stands ashamed and startled.

All of the villagers arrive to celebrate the betrothal of James and Effy. The old folk sit down at table while the young ones enjoy merry dancing. James is so distracted that he forgets to ask his bride to dance. It is she who invites him. But in the midst of the dance he perceives the Sylphide, who is visible only to him and then disappears once more. He forgets everything in trying to reach her, but she always eludes him and the guests think it is high time James was married since he stands in danger of losing his reason from sheer affectionate longing.

The dancing ceases and the bride is adorned for the ceremony. Anna gives her the ring which she shall exchange for that of her bridegroom, and everyone surrounds her with congratulations and expressions of sympathy. James alone is melancholy. He stands apart from the others with the betrothal ring in his hand. The Sylphide emerges from the fireplace, snatches the ring from him, and signifies with an expression of utter despair that she must die if he marries Effy.

The bride is ready. She has given her girlhood friends a parting embrace. They summon the bridegroom, but he is nowhere to be found. General astonishment. Gurn has seen him flee to the hills with a woman. Effy is plunged in grief. Anna expresses indignation; everyone, anger and disapproval.

Gurn triumphantly mentions what Madge had predicted for him. He still talks of love and now finds support among the young girls. Effy is overwhelmed with grief and despair. She is indifferent to all consolation and leans helplessly on Anna's breast. Gurn kneels at her feet and all express the liveliest sympathy.

Act Two

The forest and night. A dense fog permits only a glimpse of the foremost trees and cliffs. To the left, the entrance to a cave.

Madge prepares for a meeting with other witches. They come from all quarters, each with lamp and broomstick, each with her familiar spirit. They dance about the fire in a circle, hail Madge, and by way of welcome empty a cup of the glowing brew she has prepared for them. Madge calls them to work. Some spin, wind, and weave a rose-colored drapery, while others dance and fence with the broomsticks. The spell is complete. They drink a farewell and the flock of witches disappear into the cave.

The fog disperses. Dawn gives way to sunrise and the landscape presents a charming blend of woods and mountains. The Sylphide leads James down from a steep mountain path, which he fearfully treads while she scarcely seems to touch the cliff with her foot. This is her kingdom. Here she will live for the one she loves, hide him from the eyes of the world, and allow him to share the joys that she prizes most highly. James is enraptured with delight and admiration. The Sylphide seems to explore each one of his wishes, brings him the loveliest flowers, and refreshes him with fruits and spring water. James regards her with rapture. He forgets everything for the one he loves and lives only to possess her. But she is more retiring than usual. She will not sit with him, easily disengages herself from his arms, and eludes him every time he ardently tries to embrace her. James is on the verge of becoming annoyed, but then she hovers about him in the most delightful attitudes. Without knowing it, James's movements take on a more airy lilt. He follows the Sylphide in her easy flight, and their dancing blends together in harmony.

Despite his love for the Sylphide and the magical power that irresistibly sweeps him away with her, the memory of Effy still returns and points out to him the injustice he has inflicted upon her. He becomes melancholy once more and he feels as drained as if he had been intoxicated.

The Sylphide perceives his state of mind and by her innocent gaiety seeks to dispel his dark thoughts. She knows a way: her sisters shall help her to cheer her beloved. At a signal they all come into view through the bushes, on the boughs, and over the cliffs. The young sylphides with wings of blue and rose color soon chase away the youth's distress. Some of them swing in airy draperies which they hang between the trees, while others stand on the tip of a bough and bend it to the ground with their weight, to have it raised into the air again by a puff of wind. Their dancing and delightful groupings arouse James's enthusiasm. He is more than ever taken with the Sylphide but she eludes his embraces and, after having disappointed him several times, she disappears at the very moment he thought to grasp her. In vain he questions the remaining sylphides. They do not answer him but fly away one after another. Anxious and grief-stricken, James cannot remain alone but rushes after the enchanting creature.

James's friends come into view on the hill. Gurn is with them. They seek and question one another about the runaway, but until now their search has been fruitless. They spread out, but Gurn discovers a hat. It belongs to James. He is about to call the others, but Madge steps out of the cave, seizes the hat, and flings it away. Gurn is frightened by the witch's sudden appearance, but she calms him, orders him to be silent and clever, as she points to the hill, from whence Effy is coming with some of her friends.

Nobody has found James and Madge now tells them of his unfaithfulness. He is lost to Effy but her prophecy will be fulfilled, for Gurn, the fine, good-hearted young fellow, is destined by fate to be Effy's husband. All the others, outraged at James's behavior, support Gurn's pleas. Effy, although deeply distressed, is nevertheless moved by the slighted Gurn's affection, and she allows him to escort her home. Madge remains alone.

James returns without having overtaken the Sylphide. His heart is a prey to regret and despair. He feels how deeply he has violated his responsibilities towards his bride, but he does not have the strength to tear himself loose from this being who, like a dream-image, charms and confuses his senses and captures his thoughts. Old Madge has been watching him secretly and approaches with feigned compassion. He readily tells her everything and says that he would gladly give his life to capture the celestial maiden if only for a single moment. "But the one you love is a *sylphide*! Naught but a talisman can bind her to you." "Give it me! In return I will bestow upon you all that I possess." "But this morning you mocked me, cast me away!" Kneeling, James begs her to forgive him for his hardness and to give him life by the possession of the Sylphide. Madge suffers herself to be moved and meaningfully hands him the rose-colored scarf: "Believe in its strength and you shall succeed! Entwine her with this blossom. Then her wings will fall and she is yours forever." Beside himself with joy and gratitude, James kisses the scarf and follows the witch to her cave with a thousand expressions of thanks.

He espies the Sylphide, sitting on a bough with a bird's nest in her hand. He waves the scarf; she climbs down and offers him her catch, but James reproaches her for her hardness towards innocent creatures. Deeply moved, she regrets what she has done and hastens to replace the nest. She now pleads for the pretty scarf, which he purposely refuses her. She begs him for it and promises never more to flee from him. Greedily, she reaches for the scarf but at the same instant he twists it about her so tightly that she cannot move her arms. The Sylphide is captured and, kneeling, asks for mercy; but James does not release the scarf before her wings have fallen off. The Sylphide puts her hand to her heart as if she felt mortally wounded. James presses her to him but she pushes him away from her. He throws himself at her feet . . . the pallor of death covers the Sylphide's brow.

James, who had thought to possess her forever and in his outburst of joy gives her a thousand caresses, suddenly stops: what has he done! The unhappy creature! By taking away her freedom has he robbed her of life? "Do not weep! You, whom I have so dearly loved! I was blessed by your tenderness but I could not belong to you, could not bestow upon you the happiness you longed for. I must die! Take your betrothal ring. Make haste, return it. You can still marry her whom you loved before me . . . Farewell! I die with the hope of your future happiness."
. . .

At this moment the fortune-teller enters to rejoice at James's despair, and counters his reproaches with the icy laughter of revenge. She points to the background, where Gurn is leading Effy to the altar. The Sylphide's strength is decreasing little by little. James lies at her feet. Her sisters surround her and in their arms she breathes forth her spirit. Sylphs and sylphides veil the beloved body and carry it away through the air. Overwhelmed with grief, the unfortunate James casts yet another look at his airy mistress and falls to the ground in a swoon.

Théophile Gautier (1811–1872)
**Fanny Cerrito in
Jules Perrot's LALLA-ROOCK
Marie Guy-Stéphan in
Arthur Saint-Léon's
LUTIN DE LA VALLÉE**
Translated from the French by Edwin Binney 3rd

Gautier, known in the annals of literature as a great poet, novelist, and journalist, and as a leader of the romantic movement in France, is the author of some of the greatest dance criticism we have as well as the librettist of a number of ballets, including the still famous **Giselle.** *Fortunately, his deep love for Carlotta Grisi did not prevent his enjoying the charms of other ballerinas, and his descriptions of their performances provide us with marvelously distinct and evocative pictures of the dancing of the mid-nineteenth century.*

To Gautier dance was "simply the art of displaying elegant and correctly proportioned shapes in various positions favorable to the development of lines." He expected the ballerina to be beautiful and had little use for the male dancer. These selections show him in his element. The first review reports from London on a star not yet seen at the Paris Opéra; the second concerns a ballerina unusually skilled in Spanish dancing, which she had actually learned in Madrid.

The ballet of *Lalla-Roock* . . . tells of a prince, fiancé of a princess who, according to custom, has never seen him. He succeeds in becoming loved by her under the name and the costume of the poet Feramorz. At the end, it appears that the prince and the poet are the same person, and everything turns out happily. This idea of a young princess whose father's court seeks to lead her to her royal fiancé, and whose love for another increases as she nears the end of her travels, is perhaps a better subject for analysis than for pantomime, and besides, traveling action is rather difficult to localize in a theatrical performance.

The first act of this ballet shows us the palace of the great Mughal with the celebrated Aurangzeb seated on his throne, the back of which is formed by a huge peacock's tail of jewels. The poet Feramorz enters to seek the princess in the name of the king, his master.

The second act . . . shows the procession of the caravan through the

SOURCES: Review of Cerrito from *La Presse*, July 30, 1846. Review of Guy-Stéphan from *La Presse*, February 1, 1853.

desert; nothing is lacking: neither the *kamsin* [wind of the Sahara] nor the spirals of uplifted sand; we even see two redoubtable camels, whose forelegs could argue with their back legs in excellent English if they became bad-tempered.

The third act contains the obligatory recognition scene, the rejoicings which occur naturally and present us with the Festival of Roses so frequently celebrated by the Persian poets. The whole thing ends with the wedding of the prince and princess, illuminated by a myriad of lamps, lanterns, candles, and candelabra.

This very legitimate canvas is embellished by Perrot with a multitude of charming dances, as he alone knows how to create.

For us, the principal attraction of this choreographic poem was Mlle Cerito [sic], whom we had not seen previously, our earlier trips to London not having coincided with seasons when she was appearing.

Mlle Cerito, and that proves the reality of her talent, has enthusiastic supporters and implacable disparagers. For the former, she is the nymph of the dance; for the others, she is a third-rate dancer whose reputation is incomprehensible. There is no middle position; she is either accepted or rejected totally.

We were curious to see the effect that she would produce on us and to discover our opinion on this reputation which Paris has not yet consecrated.

Let us begin by *le physique*, as they say in theatrical parlance, and then speak of her talent.

La Cerito is blonde; she has blue eyes which are very soft and tender, a gracious smile despite its perhaps too frequent appearance; her shoulders, her bosom do not have that scrawniness which is characteristic of female dancers, the whole of whose weight seems to have descended into their legs. Her plump, dimpled arms do not inflict tragic anatomical details upon our sight; they are used with grace and flexibility. Nothing in this pretty upper body suggests the idea of fatigue from classes or the perspiration of training. A girl taken from her family yesterday and pushed onto the stage would be no different. Her foot is small, well-arched, with a delicate ankle and a well-rounded leg; however, whether because of a belt worn too low or a torso that is actually a little too long, her waist cuts her body into two completely equal parts, which is contrary to the laws of human proportions and particularly unfavorable for a *danseuse*. All in all, she is young, fascinating, and produces a favorable impression.

The costume which Mlle Cerito wore, without being of a rigorous exactitude, was particularly becoming. Garlands of flowers embroidered in strong colors enlivened her white gauze skirts and gave her a spring-like air which was the most stylish and the prettiest imaginable.

As a dancer, Mlle Cerito has little or no *école*; that is immediately obvious. Let these words not be considered pejoratively: we are not "classic" in relation to the dance anymore than to anything else; we simply wish to say that Mlle Cerito owes more to nature than to her training. She dances by inspiration; her talents might even disappear, we believe, if she consecrated herself to study in the hope of perfecting herself. She would lose the *innate gift* and would not achieve the *acquired one*. Her qualities consist of freshness, casualness, naiveté, which cause a fault to be atoned for by a grace. At certain moments, one might say that she is improvising, such is the happy risk in her *pas*. As with certain singers, the timbre of whose voices are their principal charm and who would be wrong to change it through practice, Mlle Cerito has, to a certain extent, a silvery and young timbre to her dancing which fatigue might crack.

No comparison can be established between her and those dancers with whom her name is often linked: Taglioni, Elssler, and Carlotta Grisi. Mlle Cerito's place, for not being so elevated, is no less marked and honorable.

In an art which is severely regulated despite its apparent frivolity, she represents the flowering of natural capacities: caprice and fantasy.

We feel that Mlle Cerito would have great success in Paris, particularly if she limited herself to dancing three or four of these brilliant *pas* with such happy vivacity that she performs as though she were dancing in her bedroom for her own particular pleasure. . . .

The Théâtre-lyrique has just found a real success. *Le Lutin de la Vallée*, that is Saint-Léon and Mme Guy-Stéphan, for the work does not exist by itself and could be described in four lines; but it furnishes the dance with an auspicious frame and that is all that is necessary.

Count Ulric has lost a locket containing the portrait of his mother and has sworn to marry the woman who will return it to him. Katti, a poor, mute girl sheltered by the charity of dame Brigitte, has found the locket, but the old lady takes it from her while she is sleeping so that her own daughter may profit by the reward. . . . Thanks to an elf, who restores the stolen locket to her, Katti becomes the wife of the powerful Count Ulric. If this marriage seems unsuitable to you, remember that Katti is mute, which is better than a dowry, and besides, she speaks such pretty words with her feet.

Now that we've done away with the plot, and we must give it this credit that it is neither long nor complicated, let us immediately get to what is important—to the dance. . . .

Mme Guy-Stéphan exhibits as natural talent an extraordinary lightness; she bounds up like a rubber ball and comes down like a feather or a snowflake. Her foot strikes the floor noiselessly, like the foot of a shadow or a sylphide, and each jump is not echoed by a dull sound of the dancer landing which recalls the marble heels of the statue of the Commander [in Molière's *Don Juan*]. Study has given her a cleanness, a precision, a finish that are rare nowadays when real dancing is neglected for voluptuous attitudes and precarious poses for which the partner is the pivot or the springboard. Her *jetés-battus* are extremely clean; her *pointes*, which are rigid and clear, never waver; and she has remarkable elevation.

Fanny Cerrito is depicted in *Lalla-Roock* in a lithograph probably after Brandard. The diaphanous, knee-length tutu, with its delicate embroidery, reflects the spirit of romantic idealism. Cerrito, however, was called "the little realist" by those who contrasted her voluptuous grace to the ethereal quality of Taglioni. In addition to creating leading roles in works composed by her husband, Arthur Saint-Léon, Cerrito was a choreographer herself, with several ballets to her credit.

The *pas* that she dances in the moonlight with the elf of the valley, who skips on the silvery spray of the waterfall, is delightfully poetic. No one could imagine anything lighter, fresher, nor more nocturnally vaporous, nor more endearingly chaste. While the girl balances in a pose of innocence and love, the elf bounds about, hovers, and traces around her circles of benevolent magic. It is charming. To be able to compose such a dance and to execute it, one has to be Saint-Léon, an exquisite intelligence served by hamstrings of steel; one has to have both mind and legs, rare attributes, even when separated.

The madrilena, danced by Mme Guy-Stéphan, who wanted to present herself in the same evening under both her classical and her romantic aspects, brought out thunders of applause and obtained the honors of an encore. It is impossible to reunite more effectively the diverse talents of Dolores Serral, Pepita Diaz, Guerrero, Espert, Oliva and Petra Cámara [Spanish dancers whom Gautier has appreciated both in Paris and in Spain] and to translate Spanish into French in a more intelligent, faithful, and poetic manner all at once. What Elssler did for the cachucha, Mme Guy-Stéphan has done for the madrilena: to fire she has added correctness; to voluptuousness, decency; to physical abandon, ordered rationality. To restate this in a single word: to personal temperament, she has added art.

Certainly we are not suspect in such a subject; we love these passionate outbursts, this mad audacity, this swooning languor, this lascivious arching, these arms that seem to gather in every wanton desire like a hay-baler, this knee that lifts the pleat of her skirt when the dancer leans back as though dying of love—all this fiery, gracious, and yet enchanting Andalusian poetry of the *tambour de basque*, castanets, fan, sombrero, and cape. Who admires more than we the velvety eyebrows, the elongated eyes which are always lowered and open slightly like a black cloud that lets the flash of lightning shine through. . . .

Mme Guy-Stéphan has placed into this dance—so dissolute, fiery, and violent—a finesse, a classical purity, which cause it to lose none of its character; the local savor is kept but rectified and concentrated into a more delicate perfume. It is the cachucha that has acknowledged itself, criticized and organized itself. The poses are more surely designed, the steps are more clearly in rhythm; knowledge has purified inspiration and art has captured nature: this madrilena will make Paris run to the Théâtre-lyrique.

Section Four

NEW LIFE FROM RUSSIA

In the eighteenth century Catherine the Great of Russia imported ballet masters from Western Europe to arrange festivities for her court, while provincial nobles had their serfs trained in dancing to provide entertainments for their social gatherings. The capital, in particular, continued to lure talent: Didelot, Perrot, and Saint-Léon came to choreograph; Taglioni and Elssler to perform.

In the nineteenth century the Maryinsky Theatre in St. Petersburg, like the Bolshoi in Moscow, was state owned and controlled. Most of the auditorium was reserved for the court and high officials; less than a third of the seats were available to the public. Tastes were rigidly conservative. Ballets all followed the same pattern: the story was told by means of conventional pantomime gestures with loosely relevant dances inserted at appropriate points, though a *pas d'action* in each act was intended to be vaguely expressive. Women wore pink tights, *pointe* shoes, and short tutus—no matter what the period or geographical setting. For an Egyptian ballet, hieroglyphs were painted on their ruffled skirts; for a Spanish scene, a mantilla might top a fashionably coiffed head. Music was commissioned from one of several house composers, who dutifully provided tinkling tunes.

Though the Imperial Ballet dancers were Russian, native choreographers were seldom used, the prestige of foreigners being preferred. In the romantic period most of them had been content simply to restage in Russia works that they had created elsewhere, but when the Frenchman Marius Petipa assumed the post of chief choreographer in 1862 he began to enrich the Imperial Ballet with a repertory of original works. Showing no inclination to change the standard formula, he nevertheless managed to produce many ballets of the highest artistic quality.

With a slight story to tell and five acts to fill, Petipa managed in his best works to display the rich variety of styles, the beauty and vitality of the *danse d'école*. His patterns for the corps de ballet, sometimes arranged at home on a chessboard, showed tremendous diversity within the confines of the symmetrical designs he felt obliged to follow. The solo dances, known as "variations," were always built on a motif, usually a movement theme inspired either by the music or by some special quality of the performer for whom they were created; all exhibited meticulous structure and beauty of line, but each also had its own kinetic flavor and texture. For the standard *pas de deux*—always consisting of a canonical adagio for both dancers, a variation for each, and a technically brilliant, allegro coda—Petipa frequently endowed his combinations of academic steps with a distinctive character; if seldom overtly dramatic, these duets were often poetically expressive.

In the 1880's Petipa's gifts were stimulated by the importation of a number of fine artists from Italy. The first was the dramatic dancer Virginia Zucchi; it was said that there was more poetry in her back than in all the Italian poets put together. Next came the remarkable Enrico Cecchetti and—more to Petipa's taste, since he preferred choreographing for women—two splendid technicians, Carlotta Brianza and Pierrina Legnani. The last was famous for her mastery of the whipped turns known as *fouettés*, an achievement that fired the Russian artists with such zealous patriotism that soon Mathilde Kshesinskaya was also able to perform the thirty-two *fouettés* on *pointe*.

Petipa was fortunate again in his two ballets graced by the music of Tchaikovsky: *The Sleeping Beauty* (1890) and *Swan Lake* (1895). For the latter he assigned two acts to his assistant, Lev Ivanov, and it is one of these—the poetic lake scene in which the enchanted Swan Queen meets her prince—that is performed most often today. Ivanov's choreography was less conventional than his master's. The elegiac *pas de deux* in the second act of *Swan Lake* does not follow the traditional pattern; it is all adagio, all expressive movement. But it was Petipa, more classically restrained in feeling, more brilliant in technical invention, who dominated the contemporary ballet.

Before he died, Petipa wrote a note of encouragement to the young choreographer Michel Fokine, whose work he had just seen. Unlike the aging master, however, Fokine felt inhibited by balletic conventions —by the separation of pantomime and dancing, the attention to virtuosity that submerged expression, the monotony of style that allowed works set in ancient Greece or medieval France to be danced in tutus and *pointe* shoes.

In contrast to Ivanov, who did not press his beliefs, Fokine challenged the entrenched hierarchy of the Imperial Theatre to forego some of their outmoded rules, but he found them hard to convince. Failing to get permission for his dancers to appear appropriately barefooted in a Greek ballet, Fokine finally compromised by having them paint toes on the feet of their tights. But clearly he was not going to put up with this kind of despotism indefinitely.

In 1909 another young man whose independence had gotten him into trouble with the authorities of the Imperial Theatre formed a company of Russian dancers, including Fokine, to play a season of ballet in Paris. Serge Diaghilev—a connoisseur of the arts, bold, imaginative, with impeccable taste and remarkable vision—intended to overwhelm the cultural world of Western Europe. He did. Paris was thrilled, but less by Fokine's poetically evocative *Les Sylphides*, than by the exotic décors that Leon Bakst had designed for *Cleopatra* and the glamor of Alexandre Benois' setting for *Le Pavillon d'Armide*. They were stunned by the dancers—the delicate Anna Pavlova, the beautiful and sensitive Tamara Karsavina, the virile Adolphe Bolm. Most of all they cheered the phenomenal Vaslav Nijinsky, who appeared to be possessed by the characters he played and who seemed able to sustain himself in the air as long as he wished.

Diaghilev had a genius for selecting the right collaborators. In 1910 his choice fell on Fokine and Igor Stravinsky to create *The Firebird*, based on Russian legend. The following year, Benois joined them to produce *Petrouchka*, inspired by the puppets of Russian fairs. If the chic Paris audience was delighted with the picturesque crowds of peasants, merchants, and gypsies, they were also deeply moved by the tragedy of the characters. Unafraid to reverse the balletic turnout to depict the painfully introverted Petrouchka or to parody it for the movements of the stupid, egocentric Moor, Fokine converted the classical vocabulary to his dramatic purpose.

Nijinsky, when his turn came, took the dancers even further from their balletic base. In *Afternoon of a Faun* (1912) they moved with feet placed parallel and with their bodies in stiff profile to the audience as if they had been sculpted by an archaic Greek. In *Le Sacre du Printemps* (1913) their angular movements were violently distorted from the classic norm as they enacted their primitive ritual; the sacrificial dance of the Chosen Maiden was convulsively fragmented, completely breaking with the balletic concept of flow. Diaghilev had brought Marie Rambert from the Dalcroze School to help Nijinsky cope with the shifting rhythms of Stravinsky's dissonant score, but the indignant uproar of the audience made the music practically inaudible. Some critics felt that Nijinsky had scored a breakthrough greater than Fokine's, but since his works cannot be precisely reconstructed and he did not continue to choreograph, we will never really know.

Diaghilev next chose Leonide Massine, who excelled in character ballets: the eighteenth-century Italian comedy of *The Good-Humored Ladies* (1917) and the Spanish genre of *The Three-Cornered Hat* (1919). During the war years Diaghilev could not turn to Russia for fresh talent but sought new collaborators among the avant-guard artists working in Paris:

Matisse, Picasso, Satie, and Cocteau. The Ballets Russes became a cosmopolitan company, almost more renowned for its innovative music and décors than for its dancing. Then, completely reversing his direction, Diaghilev revived *The Sleeping Beauty* in 1921. Though it provided a brilliant showcase for the dancers, trained to perfection by Cecchetti, the production was a crushing fiasco. Attuned to expecting novelty from the Ballets Russes, the audience rejected this attempt to reinstate the values of classicism.

Diaghilev then promoted Bronislava Nijinska, who created the stark Russian peasant wedding of *Les Noces* (1923) with Stravinsky and the sophisticated *Les Biches* (1924) with Poulenc. The next year George Balanchine, who had managed to get out of Russia, joined the Ballets Russes. Starting with the modish type of choreography that Diaghilev then favored, he found his most congenial inspiration in the composer who had already given so much to the company—Stravinsky. Their *Apollo* (1928) had none of the obviously avant-garde tendencies that had marked other current productions; both the music and the choreography were firmly grounded in classical forms, with occasional witty deviations only accentuating the basic purity of line and sustained flow of movement. It was with *Apollo*, Balanchine claimed, that he first learned not to use all his ideas, to eliminate the unnecessary, to pare down to essentials; it became the touchstone of his style.

In 1929 Diaghilev died; an era had ended. But many of the artists he had discovered and developed were to continue to make ballet history: Karsavina and Rambert, along with two English dancers who had taken the names of Alicia Markova and Anton Dolin, and a young Irish girl who called herself Ninette de Valois, established ballet in England; Diaghilev's last male star, Serge Lifar, took over the Paris Opéra; Massine headed the Ballet Russes de Monte Carlo that toured Europe and America; Fokine and Balanchine contributed to the founding of the first two major ballet companies in the United States. It was an extraordinarily rich harvest.

Marius Petipa (1819–1910)
THE SLEEPING BEAUTY
Translated from the Russian by Joan Lawson

Born in Marseilles, Petipa came from a family of dancers. His brother Lucien partnered Carlotta Grisi in the premier of Giselle, *but Marius only got jobs in the provinces. In 1847 he was offered a one-year contract in St. Petersburg. In 1862 he was made chief choreographer, replacing Jules Perrot. In the course of his tenure he created sixty full-evening works, most of the distinguished repertory of the Imperial Ballet. He retired in 1903, bitterly disappointed by the failure of his last production,* The Magic Mirror.

The Sleeping Beauty *was proposed to Tchaikovsky by I. A. Vsevolojsky, the Director of the Imperial Theatre, and the scenario that Petipa prepared for the composer is dated 1889, the ballet receiving its premiere the following year. The plan carefully delineates the dramatic action, which was to be enacted with gestures of conventional pantomime, and specifies not only the character but often the timing and rhythm of the dances as well. There have been some arguments as to how peacefully the collaboration proceeded, since Tchaikovsky, unlike the regular ballet composers, was unaccustomed to such restricting dictation. Nevertheless, the Russian historian Vera Krasovskaya believes that the composer would have been completely sympathetic to Petipa's ideas.* The Sleeping Beauty, *she believes, is closer in form to symphony than to drama: "It is precisely the maximum coincidence of the musical and choreographic high points that determines the artistic perfection of the production."*

Prologue

SCENE I

The Christening of the Princess Aurora. A Ceremonial Hall in the Castle of King Florestan XIV. To the right, a platform for the King, Queen and the Fairies—the godmothers of Princess Aurora. Centre stage back, the door to an anteroom. Courtiers, standing in groups, wait the entrance of the King and Queen.

(1) The Masters of Ceremony place everyone in their place, so that they may take part in the customary offering of congratulations and good wishes to the King, Queen and powerful Fairies, who have been invited to be godmothers at Princess Aurora'a christening.

SOURCE: First published in *The Dancing Times* (December, 1942, and February, 1943).

(1) (During the raising of the curtain a drawing-room march for the entrance of the lords and ladies.)

(2) Catalabutte, surrounded by court servants, verifies the list of Fairies, to whom invitations have been sent. Everything has been accomplished, according to the King's command. Everything is ready for the ceremony—the Court is assembled—the arrival of the Fairies is expected at any moment.

(2) (For Catalabutte's little scene, the march is made a little more serious, yet half-comic.)

(3) Fanfare. Entrance of the King and Queen, preceded by pages and attended by the governesses and nurses of Princess Aurora; these carry the Royal Baby's cradle.

(3) (Fanfare. Broad and very festive music. The King and Queen only just reach the platform and the cradle is set down as Catalabutte announces the arrival of the Fairies.)

(4) Entrance of the Fairies. The Fairies, Candide, Fleur de Farine, Violante, Canary and Breadcrumbs enter the hall first.

(4) (Graceful music ¾. The King and Queen go to meet them and invite them to mount the platform.)

(5) Entrance of the Lilac Fairy—Aurora's principal godmother. She is surrounded by her own retinue of Fairies, who carry large fans, perfumes and hold the train of their Queen. At a sign from Catalabutte the pages run off and—

(5) (¾ broadly.)

(6) Young girls enter with brocade cushions on which are lying presents intended by the Queen of the Fairies for her godchild. The arrivals form pretty groups as they present each gift to Her, for whom they are intended.

(6) (¾ rather animated and danceable.) The pages and young girls appear dancing.

(7) The Fairies descend from the platform. Each in turn, they go to bless the child.

(7) (A little introduction for a Pas de Six.)

Pas de Six

A Sweet Adagio. A little Allegro.

Variations—

Candide.

Fleur de Farine. (Flowing.)

Kroshka (Breadcrumb). (Which interweaves and twines?)

Canary. (Who sings.)

Violante. (²⁄₄ animated.) (Plucked strings.)

The Lilac Fairy. (A sweetly happy variation.)

Coda. (¾, fast and stirring.)

(8) The Lilac Fairy, in her turn, wishes to go up to the cradle to give her gift to Aurora.

(8) (From 8–16 bars, when the Lilac Fairy wishes to go up to the cradle.)

(9) But at this moment, a loud roar is heard in the ante-room. A page runs in and tells Catalabutte that a new Fairy is arriving at the gate of the castle, one whom they had forgotten to invite to the ceremony. It is the Fairy Carabosse—the most powerful and wicked Fairy in the whole land. Catalabutte is horrified. How could he forget her; he is always so careful! Trembling he goes up to the King, to explain his shortcomings, his mistake! The King and Queen are upset. This forgetfulness of the First Lord Chamberlain will cause great unhappiness and affect the future of their dear child. Even the Fairies seem uncertain.

(9) When the noise is heard*—very animated movement.

(*Petipa repeats the words from the preceding paragraph in order to point out the position of the music more clearly. He marks these places throughout the entire programme in the same manner.)

(10) Carabosse appears in a wheel-barrow, drawn by six rats. After her come some absurd pages—cripples. The King and Queen implore her to forgive Catalabutte's forgetfulness. They will punish him in whichever way the Fairy wishes. Catalabutte, breathless with fear, throws himself at the feet of the wicked Fairy, imploring her to have mercy on him, in return for his faithful service to the end of his days. [Here and throughout the "speeches" would be rendered by pantomime gesture. Ed.]

(10) (Fantastic music.)

(11) Carabosse laughs and amuses herself by tearing out handfuls of his hair and throwing it to the rats, who eat it up. Presently Catalabutte becomes completely bald.

(11) (She laughs and amuses herself by tearing out his hair—the music must fit the situation. The pages laugh spitefully.)

(12) "I am not Aurora's godmother," says Carabosse, "but nevertheless, I wish to bring her my gift."

(12) ("I am not her godmother," the music changes and becomes cajoling.)

(13) The good Fairies implore her not to spoil the happiness of the kind Queen and persuade her to pardon the Chamberlain's unintentional forgetfulness.

(13) (The music becomes tender when the Fairies persuade her to forgive the Chamberlain.)

(14) Carabosse only laughs at them—her mirth is echoed by her crippled pages and even by her rats. The good Fairies turn away from their sister with abhorrence.

(14) (Carabosse only laughs—a slight whistling.)

(15) "Aurora, thanks to the gifts of her godmothers," says Carabosse, "will be the most beautiful, the most charming, the wisest Princess in the world. I have not the power to take these qualities away from her. But so that her happiness will never be disturbed—see how kind I am—know that if ever she pricks her finger or hand, she will fall asleep and her sleep will be eternal." (The King, Queen and entire Court are aghast.)

(15) (For this short speech—satirical, diabolic music.)

(16) Carabosse raises her wand over the cradle and pronounces her spell, then, overjoyed by her evil-doing and her triumph over her sisters, bursts out laughing. The raucous merriment of the monster is reflected by her retinue.

(16) (Pronounces her spell—a short, fantastic, grotesque dance for the crippled pages.)

(17) But the Lilac Fairy, who has still not given her gift to the child and who is hiding behind Aurora's cradle, appears from her hiding place.
Carabosse looks at her with mistrust and anger. The good Fairy bows before the cradle. "Yes, you will fall asleep, my little Aurora, as your sister Carabosse has willed," says the Lilac Fairy, "but not for ever. A day will come when a Prince will appear who, enraptured by your beauty, will plant a kiss on your forehead and you will wake from your long dream in order to become the beloved wife of this Prince and live in happiness and prosperity."

(17) (The Lilac Fairy, who has still not given her gift—music tender and a little mocking.)

(18) The infuriated Carabosse sits down in her wheel-barrow and vanishes. The good Fairies group themselves round the cradle, as if protecting their godchild from their evil sister. (Picture.)

(18) (The infuriated Carabosse—energetic, satanical music. Group around the cradle.) (Picture.)

End of Prologue

[In Act I, while a party celebrates her twentieth birthday, Aurora does prick her finger. She and the entire court fall into a deep sleep, awaiting the arrival of Prince Desiré.]

Act II

SCENE III OF THE BALLET

Prince Desiré's Hunt. (1). A woody glade, at the back of the stage, a broad river. The entire horizon is covered with thick trees. To the right of the audience is a rock, covered with plants. The sun's rays light up the landscape.

At the rise of the curtain the stage is empty. The hunters' horns are heard. It is Prince Desiré's huntsmen, hunting wolves and lynx among the pine trees. The hunters and their ladies enter the scene, intending to rest and eat on the green grass. The Prince appears almost immediately with his tutor Gallifron and some noblemen from his father's Court. The Prince and his companions are served with food.

(1) The hunting horns are heard. The music of the hunt, which changes into the motif of rest—must be very short.

(2-3) In order to amuse the young Prince, the hunters and their ladies dance a round dance, throw javelins, practice archery and invent various amusements.

(2-3) (The nobles of the King's court propose to play "Blind Man's Buff" and other games. A quick 2/4 from 48-60 bars.)

During the games Gallifron urges his pupil to join in with his companions and particularly to become acquainted with the ladies, because he must select a bride from amongst the courtiers of his kingdom. All the kings, whose kingdoms are neighbouring to his own—only possess sons. There is no Princess of Royal blood whom he could select as his bride.

(4) Gallifron, seizing the opportunity, compels the girls—the Royal courtiers—to pass before them.

(4) (Gallifron, seizing the opportunity, another motif. 16 bars before the dance begins.)

About 24 bars for each dance of these ladies.

(5) 24 bars. Dance of the Duchesses. Noble and proud.

(6) 24 bars. Dance of the Baronesses. Haughty and finicky.

(7) 24 bars. Dance of the Countesses. Coquettish and amusing.

(8) 24 bars. Dance of the playful Marquesses. They carry little darts, with which they tease the other ladies and their cavaliers.

(9) One of the marquesses proposes to dance a Farandole, because some of the local peasants can dance it. Farandole for Coda, from 48-64 bars, the heavy tempo of a mazurka.

(Note for myself.—Groups for "Blind Man's Buff." They play with the tutor. They push him with little arrows or darts. They can finish Pas de Bourrée, or a farandole step with the peasants, who have come to present fruits to the Prince.)

All these girls try to fascinate the Prince, but Desiré, with a goblet in his hand, chuckles to himself over the fruitless efforts of these numerous beauties. His heart is still whole—he still has not met the girl of his dreams and he will never marry until he has found her.

All this is spoken during the dance.

(10) Huntsmen enter to tell the company that they have surrounded a bear in his den. If the Prince wishes to kill it, it needs a very accurate

shot. But the Prince feels tired. "Hunt without me," he says to the noblemen. "I wish to rest awhile in this very pleasant place." The nobles and courtiers go off, but Gallifron, who has drunk more than one bottle of wine, falls asleep by the Prince's side.

(10) (Huntsmen enter to tell the company they have surrounded a bear. Quick ²/₄, which stops quietly as they go out. 48 bars.)

(11) Only as the hunt dies away, on the river appears a mother-of-pearl boat, adorned with gold and precious jewels. In it stands the Lilac Fairy, who is also Prince Desiré's godmother. The Prince bows before the good Fairy, who graciously tells him to rise and asks him with whom he is in love.

"You are not in love with anyone?" she asks him.

"No," answers the Prince. "The noble ladies of my country cannot capture my heart and I prefer to remain single than marry a suitable Court lady."

"If this is so," answers the Fairy, "I will show you your future bride, the most beautiful, the most charming and the wisest Princess in the whole world."

"But where can I see her?"

"I will call her vision. See if she captivates your heart and if you will love her."

(11) (Only as the hunt dies away, on the river appears the mother-of-pearl boat. Fantastic poetical music. Grand music from 48-64 bars.)

(12) The Lilac Fairy waves her wand over the rock, which opens and discloses Aurora, with her sleeping friends. At a new wave of the Fairy's wand Aurora awakens and runs on the stage with her friends. The rays of the setting sun bathe her in a rose-coloured light.

(12) (At a new wave of the Fairy's wand, Aurora awakens and runs on to the stage. A tender and happy adagio. A little coquettish adagio. Variation for Aurora and a small Coda. For the Coda the music must be muted ²/₄, like in "A Midsummer Night's Dream.")

(12b) All this occurs during Aurora's dance with her friends.

The enraptured Desiré follows behind this vision, which always eludes him. Her dance, now languid, now animated, entrances him more and more. He tries to catch her, but she escapes from his arms and appears again where he never expected to find her, amongst the swaying branches of the trees.

Finally he sees her in the opening of the rock, where she finally disappears. Overcome by his love, Desiré throws himself at his god-mother's feet.

(13) "Where can I find this divine goddess that you have shown me? Lead me to her—I wish to see her, to press her to my heart."

(13) (Where can I find this divine goddess that you have shown me? Very animated, passionate music—48 bars, which must last until the Panorama.)

(14) "Come," says the Fairy, and places the Prince in the boat, which begins to move down the river as Gallifron continues to sleep.

(Panorama.)

(14) (The boat moves quickly. The horizon becomes more and more

Collection Vera Krasovskaya

Carlotta Brianza danced Princess Aurora in the original production of *The Sleeping Beauty* in 1890, the Italian ballerina lending her virtuosic talents to the French choreographer Petipa to create one of the most remarkable of Russian ballets. In 1921 Brianza made her last appearance as a dancer in the Diaghilev production of *The Sleeping Beauty*—this time as the wicked fairy Carabosse.

austere. The sun is setting. Night comes quickly. The path of the boat is starred with silver. A castle appears in the distance, which again disappears as the river twists and turns. But now, at last, here is the castle, the end of the journey.

[Act III is the wedding of Princess Aurora and Prince Desiré.]

Michel Fokine (1880–1942)
THE NEW BALLET

Trained at the St. Petersburg school of the Imperial Russian Ballet, Fokine was inspired to rebel against the conventions of his time, first by visits to museums that showed him the beauty of the human body in nonballetic poses, and second by the performances of Isadora Duncan, who presented her natural form of dancing to Russia in 1905. His opportunity to choreograph according to his convictions came in 1909, when he joined the Diaghilev Ballets Russes for its seasons in Western Europe. After coming to the United States in 1923, Fokine restaged a number of his Diaghilev ballets for the touring Ballet Russe de Monte Carlo and for the American Ballet Theatre.

Fokine could not accept the prevailing customs of ballet production, nor could he follow the now emerging exponents of the free forms of dance that completely rejected the danse d'école. *In "The New Ballet," written in 1916 for the Russian periodical* Argus, *Fokine urges reform within the tradition. Yet he goes well beyond the position of Noverre, who claimed that ballet should unite pantomime and dance. Fokine advocated a complete unity of expression; the whole body of the dancer should portray character and feeling and this may demand the elimination, not only of virtuosity, but of standard forms which are essentially inappropriate to the theme of the particular ballet. This does not, however, imply that they are never appropriate. Here Fokine's insistence on "beauty" and the "ideal" separates him from the next step in choreographic development.*

I. On Ballet Routine

Before I discuss the traditions which hinder the natural development of the art of ballet, I wish to state that I shall consider what in my

SOURCE: From Cyril W. Beaumont, *Michel Fokine and His Ballets* (London: Beaumont, 1935).

opinion is wrong. But I shall deal with laws and traditions, and not with the talents of the artistes. It must be admitted that the creators of the old ballet possessed genius which, however, was restricted by unnecessary rules. The traditional ballet forgot man's natural beauty. It essayed to express a psychological feeling by a fixed movement, or series of movements, which could neither describe nor symbolise anything.

Not only did the spectators fail to understand the expressions of the artistes, but one artiste did not know what another was supposed to convey to him. The audience witness a number of movements but never trouble to question whether they are expressive. Some of these are familiar to them from long acquaintance. For example, it is understood that when a dancer points one finger upwards and then touches his lips with it, he is entreating a kiss; it is curious that in all ballets only one kiss is requested. If the girl to whom he makes this sign runs away from him, proudly raises her arms, points to herself, lowers her arms in front of her and then sweeps them to one side, it is intended to intimate that her would-be lover is rich while she is poor, and consequently he would soon cast her away. This incident is repeated in *Paquita, Esmeralda,* and *La Bayadère.* But this series of gestures cannot even pretend to be expressive. It is hardly likely that a man desirous of obtaining a kiss would point with his finger; but that is the traditional method of making love in a ballet. The expressiveness of the action is relatively unimportant, it is the beauty of the poses and movements, the graceful action of pointing one finger to Heaven that is all important. . . .

II. The Development of Signs

I have mentioned the above details because, in my opinion, a dance is the development and ideal of the sign. The ballet renounced expression and consequently dancing became acrobatic, mechanical, and empty. In order to restore dancing its soul we must abandon fixed signs and devise others based on the laws of natural expression. "But," it may be asked, "how can a dance be built on a sign?" Consider the *arabesque* of the good old times. "But," it may be argued, "you employed *arabesques* in *Les Sylphides*." Certainly, an *arabesque* is sensible when it idealises the sign, because it suggests the body's straining to soar upward, the whole body is expressive. If there be no expression, no sign, but merely a foot raised in the position termed *en arabesque*, it looks foolish. That is the difference between the good old, and the merely old.

Examine the prints of Cerrito, Grisi, Ellsler, and Taglioni, it will be found that their poses have a certain expressiveness. Now look through

Vaslav Nijinsky created the title role of Petrouchka in 1911. Already famous for his technical virtuosity, the dancer here proved his tremendous gifts as a dramatic artist. For this puppet-protagonist, Fokine employed turned-in positions, significant of Petrouchka's introverted character. The constricted movements contradicted the very base of the conventional classical vocabulary.

a history of dancing, on the concluding pages of which will be found the dancers of the end of the last century. Their poses are quite different. There is no sign. What does their pose express? Simply a leg extended backwards. It is neither the beginning nor end of the sign, nor its development. Instead of expressing something, the body seeks balance to avoid falling on account of the raised leg.

There is a vast difference between the dancers of the beginning of the nineteenth century, when the ballet reached its height in beauty, and those at the end of the century, when beauty was forced to give place to acrobatics. There is a complete difference in principle. Taglioni raises herself *sur les pointes* in order to be so light as to seem hardly to touch the ground. The dancer of the period when ballet was in decline uses her *pointes* in order to astonish the audience with their strength and endurance. She fills up the toe of her satin shoe and jumps on it so that the shoe hits the ground with all the strength of her muscular feet. The "steel" toe is a horrible invention of the ballet in decline. In its days of greatness, supernatural lightness was the ideal. Now, the steel toe, hard legs, and precision in execution, are the ideals.

III. The Old and the New in Ballet. The Creative Power in Ballet

I ask for the careful preservation of the beauty of the dance as Taglioni knew it. That world of fragile dreams could not support the rude acrobatic ballet and has fled from us. It will never return if we do not exert all our strength to save this highest form of the dance. But, having preserved it, this style must be employed only when it is applicable. No single form of dancing should be adopted once and for all. The best form is that which most fully expresses the meaning desired, and the most natural one that which most closely corresponds with the idea to be conveyed. For example, ballet steps executed *sur la pointe* cannot be used in a Greek Bacchic dance, on the other hand it would be unnatural to dance a Spanish dance in a Greek *chiton*. . . .

Man has always changed his plastic language. He has expressed in the most varied forms his sorrows, his joys, and all the emotions he experienced, hence his mode of expression cannot be fixed according to any one rule. The old method of production consisted in creating dances from fixed movements and poses, the mimed scenes were always expressed by a fixed manner of gesticulation, and thus the audience had to understand the theme. The most prominent creators of ballet were bound hand and foot by those laws and traditions. We must denounce this. Work of this kind is very easy for the producer and the artistes, and lightens the work of the critic. It is easy to judge whether a dancer has executed correctly the steps which he or she has performed a hundred times in other ballets. But there is one drawback to this method, a ready-made pattern does not always fit.

IV. Confusion

Creators of ballets should always endeavour to seek out that form of dancing which best expresses the particular theme, for this principle leads to great beauty. However varied the rule of ballet might become, life would always be more varied still; while ballet having no relation to reality and circumscribed by tradition naturally becomes ludicrous. The old ballet has confused periods and styles. It uses Russian top-boots and the French school of dancing in one ballet, the short ballet-skirt and historically correct Egyptian costume in another, and so forth. Is not that confusion? The style of the dance is always inharmonious with that of the costumes, theme, and period. Moreover, there is one style for classical dances, another for character dances; and all these appear in one ballet and at the same time. Such is tradition. And to give one homogeneous, harmonious thing is to sin against it, because in order to comply with ballet aesthetics it is imperative to reproduce dual styles.

V. Ballet Rules

The classical ballet came into being as a pleasure of the aristocracy and part of court ceremony. The bowing before the public, the addressing of hand movements to them, and so on, are the foundations on which the rules of ballet were built. Examine the photographs of academic dancers in, for instance, a *pas de deux*; the *danseur* always stands behind the *danseuse*. He holds her waist and looks at her back, while she faces the audience. He displays her. If I do not agree with this style of dancing, it does not mean that I ignore the school. On the contrary, I think that in order to create anything of value one must study and pass through a proper school which, however, should not be confined to the study of fixed poses and steps.

First, one must study oneself, conquer one's own body, and try to learn to feel and develop an ability to perform various movements. Ballet gymnastics are limited, they do not develop the whole body nor instil a feeling for pose and movement in all their variety. The ballet at the end of the last century was limited to several rules handed down without explanation as dogmas. It was of no avail to inquire the why and the wherefore because no one could answer such questions, they were too old. One had to accept the creed that the feet should keep to the five positions and that all movements consisted in combinations of these positions; that the arms should be rounded, the elbows held sideways facing the audience, the back straight, and the feet turned outwards with the heels well to the front. It is difficult to lose faith in these five positions in order to realise that beauty of movement cannot be limited by them.

The practice of turning the legs outward certainly develops the flexibility of the lower limbs, but exercises *en dehors* develop the feet to one side only. In order to make sure it is sufficient to look at a dancer with turned out feet in a dance requiring the feet to be in a natural position. It is obvious that she is ill at ease. Her feet are not under control. I appreciate the "turning out" of the feet in preliminary exercises, but as soon as the exercises are finished the "turning out" should cease, except in Siamese, Hindu, and exotic dances, when the feet should harmonise with the angular positions of the arms. But a barefoot dance with the feet turned out is absurd.

Another failing of ballet technique is that it is concentrated in the dancing of the lower limbs, whereas the whole body should dance. The whole body to the smallest muscle should be expressive, but ballet schools concentrate on exercises for the feet. The arms are limited to a few movements and the hands to one fixed position. What variety would not be possible if the dancer renounced the mannerism of rounded arms. And the movement of the upper part of the body, to what does that lead? A straight back, that is the ideal. One must be deaf not to become furious when the teacher continually repeats for eight or nine years one and the same rule—hold up your back. What store of beauty have painters not taken from the different positions of the body? The academic dancer, however, always faces the audience in a straight line.

The conservative critics were furious because the dancers in certain of my ballets wore sandals and Eastern shoes, and only used the traditional ballet-shoe in some ballets. The admirers of academic dancing could not understand the view that *pointes* should be used as a means and not as the sole aim of ballet. *Pointes* should be employed where they are suitable and renounced without regret where they would not serve any artistic purpose. For instance, in Eastern ballets, the bare foot or a soft shoe is more pleasing than a ballet-shoe, but the dancer in *Le Cygne* does not offend when she uses her *pointes* to suggest a soaring movement. It is right if all her body express the same feeling, but wrong if she uses her *pointes* to display her "steel" toe. She degrades herself before the audience which is watching for the strength of her toes. It is a complete misunderstanding of this beautiful mode of progression.

Forgetful of its artistic aims, ballet began to use *pointes* for quite opposite means, in fact merely to display the endurance and strength of the toes. The shoe was filled up with leather, cotton wool, and cork. But this did not make any difference to anyone, because a competition began as to who could make the most turns *sur la pointe*. The dancer's toes became ugly and it became impossible for her to show her foot without the shoe. That also did not matter. If we admit that ballet should develop mime for most styles of dancing, the basis of the school should be the teaching of natural movement. One should be able to move naturally and control the body to this end. The natural dance should follow and then one could advance to the dance of artificial movement. Ballet however begins at the end. It renounces natural movement, but surely the ballet has no right to discard what it did not possess. Vrubel had the right to paint a mutilated demon because he could draw a beautiful human body. . . .

VII. Delightful Nonsense

The step from the senseless to the expressive dance does not lead to cheap drama, to the narrow dramatisation of the dance; it expresses everything that is in the human soul. "Why," it is argued, "should ballet contain expression and drama when it should be unreal and irrational?" Someone has styled ballet "delightful nonsense." I am glad that ballet is considered "delightful," but if it were not nonsense it would have gained. Expression is as necessary to ballet as any other art, even more so. If colours and sounds do not speak they are tolerable, but an expressionless human body resembles a doll or a corpse. In pictures we look for the painter's soul. We do not accept a picture which expresses nothing; how then can we tolerate a man without expression?

Léonide Massine (1896–)
THE CREATION OF "PARADE"

A graduate of the Moscow school of the Imperial Russian Ballet, Massine choreographed his first ballet for Diaghilev in 1915; his last in 1928. As artistic director of the Ballet Russe de Monte Carlo in the 1930's, he revived some of his early works but also created a controversial series of ballets to the great symphonies—which horrified some musical purists. Later Massine choreographed more of his typical period pieces for Ballet Theatre in the United States and for numerous other companies in America and abroad.

    Parade (1917) came out of Diaghilev's chic, modernist period, but its innovative contributions stemmed more from the visual concepts of Picasso and the music of Satie than from the movement invention of Massine, though his characterizations were much admired. The total effect, smart and streamlined, was

SOURCE: From *My Life in Ballet* (New York: St. Martin's Press, 1968). Reprinted by permission of St. Martin's Press and Macmillan (London and Basingstoke).

brilliant. Nevertheless, the vogue of the likes of **Parade** *did not last. As Lincoln Kirstein commented, "it was one of the first victims of the very school it launched—the cult of the contemporaneous." Notably, however,* **Parade** *was successfully revived in 1973 by the (New York) City Center Joffrey Ballet.*

During that winter of 1916–17 our studio in the Piazza Venezia was the meeting-place of an ever-widening circle of artists, which now included Pablo Picasso, whom Diaghilev had invited to Rome to collaborate on a new ballet. When he first arrived I was so busy that I had little opportunity of getting to know him, but I was intensely aware of the young Spaniard who came to watch our rehearsals, sketching the dancers and helping Bakst to paint some of the props used in the ballet. It was during the rehearsals of *Les Femmes de Bonne Humeur* that he met his future wife, Olga Kokhlova, who was dancing the part of Felicita, one of Constanza's friends.

Another member of our circle was a lean, witty, young Frenchman named Jean Cocteau, whose outrageous suggestions amused and sometimes irritated Diaghilev. But he was usually ready to listen to them, for he felt that Cocteau brought to the company a breath of *avant-garde* Paris. Now that I had finished *Les Femmes de Bonne Humeur* and *Contes Russes* I had more time to spend with them all, and soon we were seriously considering one of Cocteau's suggestions for a ballet incorporating elements of the circus and music-hall. We decided to set the scene in front of a circus tent, bringing on such characters as acrobats, tightrope walkers and conjurers, and incorporating jazz and cinematograph techniques in balletic form. Picasso was delighted by the whole concept, and suggested that the costumes should be executed in cubist style—cubism being then at its height—and he quickly produced some rough sketches, the most striking being those for the French and American managers, whom Picasso visualized as animated billboards suggesting the vulgarity of certain types of show-business promoters. For the American he devised a montage of a skyscraper with fragmentary faces and a gaudy sign reading "PARADE," which eventually became the name of the ballet.

As soon as Erik Satie, who had been commissioned to write the music for the ballet, had produced his witty, satirical score, I was able to begin work on the choreography. I found that the music, with its subtle synthesis of jazz and ragtime, offered me excellent material on which to base a number of new dance patterns. During one of our early rehearsals Cocteau told Diaghilev that he wanted to incorporate into the ballet every possible form of popular entertainment. Diaghilev agreed until the moment came when Cocteau suggested that the managers should be given lines which they would deliver through megaphones. This was going too far, even for Diaghilev, who pointed out that the spoken word was entirely out of place in a ballet. Cocteau, however, insisted that in this case the use of megaphones was perfectly valid and in tune with the cubist conception of the production. Although he lost the argument, he eventually persuaded Satie to introduce into the score a number of realistic sound effects, such as the clicking of a typewriter, the wail of a ship's siren, and the droning of an aeroplane engine. All these, Cocteau explained, were in the spirit of cubism, and helped to portray the feverish insanity of contemporary life.

We began the ballet with the entrance of the French manager, danced by Woidzikowsky, who moved in a jerky, staccato manner to match Satie's opening phrases, stamping his feet and banging his walking-stick on the floor to attract the attention of the crowd. Then came the "parade"—the name given to the efforts of fairground performers to lure the audience into their booths. A curtain was drawn, and in music-hall fashion a placard appeared announcing "Number One." This was the cue for my entrance as the Chinese conjurer, whom I envisaged as a parody of the usual pseudo-oriental entertainer with endless tricks up his sleeve. Dressed in a mandarin jacket and floppy trousers, I marched stiffly round the stage jerking my head at each step. Then going to the centre I bowed to the audience and began my act. I was at first unable to decide what sort of tricks this type of performer would do, but when I had demonstrated the opening phases of my dance to Cocteau, he suggested that I should go through the motions of swallowing an egg. The idea appealed to me. With an elaborate flourish I pretended to produce an egg from my sleeve and put it in my mouth. When I had mimed the action of swallowing it, I stretched out my arms, slid my left leg sidewards till I was almost sitting down, and with my left hand pretended to pull the egg from the toe of my shoe. The whole thing took only a few minutes, but it had to be done with the most clearly defined movements and broad mime. When I had retrieved the egg I leaped round the stage again, then paused, puckered up my lips and pretended to breathe out fire. One last march round the stage, a final deep bow, and I disappeared. My entire performance, with its exaggerated movements, broad miming, and oriental mask-like make-up, was designed to present an enigmatic figure who would intrigue the fairground public and make them want to see more of him.

The American girl who followed the entry of the second manager was intended to be a more credible character. Wearing a blazer and a short white skirt, she bounced on to the stage, crossing it in a succession of convulsive leaps, her arms swinging widely. She then did an imitation of the shuffling walk of Charlie Chaplin, followed by a sequence of

Picasso designed the costume for the Manager from New York in *Parade*. A close look at the dancer's legs provides an idea of the actual scale of the structure. The accoutrements, including such "American" symbols as the megaphone and the skyscraper, impeded the dancer no less than did the similarly identifying props of the *ballet de cour*. But three centuries made a difference in the concept of "chic."

mimed actions reminiscent of *The Perils of Pauline*—jumping on to a moving train, swimming across a river, having a running fight at pistol-point, and finally finding herself lost at sea in the tragic sinking of the *Titanic*. All this was ingeniously danced and mimed by Maria Chabelska, who interpreted Satie's syncopated ragtime music with great charm and gusto, and brought the dance to a poignant conclusion when, thinking herself a child at the seaside, she ended up playing in the sand.

The American girl was followed by a third manager on horseback, and once again we were faced with the problem of how to convey the illusion of a horse on stage. I felt that rather than attempt a realistic presentation, it would be more in the spirit of the production to use the old music-hall device of two men wearing a horse's head with a cloth draped over them. The manager was a Negro dummy in evening dress who was bounced about by the capriciously prancing horse, jumping alternately on its front and hind legs and even sitting down. The horse was followed by two acrobats—Nemchinova and Zverev—who advanced in a series of pirouettes and arabesques, and to give the illusion of a performer delicately poised on a tightrope I made Lopokova balance herself for several seconds on Zverev's bent knee. This was followed by another flurry of pirouettes, after which Zverev lifted his partner and carried her off stage.

For the finale I devised a rapid, ragtime dance in which the whole cast made a last desperate attempt to lure the audience in to see their show. The managers shouted through their megaphones, the horse clumped round the stage, the acrobats performed amazing leaps, the American girl cavorted, the conjurer smiled and bowed. But the public remained indifferent, and when it became evident that the whole "parade" had been a failure, the horse collapsed on the ground, the acrobats stood trembling with exhaustion, the girl and the managers drooped. Only the conjurer retained his oriental calm.

Parade was not so much a satire on popular art as an attempt to translate it into a totally new form. It is true that we utilized certain elements of contemporary show-business—ragtime music, jazz, the cinema, billboard advertising, circus and music-hall techniques—but we took only their salient features, adapting them to our own ends. Some critics have seen in *Parade* a foretaste of the artistic upheaval of the immediate post-war period. It may be that it was instrumental in bringing cubism firmly before the public, and that its repercussions can be traced in certain choreographic and cinematic developments of the next thirty years, and even in such recent manifestations as pop art. These are questions which are best left to the historians of art. For my part, all I can say is that in 1917 we were mainly concerned with creating something new and representative of our own age.

André Levinson (1887–1933)
THE SPIRIT OF THE
CLASSIC DANCE

Born in Russia, Levinson moved shortly after the Revolution to Paris, where
he wrote dance criticism for French newspapers and magazines. He published
several collections of his reviews as well as some notable biographies of dancers.

Levinson believed in the supremacy of pure dance, opposing Fokine, whom
he accused of sacrificing beauty of movement to expression, and to Diaghilev,
whom he derided for subordinating choreography to music and décor. This
essay provides a most precise and illuminating definition of the principles of
dance classicism. Incidentally, it serves us as a convenient summation of the
development of ballet technique up to this point in its history.

The great Noverre, called the "Shakespeare of the dance" by Garrick
and "Prometheus" by Voltaire—who is still the most vital and thorough
theoretician who has written on the subject, desired above everything
to incorporate the dance into the group of "imitative arts." Carlo
Blasis—the same incidentally who established the theory of classic
instruction—struggled manfully to evolve some plausible connection
between the spectacle of the dance and the poetry of the spoken drama.
Others have conceived the dance as strictly limited to the expression
of definite ideas—thereby sacrificing it to and confusing it with pantomime. It seems as though everyone had piled upon this art mistaken
attributes or supplementary burdens in his efforts to redeem—even if
only in a small way—the actual movements of the dance.

I can not think of anyone who has devoted himself to those character-
stics which belong exclusively to dancing, or who has endeavored to
formulate specifically the laws of this art on its own ground. . . . But
no one has ever tried to portray the intrinsic beauty of a dance step,
its innate quality, its esthetic reason for being . . . it is the desire of
the dancer to create beauty which causes him to make use of his knowledge of mechanics and that finally dominates this knowledge. He subjects his muscles to a rigid discipline; through arduous practice he bends
and adapts his body to the exigencies of an abstract and perfect form.
In the end he brings the physiological factors—muscle contraction and

SOURCE: Reprinted with the permission of the publisher, Theatre Arts Books, New York,
from *Theatre Arts Anthology*, Copyright 1925 by Theatre Arts, Inc. Copyright 1950 by
Theatre Arts Books.

relaxation—completely under the domination of the sovereign rhythm of the dance. This is what makes it so difficult to separate the gymnastic elements of the dance from its ideal essence. The technique of a dancer is not like the mechanical workings of a jointed doll; it is physical effort constantly informed by beauty. This technique is no supplementary reënforcement to his art, nor is it a mere device, designed to gain easy applause, like (according to Stendhal) the art of the versifier. It is the very soul of the dance, it *is* the dance itself.

Of all the various techniques it is that of the so-called classic dance—a term designating the style of dancing that is based on the traditional ballet technique—which has prevailed in the Western world. It seems to be in complete accord not only with the anatomical structure of the European but with his intellectual aspirations as well. We find this technique in all those countries where man is fashioned like us and where he thinks in our way. The little definite knowledge we have concerning the system of gymnastics of the ancient Greeks warrants our identifying certain of their "modes" with those of the contemporary dance. Today the universality of the classic style is disputed only by the oriental dance, that finds in the Cambodian ballet its highest and most complete expression. The superb efflorescence of the dance in Spain is in itself a vestige of an oriental civilization, repelled but not annihilated.

Opponents of the classic dance technique pretend to consider it an academic code, imposed on the dance arbitrarily by pedants and long since obsolete. It is true that it does recapitulate the experience of centuries, for we find that certain of its fundamental ideas were accepted by the dancing masters of the Italian Renaissance. It was they who first broke away from the so-called "horizontal" conception of the dance, based on outlines and figures marked by the feet of the dancer on the floor—what you might call his itinerary. The outlines of the choreographs of the seventeenth century, reproducing on paper the curving path drawn on the ground by the feet of the dancer, are the last vestiges of this "horizontal" idea, which was gradually displaced by the vertical conception of dancing—the configuration of motion in space.

. . . The five fundamental positions, which are the ABC of the dance, may seem to be the same for Feuillet, the choreographer of the "grand Siècle" and for Mademoiselle Zambelli—to mention one of the fairest flowers of contemporary classic dance. But this is not actually so. In the outlines of Feuillet that have come down to us, the feet in the first position, make an obtuse angle. In the modern they are in the same straight line in the first position, and in the other positions in parallel lines. This may seem to be a trifling detail of growth and change, when one thinks of Isadora Duncan dancing a Beethoven symphony.

But this almost imperceptible difference, this slight shift of the geometrical line, these feet pivoting at an angle of so many degrees, represents an enormously important acquisition, capable of infinite combinations and variety. This trifling detail is actually a realization of that essential principle and point of departure of classic choreography which took two centuries to prevail—that of turning the body—and more particularly the legs of the dancer—outward from its centre.

I find myself at times looking at the history of the modern dance as though it were some charming but infinitely obscure romance, that needed a key to unlock its mysteries. This key is an understanding of what a dancer means when he speaks of turning out the body. The movement of the oriental dance is concentric. The knees almost instinctively come together and bend, the curved arms embrace the body. Everything is pulled together. Everything converges. The movement of the classic dance, on the other hand, is ex-centric—the arms and the legs stretch out, freeing themselves from the torso, expanding the chest. The whole region of the dancer's being, body and soul, is dilated. The actual manifestation of this can be readily seen or even better felt in the trained body of a classical ballet dancer. The dancer spreads the hips and rotates both legs, in their entire length from the waist down, away from each other, outward from the body's centre, so that they are both in profile to the audience although turned in opposite directions. The so-called five fundamental positions are merely derivations or variations of this outward turning posture, differentiated by the manner in which the two feet fit in, cross or by the distance that separates them. In the fifth position, where the two feet are completely crossed, toes to heels, you have the very incarnation of this principle of turning outward—that is to say, of the spirit of classic dancing. The fifth position is Taglioni; the third was Camargo. A whole century of experimentation and of slow, arduous assimilation lies between the two. The orthopedic machines, true instruments of torture, that were used to turn pupils out in the days of Noverre would not be tolerated today. But it does take several years of daily exercise, beginning at the ages of eight or nine years to give a dancer the ability to perform this mechanical feat easily.

At this point, the reader may demand precisely what is gained by this hard won victory over nature. Just this—the body of the dancer is freed from the usual limitations upon human motion. Instead of being restricted to a simple backward and forward motion—the only directions in which the human body, operating normally, can move with ease and grace, this turning outward of the legs permits free motion in any direction without loss of equilibrium; forward, backwards, sideways, obliquely or rotating. The actual extent of motion possible is considerably augmented, and since the feet are thus made to move on lines parallel to each other there is no interference and many motions otherwise impossible are thereby facilitated. As a good example of this, I might cite the *entrechat*—that exhilarating movement where the dancer leaps high in the air and crosses his legs several times while off the ground. This effective "braiding" movement necessitates the turning outward of the body—otherwise the dancer's legs would block each other.

What a tiresome recital, you may be saying and all of this in trying to talk about so elusive and illusive a thing as the dance! But I assure you it is justified, for the very illusion of this enchanting art—which seems to ignore all natural laws—depends on an intelligent ordering of physical effort. The dancer then is a body moving in space according to any desired rhythm. We have seen how the turning outward of the body increases this space to an extraordinary degree, pushing back the invisible walls of that cylinder of air in the centre of which the dancer moves, giving him that extraordinary extension of body which is totally lacking in oriental dancing and multiplying to an infinite degree the direction of the movement as well as its various conformations. It surrounds the vertical of the body's equilibrium by a vortex of curves, segments of circles, arcs; it projects the body of the dancer into magnificent parabolas, curves it into a living spiral; it creates a whole world of animated forms that awake in us a throng of active sensations, that our usual mode of life has atrophied.

I have not tried to explain clearly more than one of the salient and decisive characteristics of the classic technique. The rich development of the dance that increases its sway from generation to generation corresponds to the gradual elaboration of this principle of turning outward.

If at the beginning of the classic period the dance served merely to give law and style to the carriage and deportment of the perfect courtier, or if at the time of the *"fêtes galantes"* it was still skipping and mincing, it has gradually became exalted and transfigured until it is now called upon to express the loftiest emotions of the human soul.

When once the enthusiasm of the romantic period had created the idea of the dance of elevation, it was only one step further to make the dancer rise up on his toes. It would be interesting to know at exactly what moment this second decisive factor entered in. The historians of the dance, unfortunately, are not concerned with telling us. It is however evident that this reform was at least a half century in preparation. The heel of the shoe raised up, the instep arched, the toe reached down—the plant no longer was rooted to the soil. What happened was that the foot simply refused to remain flat any longer. It strove to lengthen out the vertical lines of its structure. It gave up its natural method of functioning to further an esthetic end. And thus it is that when a dancer rises on her points, she breaks away from the exigencies of everyday life, and enters into an enchanted country—that she may thereby lose herself in the ideal.

To discipline the body to this ideal function, to make a dancer of a graceful child, it is necessary to begin by dehumanizing him, or rather by overcoming the habits of ordinary life. His muscles learn to bend, his legs are trained to turn outward from the waist, in order to increase the resources of his equilibrium. His torso becomes a completely plastic body. His limbs stir only as a part of an ensemble movement. His entire outline takes on an abstract and symmetrical quality. The accomplished dancer is an artificial being, an instrument of precision and he is forced to undergo rigorous daily exercise to avoid lapsing into his original purely human state.

His whole being becomes imbued with that same unity, that same conformity with its ultimate aim that constitutes the arresting beauty of a finished airplane, where every detail, as well as the general effect, expresses one supreme object—that of speed. But where the airplane is conceived in a utilitarian sense—the idea of beauty happening to superimpose itself upon it, the constant transfiguration, as you might call it, of the classic dancer from the ordinary to the ideal is the result of a disinterested will for perfection, an unquenchable thirst to surpass himself. Thus it is that an exalted aim transforms his mechanical efforts into an esthetic phenomenon. You may ask whether I am suggesting that the dancer is a machine? But most certainly!—a machine for manufacturing beauty—if it is in any way possible to conceive a machine that in itself is a living, breathing thing, susceptible of the most exquisite emotions.

Section Five

THE MODERN DANCE: MOVING FROM THE INSIDE OUT

Despite the vitality of its frontier life, its belief in rugged individualism, and its concern with a national identity, the United States long looked to Europe for its culture. Throughout the nineteenth century most of its choreographers and dance soloists came from abroad.

After the demise of the romantic ballet, touring groups carried spectacles like *The Bower of Beauty* and *The Oriental Dream* from coast to coast. Native themes were either ignored or glossed over with fantasy; when a ballet with a local setting was performed in San Francisco in 1854, the leading role was that of Fairy Minerali, Queen of the Gold Mines.

Ballet technique was considered appropriate to any subject, but by the latter part of the century it had become corrupted. Since the popular productions relied more on scenic effects than on actual dancing, members of the corps de ballet did not need much skill; most of the time they just marched in various formations, more or less in time with the music. *Barre* work was abandoned. Albert W. Newman, wearing silk hose and satin knickers, taught his pupils meanings for the five positions: first, attention; second, assurance; third, modesty; fourth, pride; fifth, artistic finish. The idea could have been influenced by the theories of François Delsarte, whose American disciples were teaching that each bodily gesture had an emotional significance. The system, originally designed for opera singers, had no real impact on ballet, but it was to have repercussions on freer forms of dance.

For other forms were emerging. The time had come for America to assert its independence. Some of the first stirrings were isolated experiments, but they served to dent the sterile pattern and to open the eyes of audiences to fresh ideas. Others, more concerted, were to change the nature of theatre dance throughout the Western world.

In the early 1890's Loïe Fuller was a minor and not very successful actress who happened one night to wear an Indian silk skirt on the stage. Fascinated by its shimmering, she started to devise solo numbers in whch she manipulated gauzy fabrics to produce amazing shapes of color and light. Though Fuller soon settled in Paris, she returned to tour America, where observers saw her extraordinary experiments with electric lighting, which seemed to turn her figure into "a golden drinking cup, a magnificent lily, a huge glistening moth." As a dancer, Fuller had no particular technical equipment, but she created a novel form of movement and revealed a tremendous potential for dance in the imaginative uses of lighting.

From Canada came Maud Allan, who wanted to revive the forms of ancient Greece. When she danced in New York in 1910, the critic Carl Van Vechten described her floating "from one pose to the next, emphasizing the plastic transitions with waving arms and raised legs and sundry poses of the head." This sounds rather like balletic flow, but Allan was bare-legged, clothed in a soft tunic, and had no virtuosity to offer. Yet this was dancing; the range of the art was expanding.

Also inspired by Greece but a more zealous missionary was Isadora Duncan. Completely opposed to the ballet—which she denounced as unnatural and harmful in its system of training, empty and unworthy in its theatrical form—she conceived of a dance that would come from the intuitions of the spirit rather than from formal structures. Duncan was adamant in her belief that movement must spring from within; that the dancer, inspired by nature or by music, would naturally respond with beautiful gestures if her soul was not inhibited by technical codes and social taboos. Duncan's own movements were ingenuous: in the early dances they were leaps and runs of spontaneous joy; later there were portraits of grief, drawn from personal tragedies, as well as noble images of humanity's struggles and conquests. One witness recalled an entire dance built simply on rising from the floor; it seemed as if the repressed of the world had shed their chains and triumphed over all tyranny. Since Duncan's art was so dependent on individual sensitivity, she founded no lasting school. In her technique, there were no seeds for development. Yet the impact of her performing was enormous. Even more important in its influence was her concept of dance as an expression of personal emotion: not a representation of the feeling of a dramatic character, but a lyric outpouring of passion.

Meanwhile Ruth St. Denis was channeling her personal emotions into a different kind of dance. Where Duncan expressed her feelings directly and immediately, St. Denis objectified hers in dramas of Eastern ritual; where Duncan danced chiefly as a soloist with simple blue curtains as her only background, St. Denis required a company and all the devices of spectacle: elaborate costumes, models of shrines and pagodas, and arrays of colored lights. Though audiences were undoubtedly attracted by the visual splendors of the productions, these were to St. Denis only the means of embodying her spiritual vision. She relied on them more than on her movement, which was minimal: an evocative walk, a subtle turn of the head, marvelous undulations of the arms. Though these Oriental works were the mainstay of the repertory of the Denishawn company, led by herself and her husband Ted Shawn, other genres were eventually added. Shawn created pieces based on American folk material. His wife ventured into abstractions designed to follow the rhythms and melodic structures of the musical scores that inspired them; for her this was another form of emotional objectification. When she turned to more specifically religious works, this time outside the Oriental context, Shawn developed a group of men dancers to show America that the male performer merited attention equal to the female.

The Denishawn company took dance seriously; they challenged the view that dance was a mere superficial form of entertainment, providing exhibitions of its power to depict, in St. Denis' phrase, "the most noble thoughts of man." But in its way the company was as escapist in concept as the romantic ballet had been; its ideas were realized under guises of ancient legends of exotic lands; its forms were borrowed from distant rituals, from folk tales of the past, from the universal abstractions of music. Even while Denishawn was cheered, fresh forces were visible in other areas of American art: painters and writers were coping with new ways of viewing the contemporary world; musicians were destroying long-respected foundations of tonality; the insights of Freud were changing man's way of regarding himself and his creativity. The philosophy of Denishawn could not last, but before it died it had helped to release dance from its previous confinement to the role of an innocuous amusement.

The next generation, bred within Denishawn, began again with the need to express personal experience. But the experience they had to express was more realistic, closer to the actualities of the society in which they lived, tougher because of its commitment to deal with the sometimes disagreeable facts of the present. To present such experience, these dancers dispensed with the ornate costumes of Denishawn, as Denishawn had dispensed with the pretty prancings of the decadent ballet. In its "black woolens" period, American dance was austere, using sharp, angular, but telling movement to speak its message.

When she left Denishawn, Martha Graham stated: "Life today is nervous, sharp, and zigzag. This is what I aim for in my dances." Spurred by her musical director Louis Horst, she listened to the new music, visited the avant-garde art galleries, and observed the Indian ceremonials of the Southwest. Like the painters who were studying primitive art, Graham was looking for a movement style at once basic to man's nature and attuned to the rhythms of contemporary life. In the beginning her style was unrelentingly strong, earthbound, percussive. There were ritual dances like *Primitive Mysteries* (1931) and dances rooted in her American heritage like *Letter to the World* (1940), which probed the life of Emily Dickinson. There were studies of Greek myth—prototypes of universal experiences of passion, guilt, and redemption; the cycle was climaxed by *Clytemnestra* (1958). Then there were some lyrical works like *Diversion of Angels* (1948), and in time the technique too became somewhat softened with rounded arms, a spiraling torso, and a lighter attack. But a tension, like animal alertness, was always present—the dancer always poised on the brink of danger and discovery.

Where Graham looked inward, to the individual's relation to his own feelings and experiences, her former colleague in Denishawn Doris Humphrey looked out at the individual's relation to the world around him. Humphrey found an arena of conflict, of striving competition, in which the person longs at once for the risk of adventure and the security of the hearth. Optimistically, though, she envisioned a potentially harmonious society, a conquest of opposing forces. Because Humphrey was intensely musical, she realized her dramatic concept in rhythmic as well as spatial forms—a fall forced by the pull of gravity, a mustering of energy to recover balance, a resolution on an exultant breath of triumph. She saw the design in the forces of nature in such works as *Water Study* (1928) and *Life of the Bee* (1929). She found material in religious sects like *The Shakers* (1931) and in the life of a bullfighter, as in *Lament for Ignacio Sánchez Mejías* (1946). But she could also dispense with specific content, creating works like *Passacaglia* (1938) that simply made visible the majestic measures of Bach.

Humphrey's partner, Charles Weidman, showed with autobiographical sketches like *And Daddy Was a Fireman* (1943) that the concern for expressing personal experiences could have its lighter side. Yet his powerful *Lynchtown* (1936) was also drawn from a childhood experience. A skilled mime, Weidman's best choreography was dramatic and shone especially in his witty sketches based on James Thurber's *Fables for Our Time* (1948). Together, Humphrey and Weidman created a rich repertory of wide-ranging styles, unusually diversified in these days of asceticism but always loyal to the principle of starting with the emotion to be portrayed, then finding the movements that would best portray it.

Working along lines similar to the self-exiles from Denishawn was a renegade from the Metropolitan Opera Ballet, Helen Tamiris. She too felt that dance had to be revitalized, had to find fresh movement to express contemporary life. But she was especially involved with the specific social issues of her time, showing her sympathy for the American Negro in *How Long Brethren?* (1937) and for the Spanish Loyalists in *Adelante* (1939). Tamiris stated her beliefs: "We must not forget the age we live in. . . . Each work of art creates its own code. . . . The dance of today must have a dynamic tempo and be valid, precise, spontaneous, free, normal, natural, and human."

These were the leaders of the American modern dance—a most unsatisfactory name, but the one that has been accepted. John Martin, dance critic of *The New York Times*, called it "expressional dance," and this is more accurate. What gave these choreographers their identity was a method: Humphrey called it "moving from the inside out," starting not with traditional steps but with an emotional concept; then seeking the way through the body to communicate that concept. Of the previous rebels, only Fokine had sought to expand the existing vocabulary to accommodate dramatic needs. The modern dance was not satisfied with this degree of change; its exponents had first to eliminate all previous forms, then start—as from the beginning—with the body and its natural impulse to express its feelings in movement. Because the choreographers differed from one another in temperament, in areas of concern, in approach to movement stylization, the modern dance was essentially heterogeneous. Only the motivation was constant.

Though the American modern dance was a largely independent phenomenon, a similar—though distinct—form had risen in Central Europe. In Switzerland in the years following World War I, Rudolf von Laban had started experimenting with the range of movements the body could enact in space and time. Codifying the possible degrees of shape, direction, and energy involved, he went on to explore the principles that determine the expressiveness of human movement. A scientist by nature, Laban began with motion rather than emotion. His own choreographic efforts were limited; his students adapted his ideas for the stage.

The most significant dancer to study with Laban was Mary Wigman. She viewed Laban's theories dramatically: space became her environment, friendly or hostile, to be indulged in or conquered. From the confrontation with space sprang both the spatial design and the rhythms of the dance. Wigman wrote of the dancer who "disturbs the unseen body of space"; "a movement of the arm changes and forms it." From such encounters came dance themes: the celebration of *Festive Rhythm*; the rebellious struggle of *Song of Fate* with its "long strides into the dark and empty space."

Wigman was primarily a solo dancer. Kurt Jooss, on the other hand, who also studied with Laban, worked with a company because he chose to express his ideas through choreographed dramas. Not inclined to deal abstractly with rhythm or design, Jooss used his master's theories to portray specific characters and conflicts. Most famous of his works is *The Green Table* (1932), a bitter denunciation of peacemakers whose hypocritical diplomacy leads only to war, where the only victor is Death—personified by a figure who relentlessly stalks his victims until all have succumbed.

The promise of the German modern dance was cut off by World War II. But in 1931 Hanya Holm had arrived in New York, sent by Wigman to open a school of German modern dance technique. Through the 1930's Holm did some notable choreography for her own concert group, though the greater part of her present reputation rests on her brilliant contribution to the Broadway musical stage. She also continued to teach and in time her students were to bring the influence of their Wigman-rooted ideas to bear on the development of the American modern dance.

Isadora Duncan (1878–1927)
THE DANCE OF THE FUTURE

Born in San Francisco, Duncan learned happily from her music-teacher mother, but quit her ballet classes after a few lessons because she found the movements ugly and unnatural. Dancing in sandals and a simple tunic, she made little impression in the United States, but quickly found admirers in Europe. In 1905 Duncan appeared in Russia, where Fokine was impressed although he could not agree with her rejection of classical technique. Though she danced occasionally with the pupils of the school she had established in Berlin, Duncan performed most often alone, with a single piano to accompany her with the music of Bach or Schubert. Many derided her simplicity, but Karl Federn described the reaction of many more: "Her entrance, her walk, her simple gesture of greeting are movements of beauty. She wears no tights, no frilled ballet skirts, her slender limbs gleam through the veils and her dance is religion."

"The Dancer of the Future," written about 1902, is typical of Duncan's statements about her art. What Levinson called "idealization" was deformation to her, but Fokine agreed with her about the beauty of Greek sculptures. The question of ballet versus modern dance is far from a simple one.

If we seek the real source of the dance, if we go to nature, we find that the dance of the future is the dance of the past, the dance of eternity, and has been and will always be the same.

SOURCE: Reprinted with the permission of the publisher, Theatre Arts Books, New York. Copyright 1928 by Helen Hackett, Inc. Renewed. Copyright © 1969 by Theatre Arts Books.

The movement of waves, of winds, of the earth is ever in the same lasting harmony. We do not stand on the beach and inquire of the ocean what was its movement in the past and what will be its movement in the future. We realize that the movement peculiar to its nature is eternal to its nature. The movement of the free animals and birds remains always in correspondence to their nature, the necessities and wants of that nature, and its correspondence to the earth nature. It is only when you put free animals under false restrictions that they lose the power of moving in harmony with nature, and adopt a movement expressive of the restrictions placed about them.

So it has been with civilized man. The movements of the savage, who lived in freedom in constant touch with Nature, were unrestricted, natural and beautiful. Only the movements of the naked body can be perfectly natural. Man, arrived at the end of civilization, will have to return to nakedness, not to the unconscious nakedness of the savage, but to the conscious and acknowledged nakedness of the mature Man, whose body will be the harmonious expression of his spiritual being.

And the movements of this Man will be natural and beautiful like those of the free animals.

The movement of the universe concentrating in an individual becomes what is termed the will; for example, the movement of the earth, being the concentration of surrounding forces, gives to the earth its individuality, its will of movement. So creatures of the earth, receiving in turn these concentrating forces in their different relations, as transmitted to them through their ancestors and to those by the earth, in themselves evolve the movement of individuals which is termed the will.

The dance should simply be, then, the natural gravitation of this will of the individual, which in the end is no more nor less than a human translation of the gravitation of the universe.

The school of the ballet of today, vainly striving against the natural laws of gravitation or the natural will of the individual, and working in discord in its form and movement with the form and movement of nature, produces a sterile movement which gives no birth to future movements, but dies as it is made.

The expression of the modern school of ballet, wherein each action is an end, and no movement, pose or rhythm is successive or can be made to evolve succeeding action, is an expression of degeneration, of living death. All the movements of our modern ballet school are sterile movements because they are unnatural: their purpose is to create the delusion that the law of gravitation does not exist for them.

The primary or fundamental movements of the new school of the dance must have within them the seeds from which will evolve all other movements, each in turn to give birth to others in unending sequence of still higher and greater expression, thoughts and ideas.

To those who nevertheless still enjoy the movements, for historical or choreographic or whatever other reasons, to those I answer: They see no farther than the skirts and tricots. But look—under the skirts, under the tricots are dancing deformed muscles. Look still farther—underneath the muscles are deformed bones. A deformed skeleton is dancing before you. This deformation through incorrect dress and incorrect movement is the result of the training necessary to the ballet.

The ballet condemns itself by enforcing the deformation of the beautiful woman's body! No historical, no choreographic reasons can prevail against that!

It is the mission of all art to express the highest and most beautiful ideals of man. What ideal does the ballet express?

No, the dance was once the most noble of all arts; and it shall be again. From the great depth to which it has fallen, it shall be raised. The dancer of the future shall attain so great a height that all other arts shall be helped thereby.

To express what is the most moral, healthful and beautiful in art—this is the mission of the dancer, and to this I dedicate my life.

These flowers before me contain the dream of a dance, it could be named "The light falling on white flowers." A dance that would be a subtle translation of the light and the whiteness. So pure, so strong, that people would say: it is a soul we see moving, a soul that has reached the light and found the whiteness. We are glad it should move so. Through its human medium we have a satisfying sense of movement, of light and glad things. Through this human medium, the movement of all nature runs also through us, is transmitted to us from the dancer. We feel the movement of light intermingled with the thought of whiteness. It is a prayer, this dance; each movement reaches in long undulations to the heavens and becomes a part of the eternal rhythm of the spheres.

To find those primary movements for the human body from which shall evolve the movements of the future dance in ever-varying, natural, unending sequences, that is the duty of the new dancer of today.

As an example of this, we might take the pose of the Hermes of the Greeks. He is represented as flying on the wind. If the artist had pleased to pose his foot in a vertical position, he might have done so, as the God, flying on the wind, is not touching the earth; but realizing that no movement is true unless suggesting sequence of movements, the sculptor placed the Hermes with the ball of his foot resting on the wind, giving the movement an eternal quality.

Few observers of Isadora Duncan have been able to explain the magic effect that her dancing had on audiences, and most photographers tended to snap her in poses rather than in movement. The artists tell us more. In these drawings by José Clará we seem to see Isadora as she wanted to be, as the essence of woman: "Let her dance be born of joyousness and strength and courage."

In the same way I might make an example of each pose and gesture in the thousands of figures we have left to us on the Greek vases and bas-reliefs; there is not one which in its movement does not presuppose another movement.

This is because the Greeks were the greatest students of the laws of nature, wherein all is the expression of unending, ever-increasing evolution, wherein are no ends and no stops.

Such movements will always have to depend on and correspond to the form that is moving. The movements of a beetle correspond to its form. So do those of the horse. Even so the movements of the human body must correspond to its form. The dances of no two persons should be alike.

People have thought that so long as one danced in rhythm, the form and design did not matter; but no, one must perfectly correspond to the other. The Greeks understood this very well. There is a statuette that shows a dancing cupid. It is a child's dance. The movements of the plump little feet and arms are perfectly suited to its form. The sole of the foot rests flat on the ground, a position which might be ugly in a more developed person, but is natural in a child trying to keep its balance. One of the legs is half raised; if it were outstretched it would irritate us, because the movement would be unnatural. There is also a statue of a satyr in a dance that is quite different from that of the cupid. His movements are those of a ripe and muscular man. They are in perfect harmony with the structure of his body.

The Greeks in all their painting, sculpture, architecture, literature, dance and tragedy evolved their movements from the movement of nature, as we plainly see expressed in all representations of the Greek gods, who, being no other than the representatives of natural forces, are always designed in a pose expressing the concentration and evolution of these forces. This is why the art of the Greeks is not a national or characteristic art but has been and will be the art of all humanity for all time.

Therefore dancing naked upon the earth I naturally fall into Greek positions, for Greek positions are only earth positions.

The noblest in art is the nude. This truth is recognized by all, and followed by painters, sculptors and poets; only the dancer has forgotten it, who should most remember it, as the instrument of her art is the human body itself.

Man's first conception of beauty is gained from the form and symmetry of the human body. The new school of the dance should begin with that movement which is in harmony with and will develop the highest form of the human body.

I intend to work for this dance of the future. I do not know whether I have the necessary qualities: I may have neither genius nor talent nor temperament. But I know that I have a Will; and will and energy sometimes prove greater than either genius or talent or temperament. . . .

My intention is, in due time, to found a school, to build a theatre where a hundred little girls shall be trained in my art, which they, in their turn, will better. In this school I shall not teach the children to imitate my movements, but to make their own. I shall not force them to study certain definite movements; I shall help them to develop those movements which are natural to them. Whosoever sees the movements of an untaught little child cannot deny that its movements are beautiful. They are beautiful because they are natural to the child. Even so the movements of the human body may be beautiful in every stage of development so long as they are in harmony with that stage and degree of maturity which the body has attained. There will always be movements which are the perfect expression of that individual body and that individual soul; so we must not force it to make movements which are not natural to it but which belong to a school. An intelligent child must be astonished to find that in the ballet school it is taught movements contrary to all those movements which it would make of its own accord.

This may seem a question of little importance, a question of differing opinions on the ballet and the new dance. But it is a great question. It is not only a question of true art, it is a question of race, of the development of the female sex to beauty and health, of the return to the original strength and to natural movements of woman's body. It is a question of the development of perfect mothers and the birth of healthy and beautiful children. The dancing school of the future is to develop and to show the ideal form of woman. It will be, as it were, a museum of the living beauty of the period.

Travellers coming into a country and seeing the dancers should find in them that country's ideal of the beauty of form and movement. But strangers who today come to any country, and there see the dancers of the ballet school, would get a strange notion indeed of the ideal of beauty in that country. More than this, dancing like any art of any time should reflect the highest point the spirit of mankind has reached in that special period. Does anybody think that the present day ballet school expresses this?

Why are its positions in such contrast to the beautiful positions of the antique sculptures which we preserve in our museums and which are constantly presented to us as perfect models of ideal beauty? Or have our museums been founded only out of historical and archaeological interest, and not for the sake of the beauty of the objects which they contain?

The ideal of beauty of the human body cannot change with fashion but only with evolution. Remember the story of the beautiful sculpture of a Roman girl which was discovered under the reign of Pope Innocent VIII, and which by its beauty created such a sensation that the men thronged to see it and made pilgrimages to it as to a holy shrine, so that the Pope, troubled by the movement which it originated, finally had it buried again.

And here I want to avoid a misunderstanding that might easily arise. From what I have said you might conclude that my intention is to return to the dances of the old Greeks, or that I think that the dance of the future will be a revival of the antique dances or even of those of the primitive tribes. No, the dance of the future will be a new movement, a consequence of the entire evolution which mankind has passed through. To return to the dances of the Greeks would be as impossible as it is unnecessary. We are not Greeks and therefore cannot dance Greek dances.

But the dance of the future will have to become again a high religious art as it was with the Greeks. For art which is not religious is not art, is mere merchandise.

The dancer of the future will be one whose body and soul have grown so harmoniously together that the natural language of that soul will have become the movement of the body. The dancer will not belong to a nation but to all humanity. She will dance not in the form of nymph, nor fairy, nor coquette, but in the form of woman in her greatest and purest expression. She will realize the mission of woman's body and the holiness of all its parts. She will dance the changing life of nature, showing how each part is transformed into the other. From all parts of her body shall shine radiant intelligence, bringing to the world the message of the thoughts and aspirations of thousands of women. She shall dance the freedom of woman. . . .

Ruth St. Denis (c. 1877–1968)
MUSIC VISUALIZATION

Ruth St. Denis' serious interest in dance began when she saw a poster advertising Egyptian Deities cigarettes with a picture of the goddess Isis. Though she started at once to work on an Egyptian saga, her first completed theatre piece, Radha (1906), was set in India. Later she added Isis, the Japanese Kwannon, and the Babylonian Ishtar to her galaxy of goddesses. They became well known to many parts of America through the tours she made with her husband Ted Shawn and their Denishawn company. For the Oriental tour of 1925–26, however, the pieces based on Eastern religions were left at home, replaced by works like the newly devised music visualizations.

The chatty, personal style of this article is characteristic of Ruth St. Denis' quite extensive literary efforts. Louis Horst was with the company at this time as musical director, a post he assumed the following year for Martha Graham. Though not mentioned here, Doris Humphrey assisted Miss St. Denis with the development of the music visualizations.

SOURCE: From *The Denishawn Magazine*, I, No. 3 (Spring, 1925).

Let me first define what I mean by the words "Music Visualization:" Music Visualization in its purest form is the scientific translation into bodily action of the rhythmic, melodic and harmonic structure of a musical composition, without intention to in any way "interpret" or reveal any hidden meaning apprehended by the dancer. There is a secondary form of music visualization, which naturally has not our keenest interest, wherein we definitely superimpose dramatic ideas or arbitrary dance forms which seem to relate themselves closely to the composition in emotional coloring, structural outline, rhythmic pattern, and general meaning. . . .

One experience which led me to this resolve to analyze and to arrive at fundamental truths about the relation of dance and music, was the performance of one of our music dancers purporting to interpret a symphony. I heard a large symphony orchestra playing one of the well-known symphonic works. I saw a woman moving about the stage in, at times, a rhythmic, and at other times a dramatic manner, which had in it much depth of feeling, much nobility of movement and much pure beauty of bodily line, but which had almost no connection with the musical composition to which she was dancing. That this dancer was trying to express through her movements the spirit of the work was quite evident, but in actual fact she could give but a few gestures, a few pregnant pauses, that in any way visualized, much less interpreted, the great symphonic work whose harmonies and dynamics were floating about her.

I went home from this performance very thoughtful, for the motives of her performance found a most profound agreement with my own. That is, I too asserted that only the greatest music was fit accompaniment for the deep and eternal things which I wanted to express through the dance. But her methods were obviously wrong. It could not be done that way. The result of my mediations was the conception of my Synchoric Orchestra, and, from the principles involved therein, the whole series of our music visualizations, from the *Bach Inventions* (which Mr. Shawn visualized) and which the Concert Dancers used, for two seasons, down to the *Schutt Suite for Violin and Piano*, which is new on this season's program.

In the case of the Bach Fugues and Inventions, we have the pure mathematics of the dance. In these there is no emotional coloring or intent, and therefore the music visualization of them should be without emotional coloring in movement. In a two-part Invention, two separate groups dance, each group moving to the notes of its own part only, and remaining still on the rests in that part. Dancing at the same time, the two groups imprint upon the eye a correlative image to the one given to the ear by the playing of this two-part Invention on the piano—that of two themes, each distinct in itself harmoniously mingling to produce a charming and perfect structural whole. This same principle is simply enlarged by using three groups for a three-part Invention and four groups for a four-voice Fugue, and so on, keeping always in view the relation of the groups so as to present a harmonious composition to the eye, as well as the exact beating out of the actual notes of each part by its group.

Ruth St. Denis portrays an Oriental goddess. In her dances she wanted to depict a mystical experience, particularly as she found it conceived in Oriental religions. She found it also through music. "My final use of art is impersonal," she wrote in her autobiography, "for when I dance I am really an abstraction, a creature set apart from time and space, unrelated to human things in the ordinary sense."

In other compositions, such as Beethoven's Sonata called the *Pathetique* there is obviously an emotional coloring. Some scholastic musicians argue that no emotional intent was in the composer's mind, but that sheer structural writing produced the result. However, emotional music resulted, and that must be considered in the visualization. After the abstract emotional coloring is decided upon, it must be kept in mind as influencing the quality of the gesture used throughout by the dancers.

Then, in the visualization of such a composition, these simple and obvious facts of the relation of music to movement must be obeyed:

Time value underlies all. The time in which the music is written must be recognized, and the rhythmic pattern apprehended. Then each note must have its correlative translation—an eighth note has a definite length, and its visualization must be a movement exactly as long; a quarter note is twice as long, and should be visualized by a movement twice as long.

Simple melody and simple accompaniment, obviously, would be adequately visualized as a solo dance; whereas complicated and contrapuntal writing, involving many simultaneous voices, parts or themes, should be visualized by a group of three or more dancers.

Just as there is staccato and legato in playing, so is there staccato and legato quality in bodily movement.

Dynamics must be considered. A softly struck note should be moved softly and with economy of force, while a crashing chord must be visualized with more physical energy.

The rise and fall of the melody should have some answer in the rise and fall of the body above the plane of the stage, the positions of the notes on the printed staff being in some degree analogous to the range of posture the body can control from lying flat on the stage to the highest leap above the floor.

There is sometimes a wide variety of movements that can be used equally well to visualize certain elements in the music, and here is where the selective quality of the artist comes into play. A trill in the music may be visualized as a whirl, or a vibration throughout the body accented in the arms and hands, or a *ballet emboit*, for instance. But here the quality of the movement of the visualization as a whole must govern the choice of the particular gesture. If one is visualizing an abstract composition, sonata, concerto, or etude, obviously the quality of the gesture should be kept abstract, should avoid a definite school, national or racial style—it should be universal gesture.

All of these rules are used as bases to start from. Often we depart from them ourselves for many reasons. In designing dances for entertainment purposes, the fact is borne in upon the creator that the public will stand for abstract movement only in small doses. And so, upon a sound base of rendering the value of the notes of the music into a corresponding value of movement, there is superimposed a surface idea to trick the eye of those beholders who have neither the interest nor the training to apprehend the actual visualization principles which are being applied and actually worked out in the dance which he sees. Thus in Mr. Shawn's visualization of the *Revolutionary Etude* of Chopin, he has superimposed a dramatic narrative, while at the same time the composition is visualized on rigid principles. His gesture enacting the story of the crazed revolutionist exactly parallels the melodic theme, while the whirling figures behind him symbolizing flame and fury, visualize the accompaniment. And in the *Soaring* of Schumann, the great square of silk is manipulated to give the surge of the music and to give amusement to the audience in watching its multiple forms, while the notes are just as carefully rendered by the movements of the dancers as if there were no veil. . . .

The Synchoric Orchestra, when dancing in connection with a Symphony Orchestra to visualize a symphony, would be composed of as many dancers as there were musical instruments. Each dancer would be definitely related to one certain instrument. Some arrangement of human values is desirable—such as the heavier and older dancers paralleling the heavier instruments—strong men for percussion and brass, slender youths for the wood-winds, young girls for violins, and more mature girls and women for 'cellos and basses. Each dancer would move exactly what was played by his instrument and when his instrument was silent he would be still. When all the violins played in unison, all the violin dancers would dance in a unified group, in unison of movement. A solo theme by a flute, against an accompaniment of 'cellos and basses would be seen as a solo dance movement by the flute dancer, with subordinated mass movement in the background upon the part of the dancers representing the 'cellos and basses. The whole would always maintain an architectural sense of mass composition, so that at all times the grouping was based on a sound undertaking of form.

About six years ago I visualized the two movements of the *Unfinished Symphony* of Schubert. For months I worked with more than sixty dancers who were all pupils of Denishawn, well-trained and responsive human instruments in my Synchoric Orchestra. For the obvious reason of expense, I was unable to have a symphony orchestra, but with the conductor's score, and the invaluable help of Mr. Louis Horst, our pianist-director, each instrument's scoring was studied, and the movements of that dancer worked out first separately, then in relation to the other instruments of his class, and then in relation to the form of the whole. When this was complete, we gave three performances for invited audiences in Los Angeles, and met with an extraordinary response. It is my dream to be able to give this, and other compositions of its kind, with a great orchestra. But that is a dream which must wait for someone who believes that dancing of the highest calibre is as worthy of support, and of as much benefit to mankind, as the music of a Symphony Orchestra itself.

The music of the future will have to be divided into two groups, so far as dancers and the dance public are concerned—that which is to be listened to, and that which is to be danced to. But one might say that this is true today. We have supporting music as accompaniment to singing in opera, and we have ballet music; and then we have orchestral music, symphonies, overtures, and such. Yes, but it is all the same kind of music, and the music of the dance of the future must be a different music than any we have yet heard. It must be composed for the dancers by composers who understand the fundamentals of the dance, and who have the utmost reverence for the dance as the greatest of the arts; a condition which I need not remind you does not exist today.

Beautiful, natural and noble movement can never be trained and fixed in art forms and expressed in supreme works of the dance until the music compositions are a sympathetic parallel to the capacities of the human body. At present the dancer is made to do grotesque, unnatural and futile gestures in order to meet the exigencies of an almost alien art. But until the ideal music of the future is composed upon ideal principles, we have a right to claim the use of the best, the highest and noblest works of music with which to give audible accompaniment to our noblest, best and highest thoughts as expressed through beautiful, rhythmic bodily movement. . . .

To conclude the whole matter—Visualization of Music is not the mere putting into gesture form the mechanical elements of a musical composition. But because the Creative Dancer is always striving to give expression to Divine Intelligence, and because the art of music has gone so far ahead of us in these last centuries while the dance remained the Cinderella among the arts, we have chosen the great music to aid us in making this revelation, since lesser music was not worthy of the things we have to say. We will respect and study the great music of today in order to give it adequate visualization because it says partially the same lofty things—but we believe that in order to follow the wings of the dance, music will have to soar even higher than any of its known forms.

Martha Graham (1894–)
A MODERN DANCER'S
PRIMER FOR ACTION

After serving an apprenticeship with Denishawn, Martha Graham left the company in 1923, giving her first independent concert three years later. Some called her "that arty, angular woman who moves in spasms and jerks"; others considered her a new messiah; today the almost universal verdict is "genius." In the course of her long career, Graham broke new ground in many areas of theatre dance: she commissioned scores from American composers who wrote some of their finest music for her; she had Noguchi design sculptured settings that marked a new trend in stage décor. She made works that were layered with meanings, both specific and symbolic; experimented with stream-of-consciousness structures; drove dance to cope with areas of human awareness that it had never dared to touch before.

For Graham, the simplified vocabularies of Duncan and St. Denis were no more adequate than that of the ballet. She created for dance a completely new language, the one she needed "to make visible the interior landscape." The aim of technical training, as she describes it here, is still the control of the dancer's instrument. But where the ballet class was planned to increase the independent mobility of the limbs and to develop the vertical extension of the body, the Graham exercises stress the inner core that motivates movement from the center of the torso and recognize the force that must be expended to raise the body from the floor. The turnout is either eliminated or used to only a moderate degree; control emanates from the back. The effect desired is neither courtly elegance nor ethereal lightness nor yet pedestrian naturalism, but rather a reflection of "the miracle that is a human being."

I. Certain Basic Principles

I am a dancer. My experience has been with dance as an art.

Each art has an instrument and a medium. The instrument of the dance is the human body; the medium is movement. The body has always been to me a thrilling wonder, a dynamo of energy, exciting, courageous, powerful; a delicately balanced logic and proportion. It has not been my aim to evolve or discover a new method of dance training,

SOURCE: From Frederick R. Rogers, ed., *Dance: A Basic Educational Technique* (New York: Macmillan, 1941). Copyright 1941 by Macmillan Publishing Co., Inc.; renewed 1969 by Frederick R. Rogers. Reprinted by permission.

but rather to dance significantly. To dance significantly means "through the medium of discipline and by means of a sensitive, strong instrument, to bring into focus unhackneyed movement: a human being."

I did not want to be a tree, a flower, or a wave. In a dancer's body, we as audience must see *ourselves*, not the imitated behavior of everyday actions, not the phenomena of nature, not exotic creatures from another planet, but something of the miracle that is a human being, motivated, disciplined, concentrated.

The part a modern art plays in the world, each time such a movement manifests itself, is to make apparent once again the inner hidden realities behind the accepted symbols. Out of this need a new plasticity, emotional and physical, was demanded of the dance. This meant experiment in movement. The body must not only be strong, be facile, be brilliant, but must also be significant and simple. To be simple takes the greatest measure of experience and discipline known to the artist.

It may be possible for an individual dancer to proceed instinctively along these lines, but when dance involves more than the solo figure, some uniform training is necessary. Several of us, working separately, found methods of training, evolving as we worked.

The method, however, was secondary. Training, technique, is important; but it is always in the artist's mind only the means to an end. Its importance is that it frees the body to become its ultimate self.

Technique and training have never been a substitute for that condition of awareness which is talent, for that complete miracle of balance which is genius, but it can give plasticity and tension, freedom and discipline, balancing one against the other. It can awaken memory of the race through muscular memory of the body. Training and technique are means to strength, to freedom, to spontaneity.

Contrary to popular belief, spontaneity as one sees it in dance or in theatre, is not wholly dependent on emotion at that instant. It is the condition of emotion objectified. It plays the part in theater that light plays in life. It illumines. It excites. Spontaneity is essentially dependent on energy, upon the strength necessary to perfect timing. It is the result of perfect timing to the Now. It is not essentially intellectual or emotional, but is nerve reaction. That is why art is not to be *understood*, as we use the term, but is to be *experienced*.

To experience means that our minds and emotions are involved. For primarily it is the nervous system that is the instrument of experience. This is the reason music, with its sound and rhythm, is universally the great moving force of the world. It affects animals as well as human beings.

A program of physical activity which involves only, first, exercises for strength, and second, a means of emotional catharsis through so-called "self-expression dancing," will never produce a complete human being. It is a dangerous program, for it does not fit a child or an adolescent for the virtue of living.

Living is an adventure, a form of evolvement which demands the greatest sensitivity to accomplish it with grace, dignity, efficiency. The puritanical concept of life has always ignored the fact that the nervous system and the body as well as the mind are involved in experience, and art cannot be experienced except by one's entire being.

In life, heightened nerve sensitivity produces that concentration on the instant which is true living. In dance, this sensitivity produces action timed to the present moment. It is the result of a technique for revelation of experience.

To me, this acquirement of nervous, physical, and emotional concentration is the one element possessed to the highest degree by the truly great dancers of the world. Its acquirement is the result of discipline, of energy in the deep sense. That is why there are so few great dancers.

A great dancer is not made by technique alone any more than a great statesman is made by knowledge alone. Both possess true spontaneity. Spontaneity in behavior, in life, is due largely to complete health; on the stage to a technical use—often so ingrained by proper training as to seem instinctive—of nervous energy. Perhaps what we have always called intuition is merely a nervous system organized by training to perceive.

Dance had its origin in ritual, the eternal urge toward immortality. Basically, ritual was the formalized desire to achieve union with those beings who could bestow immortality upon man. Today we practice a different ritual, and this despite the shadow over the world, for we seek immortality of another order—the potential greatness of man.

In its essentials, dance is the same over the entire world. These essentials are its function, which is communication; its instrument, which is the body; and its medium, which is movement. The style or manner of dance is different in each country in which it manifests itself. The reason for this is threefold—climate, religion, and social system. These things affect our thinking and hence our movement expression.

Although its concept was the product of Isadora Duncan and Ruth St. Denis, modern dance in its present manifestation has evolved since the World War. At that time a different attitude towards life emerged.

As a result of twentieth-century thinking, a new or more related movement language was inevitable. If that made necessary a complete departure from the dance form known as ballet, the classical dance, it did not mean that ballet training itself was wrong. It was simply found not to be complete enough, not adequate to the time, with its change of thinking and physical attitude.

In *Deaths and Entrances* (1945) the dancers are (left to right): Erick Hawkins, Martha Graham, Merce Cunningham. The "Dark Beloved" and the "Poetic Beloved" appear to the heroine, but only in her remembered vision. The dance deals with the "interior landscape" of the Brontë sisters, recalling the days of their youth from a present beset with rivalries and hatreds.

A break from a certain rigidity, a certain glibness, a certain accent on overprivilege was needed. There was need of an intensification, a simplification. For a time, this need manifested itself in an extreme of movement asceticism; there has now come a swing back from that extreme. All facilities of body are again being used fearlessly, but during that time of asceticism, so-called, much glibness was dropped, much of the purely decorative cast aside.

No art ignores human values, for therein lie its roots. Directed by the authentic or perverted magnificence, which is man's spirit, movement is the most powerful and dangerous art medium known. This is because it is the speech of the basic instrument, the body, which is an instinctive, intuitive, inevitable mirror revealing man as he is.

Art does not create change; it registers change. The change takes place in the man himself. The change from nineteenth- to twentieth-century thinking and attitude toward life has produced a difference in inspiration for action. As a result, there is a difference in form and technical expression in the arts.

2. Posture, Movement, Balance

One of the first indications of change, because it is the total of being—physical, emotional, mental, and nervous—is posture.

Posture is dynamic, not static. It is a self-portrait of being. It is psychological as well as physiological.

I use the word "posture" to mean *that instant of seeming stillness when the body is poised for most intense, most subtle action, the body at its moment of greatest potential efficiency.*

People often say that the posture of this dancer or that dancer or of all dancers is not natural. I ask, "Not natural to what?—natural to joy, sorrow, pain, relaxation, exaltation, elevation, fall?"

Each condition of sensitivity has a corresponding condition of posture. Posture is correct when it is relative to the need of the instant.

There is only one law of posture I have been able to discover–the perpendicular line connecting heaven and earth. But the problem is how to relate the various parts of the body. The nearest to the norm, as it has been observed and practiced over centuries, has been the ear in line perpendicularly with the shoulder, the shoulder with the pelvic bone, the pelvic bone in line with the arch of the foot.

The criticism that the posture of some dancers is bad because they appear to have a "sway back" is usually not justified, for a "sway back" is a weak back. Often the development of the muscles for jumping, leaping, and elevation, all of which concentrate in the hips and buttocks, is so pronounced as to give the appearance, to the uninformed critic, of "sway back."

Through all times the acquiring of technique in dance has been for one purpose—so to train the body as to make possible any demand made upon it by that inner self which has the vision of what needs to be said.

No one invents movement; movement is discovered. What is possible and necessary to the body under the impulse of the emotional self is the result of this discovery; and the formalization of it into a progressive series of exercises is technique.

It is possible and wise to teach these exercises even to the person who has no desire to dance professionally. It must, however, be emphasized that performance of these exercises is not a mere matter of "having a good time," but of achieving a center of body and mind which will eventually, but not immediately, result in a singing freedom. Throughout the performance of these technical exercises, a woman remains a woman, and a man a man, because power means to become what one *is*, to the highest degree of realization.

As in any other architectural edifice, the body is kept erect by balance. Balance is a nicety of relationship preserved throughout the various sections of the body. There are points of tension which preserve us in the air, hold us erect when standing, and hold us safely when we seem to drop to the floor at incredible speed. We would possess these naturally if they had not been destroyed in us by wrong training, either physical, intellectual, or emotional.

Contrary to opinion, the dancer's body is nearer to the norm of what the body should be than any other. It has been brought to this possible norm by discipline, for the dancer is, of necessity, a realist. Pavlova, Argentina, and Ruth St. Denis all practiced their art past the age of fifty.

3. The Aim of Method

There is no common terminology for describing the technique of modern dance. Furthermore, to describe two or three exercises would give an accent to these few beyond their importance. Therefore, rather than being a description here of actual specific practice of exercises, this is intended as an exposition of the theory behind the practice of the technical training I employ.

The aim of the method is coordination. In dance, that means unity of body produced by emotional physical balance. In technique, it means so to train all elements of body—legs, arms, torso, etc.—as to make them all equally important and equally efficient. It means a state of relativity of members in use that results in flow of movement. I have discovered whatever it is that I have discovered through practice and out of need. My theory, if it can be called such, had its origin and has its justification in practical experience.

What I say is based on one premise–dance is an art, one of the arts of the theatre. True theatricality is not a vain or egotistic or unpleasant attribute. Neither does it depend on cheap tricks either of movement, costume, or audience appeal. Primarily, it is a means employed to bring the idea of one person into focus for the many. First there is the concept; then there is a dramatization of that concept which makes it apparent to others. This process is what is known as theatricality.

I believe dancing can bring liberation to many because it brings organized activity. I believe that the exercises I use are as right for a lay person as for a professional dancer, because they do no violence anatomically or emotionally. The difference in their use for the lay person and for the professional dancer is not in their basic approach but in the degree and intensity of their application. I have always thought first of the dancer as a human being. These exercises, though their original intention was the training of professionals, have been taught to children and adolescents as well.

What follows might be termed a "Primer for Action."

4. Primer for Action

A. An Attitude Toward Dance.
   1. There must be something that needs to be danced. Dance demands a dedication, but it is not a substitute for living. It is the expression of a fully aware person dancing that which can be expressed only by means of dance. It is not an emotional catharsis for the hysterical, frustrated, fearful, or morbid. It is an act of affirmation, not of escape. The affirmation may take many forms—tragedy, comedy, satire, lyric or dramatic.
   2. There must be a disciplined way of dancing. This means learning a craft, not by intellection, but by hard physical work.
B. A Dancer's Attitude Toward the Body.
      The body must be sustained, honored, understood, disciplined. There should be no violation of the body. All exercises are but the extensions of physical capabilities. This is the reason it takes years of daily work to develop a dancer's body. It can only be done just so fast. It is subject to the natural timing of physical growth.
C. An Attitude Toward Technique.
      Technique is a means to an end. It is the means to becoming a dancer.
   1. All exercises should be based on bodily structure. They should be written for the instrument, a body, male *or* female.
   2. As the province of dance is motion, all exercises should be based upon the body in motion as its natural state. This is true even of exercises on the floor.
D. Technique Has a Three-Fold Purpose.
   1. Strength of body.
   2. Freedom of body and spirit.
   3. Spontaneity of action.

E. Specific Procedure in Technique.

All exercises are in the form of theme and variations. There is a basic principle of movement employed which deals specifically with a certain region of body—torso, back, pelvis, legs, feet, etc. The theme of the exercise deals directly with its function for body control. It is stripped of all extraneous movement or embellishments. The variations become increasingly wider in scope, moving from the specific to the general movement which embraces the use of the entire body. Variation still keeps, however, no matter how involved it becomes, its relationship to the theme.

F. Four Main Classes into Which Technique Is Divided.

1. Exercises on the floor.

All exercises on the floor are direct preparations for standing and elevation later. The first principle taught is body center. The first movement is based upon the body in two acts of breathing —inhaling and exhaling—developing it from actual breathing experience to the muscular activity independent of the actual act of breathing. These two acts, when performed muscularly only, are called "release," which corresponds to the body in inhalation, and "contraction" which corresponds to exhalation. The word "relaxation" is not used because it has come to mean a devitalized body.

In the professional class, the floor exercises take approximately twenty minutes. They comprise: a. stretching; b. back exercise; c. leg extensions.

N.B. No stretch is made by pushing the back of the student to the floor. The down movement is never helped. The spine is never touched. The leg is never stretched suddenly or forcibly by pressure. The hand never tries to straighten the knee by pressure. The leg is straightened only by slow and gradual extension.

2. Exercises standing in one place.

a. All exercises for the legs—bends, lifts, extensions, front, side, and back.

b. Hip swings.

c. Feet exercises.

d. Turns in place.

N.B. In all lifts and *pliés*, the relationship of knee to foot is closely observed. There must be no strain on knees or arches at any time. In all exercises on contraction, the shoulders and pelvic bone have a definite relationship in order to avoid all abdominal strain.

3. Exercises for elevation.
   a. Jumps in place.
   b. Open space work.
      Walks in rhythms.
      Runs.
      Turns across the floor.
      Turns in the air.
      Leaps.
      Skips.

   N.B. No elevation is attempted until at least one half hour of preliminary work is done to permit the body to become fluid. All elevation is without strain. The legs and back are strong and the body centered from the exercises which have gone before.

4. Exercise for falls.

   This exercise is a series of falls forward, side, and back in various rhythms and at various speeds. The body never strikes the floor by landing on the knees, on the spine, on a shoulder, or on an elbow or head. The joints must not be jarred or any vital part struck. Falls are used primarily as preliminary to and therefore as a means of "affirmation." In no fall does the body remain on the floor, but assumes an upright position as part of the exercise. My dancers fall *so they may rise*.

Doris Humphrey (1895–1958)
NEW DANCE

In 1928 Doris Humphrey left the Denishawn company, feeling that she had learned to dance in the styles of nearly all kinds of people—except twentieth-century Americans. The group that she formed with Charles Weidman was dedicated to the contemporary idiom, although they conceived that idiom with less violent intensity than Graham. The tours of the Humphrey-Weidman company, mostly to college campuses that became known as the "gymnasium circuit," took their work to young people throughout the country. After her retirement as a dancer in 1944, Humphrey became artistic director of the José Limón company, creating some of her finest works for her Mexican protégé.

The plan of New Dance (1935) is representative of one vein of her work, a piece in which the drama was inherent in the movement, needing no overlay of literary subject matter; and it reveals the meticulous care with which Humphrey worked out expressive spatial patterns. Unfortunately, it does not show the equally perceptive attention she paid to rhythmic design, design made to reflect the intricate manner in which the individual weaves his personal paths in counterpoint to the group, yet always in harmony with it.

There is a great difference between the modern dance as it is presented today and as it was presented as little as five or six years ago. When I gave my first recital in New York apart from the Denishawn company, the stage was bare, there was only one pianist for the music, and costuming was at a minimum. Now, however, the modern dance leaves this period of barrenness and comes forward as a new theatrical form.

In the past two seasons, Charles Weidman and I have developed our forms away from the recital stage, where each dance was about five minutes long, and have composed long ballets, consecutive in idea. More significant than this is the fact that these new dances are the comment of two American dancers on contemporary life. This comment naturally brings them close to the theatre, but this is a theatre of movement rather than of words.

It might be interesting to describe one of them in some detail, since the manner of building will show how a large, complex theme may be presented entirely through movement, and, I believe, more forcibly than could be done through words.

SOURCE: From Selma Jeanne Cohen, *Doris Humphrey: An Artist First* (Middletown, Conn.: Wesleyan University Press, 1972).

I have composed a trilogy of which the general theme is the relationship of man to man. There are three long works which would take an evening and a half for presentation. One is in symphonic form and two are in dramatic form. The first, *New Dance*, represents the world as it should be, where each person has a clear and harmonious relationship to his fellow beings. The second, *Theatre Piece*, shows life as it is today—a grim business of survival by competition. Much of this is done in satire. The third, *With My Red Fires*, deals with love between man and woman, and between two women.

Let me describe *New Dance* for you. It was to be a dance of affirmation from disorganization to organization. It begins with two dancers with the group standing on the blocks in the corners as audience. For this Introduction, since I wished at first to convey a sense of incompletion, I chose the Broken Form, by which I mean an unfolding continual change, with contrast but very little repetition. This is the same form that Mr. Weidman and I used in *Rudepoema*, where a movement was done several times and then discarded, giving way to new ones.

By this means I was able to present the main themes of the whole composition, which were elaborated in the remaining sections of the dance: First Theme, Second Theme, Third Theme, Processional, Celebration, and Variations and Conclusion. I used lateral lines, perpendiculars —in fact, as many varieties as possible to convey the sense of a jetting forth of movement as yet disorganized.

The movements used in this Introduction were by no means spontaneous. I had a very clear reason for them. They were mainly feet and leg themes; I consciously eliminated any free use of the hands, arms, head, and torso. My main theme was to move from the simple to the complex, from an individual integration to a group integration, and therefore I thought it best at first to confine myself to movement which was in a way primitive. The primitive urge for movement—in fact, all early dancing made use of steps and leg gestures but scarcely ever used the rest of the body with any emphasis. Therefore, until the group integration had been achieved, the feet and leg themes seemed more expressive.

There are two essential movements of the body: the change of weight and the breath-rhythm. After the various themes had been stated in the Introduction, I used this essential changing of weight as the basis for the First Theme. The Second Theme used the breath-rhythm.

The Third Theme, which was composed by Mr. Weidman, used both of these in a single section. My only function in this was to explain the general idea: that it must be a loose form, broken, unbalanced, not symmetrical, and it must have an inconclusive ending. Each of these themes was in this sense inconclusive, because each was only a part

Photo, Edward Moeller, Collection Charles H. Woodford

The sculptural molding of the dancers in the second theme of Doris Humphrey's *New Dance* clearly shows in this grouping where the central figure relates the opposing forces by letting her own body strike a balance between the contrary pulls of the two spatial directions. The dancers are (left to right): Edith Orcutt, Katherine Litz, Letitia Ide, Doris Humphrey, Ada Korwin, Beatrice Seckler, Miriam Krakovsky, Joan Levy.

of a whole. I would never perform any of these sections as separate pieces, except the Variations and Conclusion which is a summation of them all, because there is a dramatic idea behind them of which each theme expresses only a fraction.

This dramatic idea played a large part in determining what movements and what forms were necessary. After Mr. Weidman and I, as leaders and integrators, had stated our themes together and alone, it was necessary to bring the women under my orbit and the men under Mr. Weidman's before they could be finally fused.

The Broken Form would do no longer. Those themes which were stated had to be conveyed to a group, and a group never accepts immediately en masse. For the First Theme, then, I used the Cumulative Form. The leader molds the group; the women are gradually drawn into the movement. One dancer may cross the stage and return; when she crosses again, two or three more follow her until finally the whole group is doing that particular movement-phrase. This section ends inconclusively.

In Second Theme, the leader again tries to unify the group. The dance ends in a revolving pulsation, but is again not cohesive enough to make a compact whole. It is inconclusive because there are only women. In Third Theme, the men take the stage and are compelled and molded by Mr. Weidman as leader. Now all themes have been stated for the groups and to finish them the two groups must be brought together.

Processional uses the Cumulative Form once more and in movement brings the themes to a head; in dramatic idea brings the whole group to an integrated whole. I chose a slow tempo for this because that gives a sense of greater control and, theatrically, is obviously in sharp contrast to the preceding sections. The men never deviate from a perpendicular but the women are fluid and make a wavering line. It was here that I used symmetry for the first time as the best way to express cohesion and completion.

The groups have now fused and break into a Celebration, which is built in fugue form, joyous in character. The fugue was eminently suitable to express a harmonious chorus wherein no member was more important than another. It is a short theme and goes directly into a square dance, which is again consciously symmetrical. I could have used several symmetrical forms here, but chose the square dance because at a moment of climax forward movement is the most powerful. Other forms do not have that direct impact. The ballet, incidentally, has used the square a great deal but rarely uses all four sides. It confines itself to the side from the back of the stage to the front and then weakens that impact by almost walking around the other three to get back to its starting point.

Having thus unified the men's group and the women's group, one more section was necessary in order to express the individual in relation to that group. Too many people seem content to achieve a mass-movement and then stop. I wished to insist that there is also an individual life within that group life.

All previous action had taken place within an arena marked by masses of blocks along the side of the stage. Mr. Weidman and I had stated our themes in this arena before the watching crowd and had finally brought that crowd down into our field of activity. It was obvious, now that all were working in unison, that the arena was useless since there was no longer any conflict between those who do and those who watch. In order to focus the dance and fully convey that sense of unity, the curtain was lowered momentarily while the blocks were moved into a pyramid in center stage. The whirling star pattern was used around this pyramid to avoid monotony. I could have allowed the two lines of dancers to remain in one place to form a path for the new dancers who now came in and performed briefly their own personal themes. However, by having this line whirl and by having the new dancers enter from different directions, a deadness was avoided and a greater space and excitement was achieved. In this section, Variations and Conclusion, I used the Repetitional Form where the group performs the same movement. The brief solos are in Broken Form against the *basso sustenuto* of the group.

It is this method of work, which I have described for *New Dance*, that broadens the field of the modern dance, gives it a new life and a new potency. Solo dances flow out of the group and back into it again without break and the most important part is the group. Except for an occasional brilliant individual, the day of the solo dance is over. It is only through this large use of groups of men and women that the modern dance can completely do what it has always said it would do. It has not done it before mainly because a new technique and new forms had to be evolved. We were forced to work from the ground up.

Now we have reached sufficiently firm ground to be able to add those embellishments which we had been forced to discard in our search for a new technique of movement. *New Dance* and the other two works which I have not described are no longer a series of episodes strung along in a row, as too many attempts at large forms have been. They are a cohesive form in the way that symphony is and need neither music nor story as crutches to support them.

Mary Wigman (1886–1973)
THE PHILOSOPHY OF
MODERN DANCE

Wigman first studied eurhythmics with Dalcroze, then worked in movement with Laban. As if in revolt against her first teacher, her early compositions were executed in silence—her way of asserting the independence of the art of dance. Her choreographic career, which began with the Witch Dance *of 1914, extended into the 1960's. Centered in Germany, where she maintained her own school, Wigman also toured in Europe and the United States. Though the American modern dancers were intrigued by her work, the two nationalities actually developed their forms quite independently.*

The critic Margaret Lloyd described Wigman's dance as "largely an ecstasy of gloom, stressing the demonic and macabre, as if to exorcise through movement the secret evils in man's nature." Though this description succeeds in characterizing a majority of her pieces, it does not recognize the lighter, lyrical side of her repertory seen in dances like Shifting Landscape *(1930). The emphasis on the somber is confirmed, however, in this article with its references to Wigman's concern with man and his fate, and with its contrast of ballet and modern dance, the latter admitting the dark and earthbound qualities of the dancer's movement.*

The dance is one of many human experiences which cannot be suppressed. Dancing has existed at all times, and among all people and races. The dance is a form of expression given to man just as speech, philosophy, painting or music. Like music, the dance is a language which all human beings understand without the use of speech. Granted, the dance is as little an everyday expression as music: the man who begins to dance because of an inner urge does so perhaps from a feeling of joyousness, or a spiritual ecstasy which transforms his normal steps into dance steps, although he himself may not be conscious of this change.

In short, the dance, like every other artistic expression, presupposes a heightened, increased life response. Moreover, the heightened response does not always have to have a happy background. Sorrow, pain, even horror and fear may also tend to release a welling-up of feeling, and therefore of the dancer's whole being.

SOURCE: From *Europa*, I, No. 1 (May-July, 1933).

There is something alive in every individual which makes him capable of giving outward manifestation, (through the medium of bodily movement) to his feelings, or rather, to that which inwardly stirs him. . . .

I feel that the dance is a language which is inherent, but slumbering in every one of us. It is possible for every human to experience the dance as an expression in his own body, and in his own way.

What we expect from the professional dancer is the creative dance in its most intense representation. We never insist upon such an intense representation from the lay-dancer. The professional dancer is distinguished for his particular qualifications, and for his artistic contribution to the dance. He must have the divine capacity to portray the difficult language of the dance: to recreate and objectify what he feels inside of himself.

The same desire for artistic liberation, for exaltation, for personal ecstasy, for bodily movement, in short, for activating his own imagination is also present in the non-professional dancer, and therefore gives him the right to seek for himself the intense expression of the dance.

We all know that the body is an end in itself. The dancer must learn, however, when and how to control his body. He ought not to regard his body simply for itself. He must transform and cultivate it as an instrument of the dance. The dance begins where gymnastics leave off. There are subtle differences between these two forms, and it is somewhat difficult to demarcate between them. Suffice it to say, the differences are neither in the kind or in the style of bearing, but rather in those unexplainable disparities which cannot be easily put into words. The single gestures, isolated in themselves, do not make the dance, but rather the manner in which the gestures are connected in and by movement: the way in which one form of movement is organically developed from its preceding movement, and the manner in which it leads as organically into the next movement. That which is no longer apparent or obvious, which may be said to "lie between the lines" of dancing, is what transforms the gymnastic movement into that of the dance.

To recapitulate: dancing is a simple rhythmic swinging, or ebb and flow, in which even the minutest gesture is part of this flow, and which is carried along the unending tide of movement.

The dance always remains bound by the human body, which is, after all, the dancer's instrument. However, with the emotion which stirs him, and the spirituality which uplifts him, the dance becomes more than mere physical movement in space, and the dancer more than its mobile agent. From then on, it represents the internal experiences of the dancer. To put it another way: we dance the mutation or change of our spiritual and emotional conditions as they are alive in our own body, in a rhythmic to and fro.

Chàrlotte Rupolph in Mary Wigman's
The Language of Dance, Wesleyan University Press

Mary Wigman has described her experience of creation: " . . . the hand seizing the mantle which clung to the body, stretching high, rearing up, then with three long strides into the dark and empty space, a rhythm compelling the arm to reach up—the movement theme for *Song of Fate* was born. I could hear the cry of despair within me. Behind it was the proud and defiant: 'Nevertheless!' " (*The Language of Dance*)

The idealistic substance of the dance, and of the dance creation, are the same as that of other creative and interpretative arts. In any event, it treats of man and his fate,—not necessarily the fate of men of today, nor of yesterday, nor even of tomorrow. But the fate of man caught in his eternal and perpetual web forms the old and yet ever new theme of the dance-creation. From the crudest reality to the sublimest abstraction, man is personified in the dance. All his struggles, griefs, joys are thus represented. Man himself forms the general theme for a limitless and ever significant congeries of variations.

"What idea do you think of when you dance?" A question which is often asked me, and which is difficult to answer. For the process which we call thinking has really nothing to do with the dance. The idea for a dance may come to a creative artist in his sleep, or at any moment of the day; that is to say, it is suddenly there. The idea finds root in one's consciousness without the conjuration of thought. Just as a melodic theme comes to a composer without his knowing why or where, so an idea of movement, a dance-theme, occurs just as spontaneously to the dancer. It often happens that the dancer carries the germ of the dance-theme inside of himself for a long time before it is released. It gives him no peace until it begins to take shape and form as movement. Once this theme, which is the eventual starting point of the entire dance, is at hand, the real work on the dance-creation begins; its composition and its interpretation. This formative period keeps the dancer in a constant state of excitement until the idea of the dance has reached its final point, until it has matured into a work of art. When this moment has arrived, the dance-creator becomes the dance-interpreter. It is absolutely necessary then that the dancer portray the dance in a way that will convey the meaning and force of the inner experiences which have inspired him to conceive this dance.

The primary concern of the creative dancer should be that his audience not think of the dance objectively, or look at it from an aloof and intellectual point of view,—in other words, separate itself from the very life of the dancer's experiences;—the audience should allow the dance to affect it emotionally and without reserve. It should allow the rhythm, the music, the very movement of the dancer's body to stimulate the same feeling and emotional mood within itself, as this mood and emotional condition has stimulated the dancer. It is only then that the audience will feel a strong emotional kinship with the dancer: and will live through the vital experiences behind the dance-creation. Shock, ecstasy, joy, melancholy, grief, gayety, the dance can express all of these emotions through movement. But the expression without the inner experience in the dance is valueless.

A definite change in dancing, particularly in Germany, has been taking place these past twenty years. The revised mode of terpsichorean expression we designate as the "modern dance" in contrast to the "classic dance" or the ballet.

The ballet had reached such a state of perfection that it could be developed no further. Its forms had become so refined, so sublimated to the ideal of purity, that the artistic content was too often lost or obscured. The great "ballet dancer" was no longer a representative of a great inner emotion, (like the musician or poet) but had become defined as a great virtuoso. The ballet-dancer developed an ideal of agility and lightness. He sought to conquer and annihilate gravitation. He banned the dark, the heavy, the earthbound, not only because it conflicted with his ideal of supple, airy, graceful technique, but because it also conflicted with his pretty aesthetic principles.

Times, however, became bad. War had changed life. Revolution and suffering tended to destroy and shatter all the ideals of prettiness. Traditions, aged and cherished, were left behind. How could these old and broken-down traditions remain firm throughout this awful period of destruction? Youth seeking for some spiritual relief could no longer turn to these anile panaceas. And so youth destroyed whatever appeared static, superfluous and moribund; and in its stead set up its own spiritual demands, its own material challenges.

What this new youth demanded of life and mankind, it also demanded from the artistic expression of its time, namely, the honest reflection of its own emotional experiences in symbols of artistic creation and interpretation. It demanded this positive reflection from its literature, drama, poetry, painting, architecture, music and the dance. All of these new things were direct outgrowths from its spiritual restiveness, its material challenges.

It is therefore easy to understand why this new youth should be attracted to the modern dance, the latter being one of the things which grew out of the youth's new world. The modern dance is the expression of youth and of today, and it is as positive in its expression as all the other modern arts. . . .

Section Six

THE EXTENSION OF THE CLASSICAL TRADITION

The Diaghilev Ballets Russes left few traces of its impact in Soviet Russia, which for some time after the Revolution was isolated from the stream of Western developments in the dance. Contemporary with Fokine, however, and advocating some of the same principles, was Alexander Gorsky, who led the ballet in Moscow from 1900 to 1924. Influenced by Stanislavsky, he produced narrative ballets marked by realism and historical accuracy. Early in the new regime, authorities encouraged the ballet to abandon its tzarist repertory in favor of works depicting the industry and happiness of the workers. Choreographers reserved classical technique, like *pointe* work, for decadent characters; the heroic protagonists were given movements drawn from folk dance styles. Such works, however, did not prove popular, and the Russians soon found that they could preserve their heritage, both in repertory and technique, and still create ballets that were attuned to Soviet thought. Following the ideas of Gorsky, the Kirov Ballet in Leningrad and the Bolshoi in Moscow developed choreography that was vigorously dramatic, whether it retold ancient legends or dealt with contemporary themes.

In the state-supported schools the legacy of the *danse d'école* was maintained but extended; jumps reached breathtaking heights; the body became incredibly flexible; a partner supported his ballerina with a single hand and held her high above his head. The Bolshoi did all this with athletic exuberance; the Kirov was softer but no less spectacular. Many dancers of extraordinary technical accomplishment came from these schools, but the most famous was the expressive ballerina Galina Ulanova. She was a beautiful and touching Giselle, but her most remarkable creation was the poetic heroine of Leonid Lavrovsky's *Romeo and Juliet* (1940), a role later taken by her flamboyant and virtuosic successor at the Bolshoi, Maya Plisetskaya.

The graduates of the two major ballet schools have served many companies, for in the Soviet Union numerous provincial cities have their own groups led by dancers trained in Moscow or Leningrad, while folk ensembles, like the brilliant one directed by Igor Moiseyev, get their personnel from these same sources. The tradition remains respected and productive.

In Western Europe, the same tradition spread from the scattering of the Diaghilev company. The first country to profit substantially from the dispersal was England, where Marie Rambert established a school and a small company in the early 1920's and Ninette de Valois soon followed. Rambert had an uncanny way of spotting choreographic talent and grooming it; de Valois chose the right people—including some prepared by Rambert—and structured a formidable organization that eventually emerged as Britain's Royal Ballet.

Of the two choreographers that Rambert was nurturing in the early 1930's, de Valois picked Frederick Ashton to lead her company. His work was clean, precise, and concentrated on design—a fine foil to her own style, which was strongly dramatic. Before long she let his growing list of contributions overshadow her own ballets like *The Rake's Progress* (1935), in which Hogarth's drawings of rowdy eighteenth-century London had provided her theme. Ashton's inspirations came less often from stories or characters (though he did use them) than from dancers, chief among them England's great lyrical ballerina Margot Fonteyn. Her musicality, her lovely classical line, and her intuitive ability to infuse the purest movements with overtones of feeling illuminated such Ashton ballets as *Daphnis and Chloë* (1951) and *Ondine* (1958). The taste of de Valois and Ashton, supported by the elegance of Fonteyn, prompted revivals of *Sleeping Beauty* and *Swan Lake*, which no longer impressed the British public as old-fashioned as they had in Diaghilev's time. Unlike the Ballets Russes, the English company was not innovative. De Valois concentrated, instead, on meticulous execution and production; evolving a distinctive style, gracious and refined, that suited the British temperament and won admirers abroad as well.

De Valois did not bid for Rambert's second choreographer, whose mettle was very different. From the beginning, Antony Tudor was dramatically oriented but not in terms of the conventional story ballet. In *Jardin aux Lilas* (1936) his Victorian characters expressed nothing directly; their movements intimated their feelings but never broke through the bounds of social constraint or classical technique. Still more modern in concept were the bleak dances of mourning in *Dark Elegies* (1937). But Tudor did not remain in England; he went to America.

In the United States interest in classical ballet, rather than ballet spectacle, had begun to revive after the tours of Anna Pavlova. In 1933 the Ballet Russe de Monte Carlo, with Massine as its chief choreographer, paid the first of a series of successful visits. The country was enchanted with the glamorous aura of the company and with its dancers, headed by the chic Alexandra Danilova and a set of teenage ballerinas, all émigrées from Russia. The few Americans who managed to get into the company were given Slavic stage names so as not to disturb the image. Massine, however, made a gesture: he tried his hand at a bit of Americana with *Union Pacific* (1935); his earlier ballets were much more successful.

Meanwhile a few Americans were trying to establish the art on a more indigenous base. Catherine Littlefield created *Barn Dance* (1937) for her Philadelphia Ballet; in Chicago, Ruth Page composed *Frankie and Johnny* (1938) on an American ballad theme; Lew Christensen from Utah did *Filling Station* (1938). But the progress was slow. In the end, it was a Russian who led the first American company to attain international stature.

In 1933 Lincoln Kirstein had invited George Balanchine to the United States, providing him with a small group of native dancers. Apart from a bow in their direction with *Alma Mater* (1935), Balanchine's repertory for the American Ballet consisted of works in his neoclassical style—soundly grounded on traditional technique, musically based, without specific story or character content, designed simply to reveal the beauty of the *danse d'école*. At one point a small touring segment, the Ballet Caravan, let young choreographers try other approaches, notably with Eugene Loring's *Billy the Kid* (1938), which was probably the first major ballet using American material. But on the whole the Balanchine style dominated. Lacking the spectacular productions of the Ballet Russe, Kirstein's company attracted comparatively small audiences and its activities were suspended in 1941.

Meanwhile, from a small group directed by Mikhail Mordkin grew the idea of an ambitious scheme: a gallery of the masterpieces of the past and the classics of the future. In 1940 Ballet Theatre made an auspicious debut with productions of such established works as *Giselle* and *Les Sylphides*, the previously unknown ballets of Tudor, and premieres by Eugene Loring and Agnes de Mille besides. But the epoch-making works were yet to come. In 1942 the eventful ballet was Tudor's *Pillar of Fire*, portraying sexual frustration without romantic glosses; then his *Romeo and Juliet*, perceived in the imagery of a quattrocento painter. In 1944 it was Jerome Robbins' *Fancy Free*, with three sailors cavorting to the jazz rhythms of Leonard Bernstein; then his *Interplay* (1945), sophisticated children's games on *pointe*. Where Tudor used classical technique but manipulated it to serve his dramatic needs, Robbins drew on the traditional language when it suited his purpose but ignored it when tap dancing or stylized natural gesture suited him better. In 1946, when Ballet Theatre was known for its innovative repertory and for its stars —Alicia Alonso, Anton Dolin, André Eglevsky, Nora Kaye, Alicia Markova, Igor Youskevitch—Balanchine and Kirstein founded Ballet Society, which two years later became the New York City Ballet.

Ballet Theatre, now directed by Lucia Chase and Oliver Smith, still found important works to present; there were de Mille's *Fall River Legend* (1947) and Herbert Ross's *Caprichos* (1949), for example. These were compelling, dramatic ballets, but they did not break new ground. In 1949 Robbins left to join the New York City Ballet, and in 1950 Tudor dropped out also. In later years the company was less fortunate in its search for new choreographers—until 1967, when it took on Eliot Feld, a young protégé of Robbins. The emphasis of Ballet Theatre turned to revivals; a new production of the complete *Swan Lake*, the Danish *La Sylphide*—and to foreign stars: Erik Bruhn from Denmark, Carla Fracci from Italy, Natalia Makarova from Russia.

Meanwhile Balanchine developed the New York City Ballet. Some concluded, and he did not deny, that economics influenced his choice of presenting ballets without décor—just a skillfully lit cyclorama; and without elaborate costumes—usually just leotards or tunics for the women, black tights and white shirts for the men. But he had aesthetic reasons as well: the conviction that nothing should interfere or distract from the purpose of ballet—the vision of the body dancing. Balanchine chose the kind of bodies he wanted; "like toothpick," he said of women. He was inspired by his ballerinas: Diana Adams, Melissa Hayden, Tanaquil LeClerq, Maria Tallchief, then Allegra Kent, Patricia McBride, Violette Verdy, Suzanne Farrell, Kay Mazzo. He was less attentive to the men, although some—Arthur Mitchell, Jacques d'Amboise, Edward Villella, Helgi Tommasson, Peter Martins—were too good to ignore. He trained all his dancers to fleetness and precision; the British called them "athletic" while the French spoke of "le style frigidaire."

Balanchine enriched the New York City Ballet's repertory annually. Apart from a few deviations into extended dramatic works like *The Nutcracker* (1954)—which set a nation-wide fashion for Christmas ballet seasons—and *Don Quixote* (1965), he kept most often to his abstract, neoclassical style, choosing music that suited his taste. He described his favorite music as "pure and heartless"; to match it he used "purified gesture—gesture with all the bugs taken out." He turned frequently to Stravinsky, continuing the line of collaboration begun with *Apollo* —*Orpheus* (1948), *Agon* (1957), and the trio of 1972 triumphs: *Duo Concertant*, *Symphony in Three Movements*, *Violin Concerto*. The musical titles were indicative of his desire to present ballet as the art of dancing in time, needing no extraneous references to dramatic action. A theoretical descendent of Gautier and Levinson, rather than of Noverre and Fokine, Balanchine declared adamantly that there could be no mothers-in-law in ballet; movement was its own self-sufficient reason for being.

Though Balanchine has created most of the New York City Ballet's repertory, Jerome Robbins has contributed some of his finest compositions to it. His later works, including *Dances at a Gathering* (1969) and *Goldberg Variations* (1971), were pure dance, classically based, yet suggestive of human relationships—a touch of teasing, of rivalry, of nostalgia. But only a transitory glimpse. "Keep it cool, very cool," he told the dancers. But the effect was nothing like Balanchine's; the Robbins ballets, despite his apparently contrary assertions, were infused with warmth. Using the full range of the dancers' technical skills, they brought a new kind of drama—subtle and understated—to the *danse d'école*.

The third major force on the American ballet scene began in 1954 with a small group led by Robert Joffrey and became the official City Center Joffrey Ballet twelve years later. Though he had been a most promising choreographer, Joffrey created fewer ballets as the company grew, though *Astarte* (1967) caught national attention for its effective use of live dance combined with film for the presentation of an erotic *pas de deux*. Joffrey's assistant, Gerald Arpino, has attracted less critical acclaim but considerable popular enthusiasm, especially for his timely pieces set to rock music. Of special importance have been Joffrey's commissions of a number of significant revivals including Jooss's *The Green Table* and Massine's *Le Beau Danube* and *Parade*.

In Europe also the picture has changed rapidly. In France, where for many years Serge Lifar ruled the Paris Opéra, rebels broke away. One of the first was Roland Petit, who created a chic version of *Carmen* (1949) and other popular works for his own company; in the 1960's Maurice Béjart, hailed as a guru by the younger generation, staged enormous arena productions with his Brussels-based Ballet of the Twentieth Century. The Royal Danish Ballet, long the isolated custodian of Bournonville, began to modernize its training and repertory in the 1950's, striving to keep its traditions alive at the same time. The Royal Swedish Ballet also brought in foreign teachers and choreographers, while Jooss-trained Birgit Cullberg formed her own company along less classical lines. Germany, where ballet had never taken a strong hold, turned from its native modern dance pioneers to import ballet choreographers for its opera houses, the Englishman John Cranko bringing the Stuttgart Ballet to a place of international prominence. Not to be outdone, England took the Russian Rudolf Nureyev into its Royal Ballet, which, under his dynamic influence, acquired a new pungency that revitalized the company's by now sedate image. The English style spread abroad when Celia Franca left de Valois to head the National Ballet of Canada in 1951.

Agrippina Vaganova (1879–1951)
THE CONSTRUCTION OF THE LESSON
Translated from the Russian by Anatole Chujoy

Considered the founder of the Soviet system of ballet education, Vaganova was trained in the school of the Maryinsky Theatre. She retired as a performer in 1916 and began teaching shortly thereafter. Her Basic Principles of Classical Ballet, *first published in 1934, has been translated into many languages.*

Since Adice the ballet lesson has become more complicated, involving a greater variety of exercises, but still following the same general pattern. The developpés *at the* barre *are a significant addition, for the twentieth century has placed more emphasis on the control and height of the extended leg. The stress on allegro is also an important change. Coordination and flow of movement seem now to have replaced Adice's accent on brute endurance.*

. . . In adagio the pupil masters the basic poses, turns of the body and the head.

Adagio begins with the easiest movements. With time it gets more and more complicated and varied. In the last grades, difficulties are introduced one after another. Pupils must be well prepared in the preceding grades to perform these complicated combinations,—they must master the firmness of the body and its stability,—so that when they meet still greater difficulties they do not lose their self-control.

A complicated adagio develops agility and mobility of the body. When, later in allegro, we face big leaps, we will not have to waste time on mastery of the body.

I want to dwell on allegro and stress its particular importance. Allegro is the foundation of the science of the dance, its intricacy and the bond of future perfection. The dance as a whole is built on allegro. . . .

When the legs of the pupil are placed right, when they have acquired the turnout, when the ball of the foot has been developed and strengthened, when the foot has gained elasticity and the muscles have toughened,—then may we approach the study of allegro.

We begin with jumps which are done by a rebound of both feet off the floor, changement de pieds and echappé. To make them easier they

SOURCE: From *Basic Principles of Classical Ballet* (New York: Dover, 1953). Reprinted by permission of Dover Publications, Inc.

are done in the beginning at the bar, facing it and holding on with both hands.

The next jump to be done is the assemblé, rather complicated in structure. This sequence has deep and important reasons.

Assemblé forces the dancer to employ all muscles from the very start. It is not easy for the beginner to master it. Every moment of the movement has to be controlled in performing this pas. This eliminates every possibility of muscular looseness.

The pupil who learns to do assemblé properly not only masters this step but also acquires a foundation for the performance of other allegro steps. . . .

In the higher grades, when it becomes necessary to make the lessons more and more complicated, all steps may be done en tournant. Beginning with simple battement tendu and ending with the most intricate adagio and allegro steps, everything is done en tournant, affording the developed and strong muscles harder work. . . .

There is nothing bad about the exercises being tedious in their monotony, although this monotony can be broken by doing the movements in different time, four-four and two-four, so that the pupils do not do them mechanically but follow the music.

In these classes a foundation is laid for the development of the muscles, the elasticity of the ligaments; a basis is instilled for the elementary movements.

All this is accomplished by systematic repetitions of the same movement a great number of times in succession. For example, it is better to do a step eight times in succession than two or four combinations in eight measures. Few, scattered movements will not achieve the aim. The teacher must be absolutely certain that the pupil has mastered the movement, that it becomes part of her and that it will be done correctly in any combination, before he may complicate the lesson without harm to the pupil. . . .

Sample Lesson

The following is a sample lesson suitable for advanced classes. The entire lesson is given on half-toe.

EXERCISE AT THE BAR

1. *Plié* in five positions. (Two measures in $^4/_4$.) One slow in $^4/_4$; one fast in $^2/_4$, on the other $^2/_4$ rise on half-toe.

2. *Battements tendus.*

Front: in ¼—two with *plié*, two without *plié*; three in ⅛ (on the fourth ⅛—rest); seven in ¹/₁₆ (on the eighth ¹/₁₆—rest).

To the side: the same.

Back: the same.

Again to the side: the same.

Repeat these eight measures.

The same exercise from the other foot (*).

3. *Battements fondus* and *frappés* (combination). Eight measures ⁴/₄.

Front: one *fondu* slow in ²/₄, two fast one in ¼.

To the side: the same.

Back: the same

Again to the side: the same.

Two *frappés* slow in ¼, three fast ones in ⅛ (rest on the fourth ⅛).

Do it four times.

Repeat the whole combination beginning to the back.

The same exercise from the other foot.

4. *Ronds de jambe.* Two measures in ⁴/₄.

Three fast *ronds de jambe par terre en dehors* in ³/₈; on the fourth ⅛ rise on half-toe, open leg in 2nd position. Three *ronds de jambe en l'air en dehors* in ³/₈; rest on the fourth ⅛; four *ronds de jambe en l'air en dehors* in ⁴/₈. *Plié sur le cou-de-pied* and *tour en dehors* in ⁴/₈.

Repeat entire figure *en dedans*.

The same exercise from the other foot.

5. *Battements battus* and *petits battements.* Eight measures in ⁴/₄.

Four times in ⁴/₄ double *battement battu* with a rest in pose *effacé* front in *plié* after each ¼. During the next measure, *battements battus* are done successively with a rest on the fourth ¼ in pose *effacé* front in *plié*. Four times in ⁴/₄ one *petit battement* with a rest in 2nd position after each ¼. One measure successive *petits battements* with a rest in 2nd position in *plié* on the fourth ¼.

Four times in ⁴/₄ one *petit battement* with a rest in pose *effacé* back in *plié* after each ¼. One measure successive *petits battements* with a rest on the fourth ¼ in pose *effacé* back in *plié*. Repeat the described two measures of *petits battements* with a rest in 2nd position.

The same exercise from the other foot.

6. *Developpé.* Two measures in ⁴/₄.

Carry out right leg front with point to the floor, doing *demi-plié* with left leg (first ¼), raise right leg to 90°, straightening the knee of the left leg (second ¼), small, short *balancé* with the raised leg (third ¼),

(*) Each movement of every exercise at the bar is always done from one foot and then from the other.

carry the leg to 2nd position (fourth ¼). Bend leg in knee (first ¼), open in 2nd *arabesque* (second ¼), raise on half-toe, fall on raised leg back in *demi-plié* extending the toes of the left leg front (third ¼), rise on it quickly on half-toe, raising right leg in *attitude croisée* (fourth ¼). Do the entire combination in reverse order, from the back.

Third figure—in 2nd position, all poses to the side. The concluding pose will be in the first case *écarté* back, in the second case—*écarté* front. The same exercise from the other foot.

This exercise may also be done in ½.

7. *Grands battements jetés balancés*. One measure in ⁴/₄.

We begin by pointing the toes and carrying left leg back. Through 1st position the leg is thrust front, then back (first and second ¼), and twice through 1st position into 2nd (third and fourth ¼).

The next time: throw the leg back, front, and into position.

The same exercise from the other foot.

The body must balance as described in *battement balancé*.

EXERCISE IN THE MIDDLE

Realizing the shortness of the lesson I recommend the following order of exercises in the middle:

1. *Petit adagio*. Combine *plié* with various *developpés* and *battements tendus*.

2. In the second *petit adagio* bring in combinations with *battements fondus* and *frappés*, and *ronds de jambe en l'air*.

3. *Grand adagio*, which contains the most difficult adagio movements for the given class.

4. For the beginning of *allegro* I try to give small jumps, i.e. low and simple ones.

5. *Allegro* with big steps.

6. For the first steps on *pointes* I select those which are done on both feet: *échappé* in 2nd position and then in 4th. This precaution is necessary because, although the students are warmed up, the new movements bring into play new muscles, and these should be prepared for the work.

7. In order to balance out all muscles and tendons which have been stimulated by the work, the lesson ends with small *changements de pieds*. To develop the flexibility of the body we do *port de bras*. . . .

GRAND ADAGIO

Pose *croisé* back with left leg, *plié*, *coupé* on left foot and *ballonné* in *écarté* front with a stop in *effacé*, right leg bent behind knee, extend it in the same direction *effacé* back, do on it two *tours en dedans sur le cou-de-pied*, stop in *écarté* back with left leg, both arms in 3rd position, turn slowly and carry the opened leg into 1st *arabesque*, the body facing [upstage]; the arms, opened in 2nd position through preparatory position are carried front with the wrists crossed. *Coupé* on left foot and *pas ciseaux* (stop on right foot), turn to *effacé* front with the left leg, *chassé* in *effacé*, fall on left leg in *plié*, after which shift to the right leg, taking the pose *croisé* in *attitude*, turn quickly *en dehors*, stand on the left foot in 4th *arabesque*, *renversé* in *écarté* back, *pas de bourrée en dehors*, two *tours en dehors* from 4th position *sur le cou-de-pied*, *pas de bourrée en dehors* and *entrechat-six de volée* with the right leg.

ALLEGRO

1. Big *sissonne* forward in *croisé en tournant en dehors, assemblé* forward and *sissonne-soubresaut* in *attitude effacée* on right foot, carry left leg on the floor front, *glissade* with the right foot to the side, and *cabriole fermée* with the right leg in *effacé*.

2. (a) *Saut de basque* and *renversé sauté en dehors*; repeat; *sissonne tombée* forward in *effacé*, *cabriole* in 1st *arabesque*, *pas de bourrée*, *cabriole* in 4th *arabesque*, *sissonne tombée en tournant (en dehors)* in *croisé* front on right foot, *coupé* on left foot and *jeté fermé fondu* on right foot to the side in 2nd position.

(b) Four *sauts de basque* diagonally with arms in 3rd position, four *chaînés* diagonally [backward], preparation in 4th position *croisé* and two *tours en dehors sur le cou-de-pied*; finish in 4th position.

3. Preparation *croisé* front with the left leg, *grande cabriole fermée* in *effacé* with the right leg and turn *en dedans* on *pointes* in 5th position. Repeat. *Sissonne tombée*: back in *croisé* from right leg, in *effacé* from left leg, with right leg *jeté en tournant en dehors* forward in *croisé*, *cabriole* into 4th *arabesque* and *pas de bourrée*. This combination may also be done in waltz-time.

Yuri Slonimsky (1902–)
OUR POINT OF VIEW

Slonimsky began to write ballet criticism at the age of seventeen and soon after started to publish a series of monographs on historical dance subjects. His first book, Masters of the Ballet of the Nineteenth Century, *appeared in 1937. Soviet choreographers have created a number of ballets based on Slonimsky's librettos.*

Here he states the basic ideology of the Soviet ballet, showing that all the glorious technique, all the moving portrayals of character, should be only means to the end of communicating "a message, ennobling and purifying." Here again the ballet art is made to serve the purposes of the state, as it was in the days of the Ballet Comique. *The Soviet ballet's use of lavish mechanical equipment (not mentioned by Slonimsky) also links it to the Renaissance genre, though now the productions are intended for all the people rather than for the select elite. Yet, like Noverre, Slonimsky wants ballet to reach the heart.*

. . . When after the Revolution of 1917 the theatres were filled with new audiences representing the widest strata of society—workers, peasants, soldiers, and office employees, the question naturally arose what attitude to adopt towards an art, existing until then on the Imperial stage. Should it be cast away as something belonging altogether to the old world, or was it in need of reform?. . . .

For several years the doors of the theatres were open to the public free of charge. People were shown the ballets of the past: both the best of our classical heritage and ballets of the type mentioned above.

The new spectators passed their own judgement. Unconditionally they favoured the best ballets of the classical legacy. The most brilliant execution of such Petipa ballets as *La Fille du Pharaon, The Talisman, Le Roi Candaule* and so forth left them completely indifferent. At the same time they came to love not only *Swan Lake, The Sleeping Beauty* and *Giselle,* but also *La Fille Mal Gardée, Esmeralda* and *Don Quixote,* and this in spite of the fact that the form of expression was often quite old-fashioned, the productions outdated and the heroes themselves—fairies, princes, magicians and kings—completely alien to them.

SOURCE: From 2nd revised edition of *The Bolshoi Ballet,* published 1960 by the Foreign Language Publishing House, Moscow, U.S.S.R. Used by permission of the Am-Rus Literary Agency.

Was this conservatism, was it backwardness? No, not at all! We our-selves did not quite understand at first that by making this selection the audiences were taking a healthy point of view on the culture of the past. . . . "Anti-Imperial" views upon ballet could not, quite natur-ally, prevail in an art dependent on the Imperial household. But they found expression—sometimes more and sometimes less obviously—al-most everywhere, practically in all noteworthy productions. All that has ever been produced for the entertainment of an empty-headed crowd is obsolete in our new ballet and should be discarded and forgotten. Such is the judgement prompted by experience. Soviet spectators have helped us to arrive at this judgement by demanding a critical approach to what we have inherited.

It became obvious that the calling of ballet, as of all arts, was to help the spectator to better understand himself and the world about him, to enrich his spiritual wealth and shape his ethical notions. Together with literature, drama and opera, ballet is a vehicle of education. . . .

Truly beautiful musical and choreographic creations boldly raise urgent problems of human existence, they always carry a message, ennobling and purifying. That is what gives them the right to immortality. Anything that fails to reach the public's mind and heart, that merely pleases the eye for a short moment, is doomed to early oblivion. These are not our words: they belong to the great Didelot. . . .

A striving to reflect the inner substance of life has become part and parcel of Soviet choreography. Soviet art cannot isolate itself from its people. This is what constitutes its novelty of principle, its entirely new mission.

It is hardly necessary to emphasise that this alone makes Soviet ballet radically different to the Imperial theatre. In those days ballet kept to the side of the road taken by literature and other arts, coming in contact with them only occasionally, whereas now it takes part in the assertion of our artistic ideals openly and directly as an equal of other arts.

Progressive art was always drawn to great literature. Literature is a wise mother that can endow its offsprings with a wealth of ideas and imagery. Its ability to penetrate beyond the surface of life cannot be equalled. Soviet ballet sees a life-giving source for further develop-ment in joining forces with literature—both classical and contem-porary. . . .

The best choreographers of the past used to dream of a union of author, musician, choreographer and designer. However, in Soviet ballet alone this alliance became a necessity and therefore a law. It is immaterial by whom the book is conceived—by the choreographer, composer or professional writer. What matters is that the dramaturgical outline of the production is sketched long before the composer conceives the first bar of the music and the choreographer—the first step of the ballet. This outline is not a framework on which music and dance are simply stretched. It finds expression in terms of musical and dance imagery. The general underlying idea of the story and, therefore, of the future production, is of primary importance in Soviet ballet. The substance of this idea is embedded in the book. And this also makes Soviet ballet an antipode of the Imperial ballet. . . .

It is well known, however, that in works of art ethics is inseparable from aesthetics. Only that is beautiful which is beautiful in thought, feeling and deed. Such is the secret of true poetry.

In championing these principles, Soviet ballet breaks with the so-called "Imperial traditions" of Russian ballet in this respect as well. The Revolution gave birth to poetry all about us, on the earth that is being transformed with our own hands, and there was no need any more to look for it in the realm of beautiful fantasy. Poetry, truth, beauty is to be found not in exaggerated praise of the past, in romantic illusions, or in escape from reality, but in fighting for its ideals. Life offers us prototypes of a positive hero at every step. He is the rank-and-file but in no way run-of-the-mill toiler, he is the creator of mankind's new history. In 1919, Maxim Gorky was dreaming of a "hero nobly self-forgetting, passionately in love with his ideal, a hero in the true, broad sense of the word."

The hero of Soviet ballet is moved by love for humanity and an infinite faith in man's moral strength, he is moved by hatred of anything that prevents a full flowering of spiritual forces, that stifles man and takes away his right to peaceful labour and personal happiness.

Our theatre asserts an inseparable bond between social and private destiny and interests. For the first time the theme of the Revolution took possession of the ballet stage. The dancers were faced with a new task: more passion and energy had to be introduced into their acting. Events of popular life lent an atmosphere of heroism and pathos to the productions. The People as the leading hero came to the foreground.

Any theme—be it fairy-tale, or historical, has to be interpreted with a contemporary vision. Otherwise there will be no authenticity, no artistic merit, no chance of "immortality" for that work of art.

The powerful current of life brought new heroes to the Soviet ballet, such as had not been known for too long a time. These heroes are compatriots and contemporaries of the spectators. No matter how much we criticised these new characters sometimes, they did invariably introduce something new into art—they endowed the heroes with great generosity, with a feeling of solidarity and fraternity, with a burning concern for the fate of the people in all the parts of the world.

Our spectator always sides with those fighting for a just cause. He shows lively interest in events taking place in any part of the universe at any period. . . .

The method of socialist realism, which is the method of Soviet art, took form gradually. Life has proved that it enables us better than any other method to depict themes from reality and to create psychologically complex and truthful characters of contemporary heroes. Realism is in no way a monopoly of Soviet ballet. It is accessible to any artist of the dance, who looks for beauty in life and for a way to the hearts of his audience.

Many foreign critics do not discriminate between two trends in art—realism and naturalism. Naturalism, in actual fact, is a bitter enemy of realism. Whereas realism selects from life that which is most important, what moves man and humanity, naturalism shows up everything that falls within its vision and so turns art into something worse than a photograph—a dreary, dull record registering facts, but incapable of conveying their inner significance. Realism catches the very heartbeat of the times. It penetrates the very core of human existence and discovers its hidden springs. It generalises events, revealing the general through the particular, finding something essential for all and for everyone in separately taken phenomena. . . .

In the course of at least a century, ballet revolved round the theme of romantic love. Now *any* great love—love for one's family, friends, children, work, creations, motherland—all this becomes part of ballet. Therefore the very scope of this art has become considerably expanded.

In pre-revolutionary ballets the characters, as a rule, were static. They did not change as the plot developed. Realism armed Soviet ballet with a versatility of characters, such as had been characteristic of drama or opera. From the beginning to the end of the performance the character grows and develops: struggle makes his love nobler and purer and his hatred stronger; new feelings, new attitudes are born in him. Thus grows the tension of passions and the tension of ideas, clashing in conflict.

Realism has made *life in dance* an absolute law of scenic behaviour. The dancer lives, breathes, thinks—all in terms of dance. That is why the dramatic narrative in a ballet is not counterposed to dance. One follows from the other, forming a single whole. . . .

We wish to live through the development of the poetic plot together with the authors and the dancers. Step by step we want to take part in their struggle for the ideal, to share with them the joy of victory or the sorrow of defeat. When the heroes' destiny is linked with that of his nation, his story can't be reduced to so many short episodes. The art of *performance* (such was the Imperial ballet) becomes an art of *living the role*. The psychological development of characters and situations which, as a rule, was absent in the old days, becomes a necessity in every production. . . .

At one time, attempts were made to tie down the system of the classical dance to a definite country or a definite class, and to treat it as a product of that given epoch. It was declared that it was as changeable as the times and styles that had engendered it, and should therefore be replaced by something else.

The past few decades have proved the fallacy of such views.

Classical dancing is the quintessence of artistically generalised human movements. It is immortal when regarded as a foundation on which choreographers, musicians, ballerinas and *danseurs* build their images. Without the classical dance as the artistic language of ballet, there is no ballet. True, once the classical dance is regarded as a set of pretty gestures and steps, it loses its meaning. The use of conventional school exercises for any situation and any image inevitably leads to formalism and naturalism. Even the most cunning pattern-creating pleasing for the moment is sterile and doomed to oblivion if it is conceived outside of content.

Contrariwise, the deeper the choreographer's perception of life, the more eloquent becomes the classical dance idiom of the characters created by his inspiration.

There are no limits to the flexibility of the classical dance, provided the choreographers know how to use it. Classical dance should, indeed, be enriched and modernised—but according to its laws and purpose (that of creating an image), rather than the choreographers' whims. Classical dancing, more readily than any other kind, blends with the music, comprising a "choreographic melody." If the very nature of classical dancing is ignored, this "melody" disappears, beauty goes too, and the ugly and deformed takes possession of the stage.

However, content must be given priority if art is to attain the maximum of expression. New content is what suggests and engenders new form. New form in itself can never give birth to corresponding content. Form-making is always sterile.

The system of classical dance is an evergreen tree of scenic expression. Anything may be grafted to it. Taking this system as a basis, the choreographer should enrich and expand it. Folk dances, grotesque acrobatics, ballroom dancing, eurythmics—all this should be made into a new alloy by force of the choreographer's imagination, an alloy best suited to the images he has in mind. It is of paramount importance to remember that stage dancing has several aspects, and the preference of one to the detriment of the rest invariably ends in disaster. Only a blend of technical virtuosity, plastic expressiveness and poetic content is capable of sustaining realism in ballet.

In ballets based on new material taken directly from life the expressiveness of dance form sometimes falls short of the content. Though quite logical at the beginning, this cannot be long tolerated. Not all Soviet choreographers display enough daring and inventiveness in their use of accepted ballet forms. However, our faith in the chosen means and methods is none the weaker for it. They are correct—therefore the imperfections will be overcome.

Frederick Ashton (1906–)
A CONVERSATION

Ashton began choreographing for Marie Rambert in London in 1926, shifting to Ninette de Valois' company nine years later. The remainder of his career has been closely associated with this company, which became Britain's Royal Ballet. Ashton was largely responsible for its repertory and style, creating for it such diversified fare as the sophisticated, witty Façade *(1931); the serenely lyrical* Symphonic Variations *(1946); the delightful frolic that was his version of* La Fille Mal Gardée *(1960); the refined and very English elegance of* Enigma Variations *(1968). He was artistic director of the company from 1963 until his retirement in 1971.*

In this interview with Clement Crisp, Ashton outlines the convictions underlying the various forms of choreography he has undertaken. His insistence on the essential comprehensiveness of classical technique is reiterated by most of the choreographers represented in this section.

CRISP: *Marguerite and Armand* has just had a tremendous success. How do you view it as part of your own output?

ASHTON: I never really think about that. The thing I feel is immense relief that it's worked, but for me every ballet that I do is a job. It's my work. That's what I have to do. I'm like somebody who sets out with his implements to go and mend frozen pipes. And you know, there's too much talk about inspiration and all that kind of thing. I mean, all very well if the muse looks in . . .

SOURCE: From *Covent Garden Book, No. 15* (London: A. & C. Black, 1964). Reprinted by permission of Clement Crisp.

CRISP: But the muse must be there at ten o'clock in the morning in the rehearsal room.

ASHTON: Exactly. If she deigns to look in all the better, but you have to get down and do the job—that's really what it amounts to.

CRISP: But I suppose there are certain ballets which are your particular favourites among your own works.

ASHTON: Yes, I think the ones I like best are the ones that I feel that have furthered my development and outlook. For instance, *Symphonic Variations*. At the time that I did that there seemed to be a clutter of ballets with heavy stories and I felt that the whole idiom needed purifying. And so I made *Symphonic Variations*, and it was a kind of testament.

CRISP: It was a breath of fresh air—re-established classical dancing as the supreme function of ballet.

ASHTON: Yes. But it's difficult to say whether I have any actual favourite. One's favourite is apt to be the last one that one does, really. But looking back on it all I'm very fond of some of my very early works. I'm very fond of *Façade*, because I think it seems to me to be a complete entity in itself. It's successful in what I set out to do—which was a parody of dances of that time. And also I think that one thing one must always guard against is that if one has to do a comic ballet, one can never say "Well now, I'm going to do a comic ballet and I'm going to be funny." That must never be so. The structure of the dance must be very solid and then you superimpose the humour if it comes naturally. And I think that in *Façade* the humour seems to come quite naturally out of the actual dances. But it must be a good dance first, and then the humour comes out of that.

CRISP: Do you feel this holds good also with *Wedding Bouquet*?

ASHTON: Yes, I think the same thing. With *Wedding Bouquet*, although it is a humorous ballet, it's rather Chaplinesque in the sense that it has an underlying sadness. And there again I think all the characters are very well rounded, and what humour there is is almost a tragic humour in a way.

CRISP: What about *Scènes de Ballet*, which has always been one of my favourites of yours; I think it says a great deal about classical ballet itself; about the formulas of classical ballet. Do you agree?

ASHTON: Yes, I do. When I was doing this ballet I immersed myself in geometry and Euclid and all those things, which was very funny, because at school I could never even understand them. And also the fact that you could make the front anywhere, not necessarily as it were where the public sit and see. So that *Scènes de Ballet*, if you were to actually sit in the wings, would still have the same effect as it has from being viewed from the auditorium. You would get a different, but logical, pattern. And this was a fascinating problem to me. I used to place the dancers in theorems and then make them move along geometric lines and then at the end I used to say "Well, Q.E.D." when it worked out. Sometimes we got into the most terrible muddles, but it was a very interesting problem for me to unravel them.

CRISP: Obviously at the time you felt very strongly about the importance of classical dancing, of the academic dance, and obviously you still do.

ASHTON: Well of course I do. I think that it's the only language really. All these other "isms" that there are, and all the modern dance, are all tributaries of the mainstream. They can be used very effectively, should be used, and one should perhaps go through periods of them in order to incorporate them. You see, the classical ballet is so rich that it can take in anything, and absorb all outside influences into itself.

CRISP: Your artistic career is now 30 years old, and more, and you still go on creating new and exciting and beautiful things. This is really because you are a classical choreographer, and you live in the classical tradition.

ASHTON: Well absolutely. I couldn't possibly live in any other and I don't think there's any hope for anybody who doesn't in the long run.

CRISP: Something that Ingres once said, that the task is not to invent, but to continue.

ASHTON: I think that as regards invention one should never consciously say "Well, now I'm going to be inventive." Of course you must search for new things, but as you're doing so you must search for new modes of expression and new movements. Naturally that is very important, because otherwise the ballet becomes a sort of cliché of classical dancing. You must have a personal idiom. Your work should be recognised. People should be able to come and say "this is a Balanchine ballet. This is an Ashton ballet. Or this is a ballet by Kenneth MacMillan." If you can say that then you know that the choreographer is good, and has something personal to offer, and a language in which he expresses himself.

CRISP: Do you feel that you've ever tried to consciously give a direction to ballet? Obviously from what you've said about *Symphonic Variations* you have. You wanted to clear away a lot of dross at the end of the war. Since then do you think you have?

ASHTON: No, not really, I've tried to give a direction to myself, I think, really more than to the actual ballet. I used the medium to express what I feel in my own ideas at the time. When I do one sort of ballet I think the way to keep oneself alive is never to follow that line up with saying "this kind of ballet has been successful. I will now do a series of this sort." I do the very contrary thing. After I

Photo, Roger Wood. Dance Collection,
The New York Public Library at Lincoln Center

In Frederick Ashton's *Symphonic Variations* the dancers are (left to right): Pirmin Trecu, Rosemary Lindsay, Michael Somes, Anya Linden, Annette Page, and Brian Shaw. The beautiful décor of Sophie Fedorovitch focussed the eye on the clean, classical lines of the choreographic design—a "testament" to the self-sufficiency of ballet technique at a time when "story" ballets were abounding.

did, say, *Symphonic Variations*, I immediately take something that is completely different, and in that way you develop yourself, I think, and increase your horizon.

CRISP: But are there certain things that ballet can't do?

ASHTON: Yes, I think there are, certainly, because ballet can't get too involved in a story, in trying to express things that can only be said by words. I think the great asset of ballet is that it can heighten beyond words certain situations and give a kind of poetic evocation, so that it becomes . . . you almost can't say what the sensation that it's given you is.

CRISP: Balanchine once said that a ballet is a shape in time and space and nothing more. I think I'm misquoting slightly. But you would agree with the basic idea?

ASHTON: Yes, I would.

CRISP: This question of big ballets. They present, I suppose, the most appalling difficulties for you.

ASHTON: In one way, they're difficult to do. On the other hand, if you have a three-act ballet, you have plenty of time to develop everything. It's a very contrary thing to *Marguerite and Armand*, which is like a pill, the whole thing is digested down to a pill. The length of a three-act ballet makes it more difficult because it will have to be more inventive and you have to keep the whole thing going and keep the interest up the whole time.

CRISP: The great disadvantage for three-act ballets is quite simply the lack of scores.

ASHTON: That is the great thing, and also the lack of stories; it's very difficult to find a story which carries right through from the first act to the last. Otherwise you tend to get a story which fizzles out by the end of the second act and the third act simply becomes a series of divertissements or dances which keep the action going to the last minute. I tend to think that really the two-act ballets are almost the best, because you get the whole thing a little bit more concise and more suited to the modern taste.

CRISP: Do you have any feelings about contemporary themes for ballets, do you think these can work?

ASHTON: Yes, I think they can work. I'm sure they can work, but they are difficult to find, and the difficulty is in dressing them I think. If you keep them on point with modern dress and mackintoshes on top I think it's apt to look ridiculous. Then on the other hand if you put them into flat shoes then the thing becomes a bit pedestrian, but I'm not at all against it, if only one could find a kind of poetic expression of modern life with brilliant and inventive collaborations, then I think of course it would be perfect but the cinema does it better. It must not be forgotten, as Mallarmé said about poetry— that it was about words and *not* ideas—the same applies to choreography. It is about movement and steps and not ideas.

Antony Tudor (1909–)
TALK ABOUT NEW BALLETS
An Interview with Jack Anderson

Though he was already nineteen when he decided to dance, Tudor won the interest of Marie Rambert because of his "poetic eyes," and he choreographed his first ballet for her in 1931. Joining Ballet Theatre in 1940, he contributed major works to its repertory for the next decade. Thereafter he mounted many of them for other companies throughout the world. Tudor speaks here after the success of Echoing of Trumpets had broken a spell of ballets that seemed to lack creative fire.

Especially significant here is Tudor's stress on the idea that "feeling must be expressed through movement." His manipulations of the classic vocabulary negated the conventional elegance and flow of its steps with rigid arms, a contracted torso, abrupt phrasing—whatever he needed to convey the fears, griefs, or frustrations of his characters. Like Fokine, he felt no need to create a completely new language, but he stretched the technique much further than Fokine to portray the crueler aspects of contemporary feeling.

The March 27 performance of the Metropolitan Opera Ballet was an important event, not only because it was one of the company's few opportunities to display itself outside the dance interludes of the standard operatic repertoire, but because the program contained the premieres of two ballets by Antony Tudor—the world premiere of *Concerning Oracles* and the American premiere of *Echoing of Trumpets*, created three years ago for the Royal Swedish Ballet and Tudor's most important ballet in many seasons.

Ask him how he came to choreograph this powerful indictment of war, then Tudor shrugs and says, "I have no idea. I have a dreadful memory about things like that." Then he pauses and starts to remember: "I suppose it began when I heard the Martinu music. I've always liked Czech composers—Dvorak, Smetana, Janacek, Martinu, and so on. You know, I often buy armloads of records and take them home and play them. If I don't like them, I give them away. If I do happen to like a particular piece of music, it may support a ballet."

Concerning Oracles was the partial result of one of these record hunts. Tudor heard a disc containing three charming compositions of Jacques

SOURCE: From *Dance Magazine* (May, 1966). Reprinted by permission.

Ibert and decided to use them for a ballet. *Echoing of Trumpets* came about several years ago when he discovered Martinu's "Symphonic Fantasies (Symphony No. 6.)"

"One passage sounded like gunshots. Another passage reminded me of a plague of locusts," Tudor says. "Now what can one do with a plague of locusts in a ballet?" Tudor turned to the Book of Revelations in the Bible and thought of choreographing a ballet about the Four Horsemen of the Apocalypse. Literal horsemen soon disappeared from the projected work. "Yet, in a way, they're still there," Tudor points out. "Once you even begin to consider the Four Horsemen as subjects for ballet, you can be very sure that whatever ballet results will deal with unpleasant things—hunger, war, things like that."

Gradually, but firmly, the ballet took its own shape. Tudor envisioned a setting enclosed by barbed wire and dominated by a ruined bridge. He says, "I suppose it symbolizes that there's no way out (I didn't realize until I actually started staging the work that the setting I had conceived closed me in as a choreographer, giving me only one place for entrances and exits)." Tudor remembered hearing of how a Nazi soldier once crushed a Greek peasant's hand into the ground to prevent him from reaching out for a crust of bread. That incident found its way into the ballet. So did Tudor's own memories of how, as a child during World War I, the family house was shelled and he was evacuated to a shelter near the Aldershot firing range. He says, "From those days I learned a lot about soldiers and how the military mind operates. I suppose it was then that I began to associate trumpets with soldiers and war and victory. In the ballet I ask: what happens *after* the echoing of trumpets? what happens when the conquering hordes have conquered? what happens to those whose wish is more and more power?"

While the Swedish title, *Ekon av Trumpeter*, can be translated as either *Echoes* or *Echoing of Trumpets*, Tudor prefers *Echoing*: "The word has a more resonant quality about it, suggesting an on-going, rather than a finished, action."

Many members of the audience have attempted to find parallels between *Echoing of Trumpets* and Tudor's earlier ballet of grief and loss, *Dark Elegies*, choreographed in 1937. The choreographer attempts to minimize these parallels: "I dearly love to steal bits from my old ballets when I choreograph a new one. But there's nothing of *Elegies* in *Echoing*." Yet he will admit that, as a composer, Martinu was influenced by Mahler (whose "Kindertotenlieder" is the score for *Elegies*) and that scores of similar moods may prompt a choreographer to create passages similar in movement quality.

Tudor also disparages another oft-repeated view of *Echoing*. Most audiences associate the ballet with World War II and there are resemblances between the plot and the historical event of the destruction of Lidice by the Nazis. Tudor denies that this is the theme of his work: "Perhaps it's more about how people always seem to want to dominate other people. Everyone knows that's a stupid thing to do. *Yet they keep on doing it.* They never stop torturing each other with a kind of mild viciousness."

Is there a *mild* viciousness?

"Oh yes. It exists. I've known some specialists in it . . . even in ballet studios." (A wicked glint appears in Tudor's eyes, then he quickly returns to discussing the psychology of war as it applies to nations, rather than dancers.) "Take the soldiers in my ballet. They don't really rape

Dance Collection, The New York Public Library at Lincoln Center

A complex web of human relationships reveals itself in Antony Tudor's *Pillar of Fire*: the freely flirtatious younger sister taunts her polite elders, while Hagar, (right) fearing she cannot win the man she really loves, accepts the man who offers himself to her. Months of discussions about the psychology of the characters preceded the actual choreographing of the ballet. Left to right, the original cast: Annabelle Lyon, Antony Tudor, Lucia Chase, Nora Kaye, and Hugh Laing.

the women in the village. They just torment them until they make the women feel degraded and, in so doing, they degrade themselves. It's this mutual degradation which, I think, prevails when people are under the conqueror's heel."

When a new work was commissioned by the Royal Swedish Ballet, Tudor arrived in Stockholm with ideas for two ballets: one to a Tchaikovsky score; the other, the ballet to the Martinu score. The Tchaikovsky idea evaporated, while "the Martinu took hold of me." He worked on the ballet for a month with the dancers, then kept it in the back of his head while he staged a work in Berlin and vacationed in Rome. In retrospect, he finds both cities were appropriate places in which to mull over a work about invasions and conquests. When he returned to Sweden he completed the ballet in five weeks. Work on the American production of *Echoing of Trumpets* was begun this past January with the assistance of Anna Marie Lagerborg, ballet mistress of the Royal Swedish Ballet.

Concerning Oracles grew out of the Ibert record with the tantalizing pieces of music on it and the sheer necessity of having to do a ballet to fill out the Met program with *Echoing of Trumpets* and Bournonville's *La Ventana*. One day Sallie Wilson, the American Ballet Theatre principal who has starred in many Tudor productions, casually suggested that he revive *Les Mains Gauches*, a little ballet about palmistry he had once staged at Jacob's Pillow. Tudor thought this would be too slight for the huge Metropolitan Opera House. Then he decided to include it as one section of a larger work about such varied forms of fortune telling as crystal gazing and card reading.

"People tell me the ballet is obscure," Tudor says. "I don't know why that should be. It's simply about fortune telling and there's nothing obscure about that. Everybody knows what fortune telling is like and what its problems are. It's inconclusive. When you have your fortune told, do you believe it? Does what you are told will happen to you really happen? . . . No, I've never been to a fortune teller myself. I never thought it necessary."

Tudor follows such a barrage of deliberately cryptic remarks with more immediately practical considerations: "The ballet is full of rough edges. One section falls apart completely. I haven't had time to study it, but I want to re-work it."

Tudor is, by reputation, one of the slowest and most painstaking of living choreographers. Tudor himself thinks this reputation is somewhat exaggerated: "Everyone remembers that my *Romeo and Juliet* was still unfinished on the night of its premiere. But who remembers that the reason why it was unfinished is that I didn't get all the rehearsal time I'd been promised? And absolutely no one remembers that I put *Dim Lustre* together in eleven days or something like that."

Regarding teaching one of his ballets to dancers, Tudor says, "I don't like to give explanations. I don't like to communicate anything to a dancer through the mind, especially—" (and here that malicious glint returns) "— especially considering what some dancers' minds are like." Sometimes Tudor will not even tell the details of his plot to the dancers.

He says, "I want my dancers to grow into their roles through the movements of those roles. Understanding, development, and growth must always come through movement. Otherwise, it's only veneer. I remember seeing a young dancer with tears in her eyes as she rehearsed *Dark Elegies*. I stopped her at once—feelings must be expressed through movement.

"If I've given you a role and you do the movements for that role *exactly* the way I tell you to do them, you will master that characterization. You can't fail." Tudor is emphatic—and almost perversely optimistic—on this point: "Yes, I mean that. If the dancers do the movement as I want it, they can't fail. But they must do it *exactly* as I want it. Yes, they may find it hard to do. But it's there inside them. Only with some people you have to dig for it harder."

In addition to conveying the emotional intensity of the choreography, Tudor wishes his dancers to convey the quality of the music in their performances. In the United States, where companies have only a minimum of orchestra rehearsals, the early performances of a ballet are usually still unsatisfactory because the dancers "still don't really *hear* the music." In Stockholm there were five rehearsals with the orchestra, at the Met only one.

All the same, "Everybody seems to want to do *Echoing of Trumpets*. The Met has exclusive American performing rights for a year. After that—well, we'll wait and see."

Jerome Robbins (1918–)
DANCES AT A GATHERING

Trained in both classical and modern techniques, Robbins joined Ballet Theatre in 1940 and the New York City Ballet in 1949. Along with creating works for these companies, he choreographed and later completely directed a number of Broadway musicals, most notably West Side Story *(1957) and* Fiddler on the Roof *(1964). Probably the most wide-ranging of contemporary ballet makers, he has done psychological dramas and comedies; ballets set to symphonies, to jazz, and to no music at all; he has filled the stage with vibrant configurations of classical movements; and with* Watermill *(1972) he set a work distinguished by its oriental sparseness and containing not a single step from the ballet vocabulary.*

When Robbins choreographed Dances at a Gathering *in 1969, he had not done a ballet since* Les Noces *in 1965. The intervening years had been devoted to an experimental project called the American Lyric Theatre Workshop which— though it left no important productions in its wake—seemed to have prepared him for a new phase of creativity, this one apparently conventional in its basic materials, but with subtle deviations from the classical base that made its imagery richer in texture, warmer in feeling. Very mid-twentieth century here is Robbins' mention of "trusting the intuition." Where previously ballet choreographers (himself included) had worked most often within the frame of a pre-established scenario,* Dances at a Gathering *seemed to grow of its own accord, by a kind of natural evolution that Isadora Duncan might well have approved. Robbins' nod to her feelings about music is significant, as is his choice of one of her favorite composers, Chopin.*

Dance Magazine was rightly proud of its coup in securing Edwin Denby to conduct this interview with Robbins. An active critic in the 1930s and '40s, Denby was writing only on rare occasions by the '60s. But those occasions were treasured by his many admirers, who found his precise yet poetically evocative descriptions of dancing unmatched by any of his followers.

Robbins' "Dances at a Gathering" is a great success both with dance fans and the general public. And it is a beautiful piece. But it wasn't planned as a sure-fire piece—it wasn't planned at all before hand, and began by chance as Robbins explains in the interview (taped shortly after the official premiere) which appears on the pages that follow.

SOURCE: From *Dance Magazine* (July, 1969). Reprinted by permission.

The ballet is set to Chopin piano pieces and the program lists ten dancers but tells you little more. The curtain goes up in silence on an empty stage. It looks enormous. The back is all sky—some kind of changeable late afternoon in summer. Both sides of the stage are black. Forestage right, a man enters slowly, deep in thought. He is wearing a loose white shirt, brown tights and boots. He turns to the sky and walks slowly away from you towards center stage. You think of a man alone in a meadow. As he walks you notice the odd tilt of his head—like a man listening, inside himself. In the silence the piano begins as if he were remembering the music. He marks a dance step, he sketches a mazurka gesture, with a kind of pensive vigor he begins to improvise and now he is dancing marvelously and, in a burst of freedom he is running all over the meadow at its edge. Suddenly he subsides and more mysterious than ever, glides into the woods and is gone. Upstage a girl and boy enter. At once they are off full speed in a double improvisation, a complexly fragmented waltz, the number Robbins speaks of as the "wind dance."

As one dance succeeds another—the ballet lasts about an hour—you are fascinated by the variety and freshness of invention, the range of feeling, and by the irresistibly beautiful music which the dance lets you hear distinctly—its mystery too. You see each dancer dance marvelously and you also see each one as a fascinating individual—complex, alone, and with any of the others, individually most sensitive and generous in their relationships. The music and the dance seem to be inventing each other. For a dance fan, the fluid shifts of momentum are a special delight. For the general theater public Robbins' genius in focusing on a decisive momentary movement—almost like a zoom lens—makes vivid the special quality of each dance, and all the charming jokes.

But it is a strange ballet.

Our talk began before the tape machine arrived. Robbins had been telling me how the ballet developed. He had been asked whether he would care to do a piece for the 25th Anniversary City Center Gala, May 8th. Delighted by the way Patricia McBride and Edward Villella had been dancing "The Afternoon of a Faun," he thought he would like to do a pas de deux for them—perhaps to Chopin music—and he accepted. As he listened to records and became more and more interested in the possibilities—it occurred to him to add two more couples—and he began rehearsal. In the course of rehearsals however, all the six dancers he had chosen were not always free, so he went on choreographing with four others, using those who happened to be free. Gradually he made more and more dances, but without a definite plan for the whole piece. When about two-thirds of the ballet was done, he invited Balanchine (who had just returned from Europe) to rehearsal. At the end of it he turned to Mr. B and said, "Don't you think it's a bit long?" Mr. B answered, "More. Make more!" He did.

Robbins said to me, "As you see, there are still never more than six dancers dancing at once." He told me that as the dances and relationships kept coming out of the different pieces of music and the particular dancers available, he began to feel that they were all connected by some underlying sense of community (he said, laughing, "Maybe just because they were dancers") and by a sense of open air and sunlight and sudden nostalgia perhaps.

We spoke of one of the many lovely lifts—this one at the end of Eddie's pas de deux with Pat where it looks as though he were lifting a sack onto his shoulder and, up on his shoulder the sack suddenly changes into a beautiful mermaid. Robbins explained how it came out of a sudden metamorphosis in the music. And he illustrated how the lift is done.

We were talking of Villella's gesture of touching the floor in the final minutes of the ballet, and Robbins mentioned that he was perhaps thinking of the dancers' world—the floor below, the space around and above. I was saying that I liked that gesture better the second time I saw it because it was slower and I wondered if he (Robbins) had changed it. At that point the tape begins:

ROBBINS: No, that's just a very subtle thing of acting and where the human being is at the time. I think two weeks ago, at the preview, Eddie was under more difficulties and pressures—down more—and perhaps that made the difference.

   I think the ballet will seem different in almost every performance, not vastly, but shades like those you saw, they will happen, depending on the dancers. You said it, I remember, way back—the dancers read (in a review) what the ballet is about, then they change because now they *know* it (they know it in words)—before they just *did* it. And that can happen—there was a modesty and a sort of not knowing in the first showing. They may start to think now that maybe they should do it more like what everyone says it is. I don't know what to do about that except to ask them not to.

   I always tell them to do it for themselves, and to think of "marking" it—Don't think of doing it full out.

. . .

DENBY: . . . You should try out your dances on the Russians. I'm sure they would like to have a dance of yours, they like to gather things—archives in their minds. It would be so much fun.

ROBBINS: I'm going to Russia. I *would* like to see if I can get it either to the Bolshoi or Kirov. I would like to see them dance this. I really would. It might finally turn out to be a peasant parody, you never know (laughter)—that folk part of it—I was surprised.

DENBY: I was surprised that people made so much of it, because the dancers are always so elegant. They might be landowners, if they were anybody in Europe.

ROBBINS: At first I also thought they were very elegant people, maybe at a picnic, maybe doing something—their own thing.

And also to me—and this I'm being very careful about—I don't want it to be a big thing—but the boys and the whole period are very hippyish.

DENBY: At first you had the beards. I was quite pleased with that.

ROBBINS: The boys still had them at rehearsal because of the long lay-off. Tony had long hair and a moustache and John Prinz had long hair and a beard and it was marvelous looking. It really affected what I was doing. I liked the boots—and the sketches are much more hippy than they appear on stage in the sense of belts and open blouses for the boys and long hair and ballooning sleeves. There is something in the nature of knowing who they are and having love and confidence in them.

DENBY: Competence. . . ?

ROBBINS: Confidence—which I feel is in the work, finally. Loving confidence in themselves and in the other people.

DENBY: That is in there very strongly.

ROBBINS: It has some strangenesses in it too, I'm sure, but I can't yet quite see it. Every now and then I look at a step and think that is a very odd step. There is a strange step that Eddie does in his solo—he should play with it the way one does this (hand gesture).

. . .

DENBY: There are things in the ballet that are a bit gruesome. And, you know, very interesting.

ROBBINS: Gruesome?

DENBY: It's partly in the lifts, partly sometimes in the way the boys treat a girl.

ROBBINS: Well, opening night there was an accident. I want to be sure you know that it was an accident. There was a place where Sally (Sara Leland) was being swung around and they fell off the lift and it turned into a—it looked like she was in outer space—like she'd been released from a capsule. She was just swirling around. Horrifying for a moment. But there are?—I don't know, I can't tell.

DENBY: It's definitely in the music. It's much stranger than one . . .

ROBBINS: Yes, than one thinks.

DENBY: Than one is supposed to think.

ROBBINS: There's a nocturne. I began late listening to one nocturne—it was like opening a door into a room and the people are in the *midst* of a conversation. I mean, there's no introduction, no preface; it's like a cut

Photo, Martha Swope

Edwin Denby writes of "the variety and freshness of invention, the range of feeling" in *Dances at a Gathering*. Here balletic virtuosity is present, but barely discernible, as we watch for subtle variations of mood—a sad smile, a backward glance, a playful jibe. The dancers exchange exuberant greetings or part with tender awareness of newly created memories. (Above) Left to right: Patricia McBride, Kay Mazzo, Sara Leland. (Below) Left to right: Edward Villella, Anthony Blum, Patricia McBride, Sara Leland.

Photo, Martha Swope

in a film; it's almost like Chopin had finished the previous nocturne, finished it properly, and there was a fade-out. And suddenly (clap) you're on somebody's face who's talking. But in the middle of a sentence! You don't even get "and then," it's right in the middle of a word and he's very strange, really quite strange. He knew a lot, I think. Much more than I thought before I began. It was fascinating that way—just like some connection happened between all those sounds that he thought of, and where I was at.

DENBY: The movement through a piece is always so interesting, and that you catch so well and do so many things with.

ROBBINS: I listened to a lot of recordings, different people playing the same piece. I used mostly Rubinstein and Novaes and some Brailowsky. I listened to some of the Dinu Lipatti. Then it was enough for me and after that I knew I would start to get confused. There are hardly any liberties taken at all—I would say none. Only one where at the end of Eddie's first dance it's marked *fortissimo*—da da da *whoosh*—I don't even know if it's Chopin's indication—I choreographed it that way—and Eddie was gone, *whoosh*. I didn't like it, it was a little obvious, like I was trying for a hand and the piece was trying for a hand, I thought there was something else there, so I took it on retard and soft, and let him take that poetic thing he does there. The dancers are beautiful.

DENBY: Gordon (Boelzner) plays it very well because he also plays it for movement, without those extra questions of pianism.

ROBBINS: There are no sentimentalities. . . . And I thought Tom Skelton did a very good job in a very little time. He did the lighting.

DENBY: Some of it looks ominous, sometimes. I mean weather. It changes. I suppose you wanted that too. I liked it.

ROBBINS: I didn't mean it to look ominous, but I suppose that vast sky, it is almost like nature changing on you. You're a little worried about what is going to happen next, it doesn't matter if it goes up or down. It's just that it changes. Everything changes.

I didn't know it was going to be that long a ballet or what it was going to be. I originally thought, we'll do it using the wings and the cyclorama because it's just going to be a pas de deux. But by the time it was all done, I thought, wow, who should do a set? Is it Jane Freilicher, or is it one of those watery sort of places, or is it—? Now I'm used to the way it is. I don't know if I want a set, or anything softer around the edges. That's a very hard line, those black wings. But once it starts, I don't suppose you are particularly aware of it any more.

DENBY: When you watch you realize that there are woods there, and you're in a meadow and there are trees.

ROBBINS: Isn't that funny, odd how that all got evoked, my names for the dances themselves, for instance, the second dance for John Prinz and Allegra (Kent), I call it "wind waltz" because to me they are like two things that are on the wind that catch up with each other. There is something about air—breezes which are clawing them and pushing them almost like two kites. And "walk waltz" or "the three girls" to me is somehow in the woods. On a Chekhov evening. It just is, I can't see it any other way. It has that quality.

DENBY: The whole piece is a Chekhov piece. There are so many things suggested and not explained. The business of looking around at the end is the trickiest. I didn't like it at all the first time. Yesterday I didn't mind it so much. It is like looking at an airplane, I think of missiles and war.

ROBBINS: They must do it very softly. That is almost one of the hardest parts to be able to do. It is very hard for them just to walk on and be confident and just raise their heads or eyes and look at something without starting to make it dramatic. I keep telling them, "Relax, don't be sad, don't get upset, just see it, just whatever you want to pick, just see. It's a cloud passing, if you want. Take it easy on it, don't get gloomy."

DENBY: It's because they all do it together.

ROBBINS: Together—right—they all follow one thing. And that upset you? You thought it was airplanes and missiles?

DENBY: The atom bomb comes in and everything else. The sort of thing about Hitler attacking Poland. Your mind gets full of ideas that you don't want, that don't have anything to do with the piece.

ROBBINS: If I had to talk about it all, I would say that they are looking at—all right—clouds on the horizon which possibly could be threatening, but then that's life, so afterwards you just pick up and go right on again. It doesn't destroy them. They don't lament. They accept.

DENBY: That's what I told myself. It must be that they are looking at clouds—clouds rarely go that fast, but it might be a storm coming up and they're wondering if it's going to happen.

ROBBINS: That section, it was the last piece I did, though. I spent about two weeks after I finished the bulk of the choreography—it was almost all done about two weeks before the 8th of May. But that last two weeks I spent in arranging, trying to get the right order. Not only who danced what, but also that sense of something happening—making the dances have some continuity, some structure, whether I knew specifically what it was or not. At one point I had the scherzo finishing the ballet and the grand waltz opening it. All different sorts of ways. It was just—it was a marvelous sort of puzzle. Here I have all these people and these situations and I know they belong to each other—now let me see how. It was almost like rearranging *things*. And suddenly a picture was there. I am surprised by a lot of it. . . . the end of it had to come out of the scherzo, that very restless piece which ends with them all sort of *whoosh* running out—disappearing like cinders falling out into the night, and it couldn't end there, either. That's not the end of it, that's not how I feel about these people—that they went *whoosh* and disappeared. They are still here and they still move like dancers. They are a community. They take—what's the Italian word?—"a passegiata"— they take a stroll, like in an Italian town, around the town's square at sundown. They may have felt a threat, but they don't panic, they stay. . . .

So coming back after the scherzo to the stage and the floor that we dance on, and putting your hand on it—if it's the earth or a ballet dancer's relationship to a wood floor—*that* somehow is the ending I knew I had to get to somewhere. Very little of this was conscious, Edwin. I don't like to make theory afterward. I'm trying to get at it—there may be seven other reasons I'm not mentioning, well, you understand. . . .

[The following day Robbins wrote a postscript from Stockholm.]

May 27, 1969

Dear Edwin:

Something bothered me terribly after we met—one of your remarks about the people looking up and watching something cross the sky at the end of the ballet. You said something about planes—A bomb—war today, etc. and it jarred me very much. I couldn't figure out "the why" right away—but then I did on the trip over. First of all I feel you are imposing a terribly out-of-context meaning to what they are seeing. The ballet stays and exists in the time of the music and its work. Nothing is out of it, I believe; all gestures and moods, steps, etc. are part of the fabric of the music's time and its meanings to me. I couldn't think of planes—A bomb, etc. Only clouds—and the flights of birds—sunsets and leaves falling—and they, the people's reactions are all very underplayed, very willing to meet whatever threat is *in the music*.

Well, those people knew their disasters—felt them, maybe felt that at a certain time their being would come to an end—but they faced it as a part of living.

I hadn't thought of *all* of this when I did it. All I knew is that they weren't afraid, had no self pity, and stayed—didn't leave.

And I do feel that last piece is the logical end of the whole ballet. To me it is very much the only possible result of all that's come before.

. . . Stockholm is lovely, limpid skies at midnight—looking clear and blue as a New York fall—It was so good to see you—*J*

George Balanchine (1904–)
WORK IN PROGRESS

After graduating from the Soviet State School of Ballet in 1921, Balanchine presented some of his choreography to unimpressed audiences in Petrograd. Managing to leave Russia, he worked with Diaghilev from 1925 to 1929, coming to the United States at the invitation of Lincoln Kirstein in 1934. Since then, Balanchine's work has been linked with the group that became the New York City Ballet. In addition to creating its extensive and distinguished repertory, he has restaged many of his works for companies abroad and is probably the most influential ballet maker in the world today.

Balanchine's choreography has been consistently based on music and classical technique. When the music was Bach or Mozart, the movement was clear, balanced, elegant; when it was Ives, Webern, or Stravinsky, the classic steps were not only extended but inverted, turned inside out or upside down, stripped of their usually smooth transitions, executed with unexpected shifts of accent or strangely distorting tempos. But the point was always the music, for unlike Tudor, Balanchine is unconcerned with expressive movement. Ballet is like a rose, he has said; it's beautiful and you admire it, but you don't ask what it means.

[Balanchine has told his interviewer, Louis Botto, that he plans to choreograph fifteen ballets for the Stravinsky Festival to be produced by the New York City Ballet in June, 1972:]

Q: Have you started work on them yet?

BALANCHINE: No. I never start until I'm in the rehearsal hall. You can't plan steps ahead of time, just as you cannot plan words when you are going to write something. It's part of your ability. You have enough vocabulary and grammar in your head when you need them—everything that's required to start writing when the moment comes. That's the same as choreographing a ballet. When that moment comes—on union time—you have all the necessary equipment and ballet grammar in your head to do your work.

Q: Some of the ballets you're doing are new versions of ballets you did in the past. Will the choreography be different?

BALANCHINE: *Le Baiser de la Fée*, which I've done before, will be completely

SOURCE: From *Intellectual Digest* (June, 1972). Copyright © 1972 by Communications Research Machines, Inc. Excerpted and printed by permission.

One of the great successes of the 1973 Stravinsky festival was Balanchine's *Violin Concerto* which showed the master at his neo-classical abstract best. Unencumbered by romantic costumes or dramatic ideas, the choreographer happily set movements to music. Left to right: Nolan T'sani, Tracy Bennett, Kay Mazzo, David Richardson, Michael Steel.

different. And the *Violin Concerto* will have nothing to do with the original version, *Balustrade*. You see, when I first did it in 1941, it had scenery and costumes by Tchelitchev, and I had to make people dance in his costumes. There were pussycats and birds, and the scenery was a big leopard. But now, it will be nothing but pure music. The other ballets I'm redoing—I don't know yet what they will be.

Q: Will most of them be plotless?

BALANCHINE: Yes—most have no plot.

Q: Do you prefer a plotless ballet?

BALANCHINE: No. It depends—if it's a good plot, fine. But a plot is a very difficult thing for the dance. You cannot dance a story. You can only do very light ideas. A very simple situation. A love story, you can do. You know—two people are in love and they dance together. A *pas de deux*. But you couldn't do a complicated story to dance. You see, if you go to see a ballet with a story, and there's nothing about it in the program, you would never understand it.

Q: Yet, your ballet of *A Midsummer Night's Dream*, despite a very complex plot, was clear. Was that because we're familiar with the play?

BALANCHINE: Well—there was nothing there. It was just entrances of two couples—who are very famous—and I made it clear that they were mixed up in Shakespeare's mind. One person runs away from another, one finds somebody else—and all of a sudden they aren't in love anymore. The ballet was a very simple thing—just a little sylph dancing and Bottom turning into a donkey. But if you didn't know the Shakespeare story, you would probably ask why? Even in Shakespeare—people probably don't know why he changed into a donkey.

Q: You and Jerome Robbins are collaborating on the choreography of *Pulcinella* for the festival. Isn't it unusual for two choreographers to work together on the same ballet?

BALANCHINE: Yes, it's unusual, but when we have so much to do—over 30 ballets—we have to help each other. Robbins and I did *Firebird* together. Sometimes when we work together, he says to me, "Would you finish this section if I can't?" And I say, "Okay." When we work on *Pulcinella*, I may say to him, "I'm busy tomorrow—will you finish it?" And he will. We have the same conception, so it doesn't matter. If my knees are okay and his back is okay, we may even dance in it—on stilts.

Q: Will most of these ballets have sets?

BALANCHINE: No.

Q: Who makes the decision on that, the choreographer?

BALANCHINE: No. Money. It depends on how much you have to spend. And the company still says "Couldn't you have done without it?" In ballet, it's really better to do without expensive sets and costumes until you know if the work is a success. If you throw away lots of money on sets and costumes and it bombs, there's nothing you can do with them.

Q: Do critics make or break a ballet as they do a play?

BALANCHINE: I don't read the critics. Even if they don't like a ballet, it doesn't make any difference. We still do it and we have a full house—whether the critics like it or not. It's the public who decides. They see it and say, I like this or I don't. On Broadway, it's different. It's *so* commercial. And the tickets are *so* expensive. The producers don't give a damn about art—only money. If the public doesn't go, they close the show.

Q: You revolutionized musical comedy in the 1930s—especially in *On Your Toes*—by making ballet an integral part of the plot. Do you think you'll ever do another Broadway musical?

BALANCHINE: No. There are young people who should do that. I'm already passé. I don't like the music or the type of theater that is popular today. You have to be young to put up with the commercialism. Let them have the ulcer. I hardly ever go to the theater anymore. I know what they're doing in musicals and it's the same thing that used to be. Nobody can do anything new.

Q: With so many new ballets to create for the festival, is it difficult to come up with something original?

BALANCHINE: I never think I'm going to do something original. You don't think that way. You just do what you want to do. That's our language. Our movements have to be performed in the composer's time. That's what makes ballet so exciting—this movement of bodies in time. That's why I call Stravinsky "an architect of time." His music provides the dancer's floor. It's the reason for us to move. Without the music we don't want to move.

Q: Does the complexity of Stravinsky's music make it difficult to choreograph?

BALANCHINE: No. It just takes longer. Nothing is difficult, really, when you know it. But it takes longer to make so many people move to certain strange divisions of time. When you're working with straight music that's divided into four bars, it's simpler.

Q: Did you prefer him to write music specifically for your ballets?

BALANCHINE: No—but if he had free time, I would ask him to write something. Once he said, "Yes—I have time. What would you like?" I said, "Just start with something—a variation—anything" and he said, "Fine." So he wrote *Danses Concertantes*, which I'm choreographing for the festival. But some of his music he didn't want people to dance to.

Q: Do you do much revising?

BALANCHINE: I revise, but not as much as a playwright in the theater. He has much more time than we have. He only uses paper and pencil. He can throw away as much of that as he wants. But we have to be very fast. You see, we're on union time. I have to invent the dance, the dancers have to learn it, and the next day we do it. You don't even have the chance to go out of town to try it out. Sometimes people ask me how long it takes to create a ballet. It's impossible to say. You have to do it in whatever time—a few days or a month—that you have with the dancers.

Q: Is ballet more of a visual than an intellectual art?

BALANCHINE: Naturally. That's all there is to it. You perceive it through the eyes. A blind person could never know what ballet is, just as a deaf person can't perceive what music is. Unless he's a musician who reads music. But if you can't read music and you're deaf, there's only silence.

Q: Does ballet reflect life?

BALANCHINE: No. It's a fantasy. It has nothing to do with life. We are not real people. We are trained to dance and perform for the idea of beautiful things, but we are not people who are playing some part of life. We're like flowers. A flower doesn't tell you a story. It's in itself a beautiful thing. We have nothing to do with people on the street. I mean offstage, yes. But onstage, we train dancers that it's all artificial. We make the body perform things that the body's not supposed to do.

Q: Then, the ballet is not an emotional art, unless it moves you by the beauty of the dancing?

BALANCHINE: Naturally. A lot of people go to the theater to see their own life, their own experience. We don't give them that in the ballet. We give them something less. When you see flowers, do you have any emotion? You're moved by the color and the beauty—but what does it mean to be moved? Some people think that you have to cry to have emotions. Suppose you don't—then people believe you're cold and have no heart. Some people are hot, some cold. Which is better? I prefer cold. I have never cried at a ballet. I never cry anytime. I don't have that type of reaction. Actually, when people cry they are only thinking of themselves. They think, I'm poor, I'm unhappy, I'm lonely, why did my girl friend leave me? And so, beautiful music that is sad or a stage situation that is ethereal suddenly attaches itself to your personal life and makes you cry.

Q: Then you never put anything from your life into your ballets?

BALANCHINE: Never. Mozart never put his miserable life into his beautiful, gay music. He didn't want to portray his life. He had a beautiful idea of music—of the sound of it.

Q: Is it true that Diaghilev was more interested in scenery than dancing?

BALANCHINE: It was a different approach. Diaghilev said there were no choreographers at that time. Fokine had left—nobody could do anything—so he saved his ballet by commissioning people like Picasso and Ravel to camouflage the fact that there was no choreography. The dancers were bad—the corps de ballet was *terrible*. When I came in, I started to do more dancing, and Diaghilev was happy to see it. He had to save himself. You see, the public in France really didn't *like* dancing. All over Europe, they *don't like* dancing. They like spectacle, scenery, costumes and association with the great Picasso, the great Derain, the great this, the great that. They just want to see one performance, then everybody goes to Maxim's. The dance is forgotten. When I did my first ballet for Diaghilev, *Le Chant Du Rossignol*, which we're reviving in the festival, he told me Matisse was designing the décor and costumes. I shrugged my shoulders. Matisse? I had never heard of him.

Q: Has ballet dancing improved since those days?

BALANCHINE: It's a different type of dancing today. We are trained now to cover more space—faster. Our ears and our eyes are better. We memorize much faster. Ensembles are more complicated. They're like a Swiss watch. If Nijinsky were alive today, he would have to start all over again as a boy to be trained in the new technique. He would learn and he would be considered a great dancer today.

Q: You are doing fifteen ballets for the festival. Will the choreography be written down?

BALANCHINE: No. I never use choreographic notation. We teach it at Lincoln Center, but I never use it.

Q: Suppose another ballet company wants to do one of these ballets?

BALANCHINE: Then, I would have to go there—or someone from my company who knows the choreography—and teach it to them.

Q: Won't these ballets be preserved?

BALANCHINE: They don't have to be preserved. Why should they be? I think ballet is NOW. It's about people who are NOW. Not about what will be. Because as soon as you don't have these bodies to work with, it's already finished. This is not a question of what the story is, or what the costumes are, or preserving the ballet of 1972 for future generations. I'm staging ballets for today's bodies. For people who are here now. And you admire the way he or she looks and how they move. It's this person today—not just *anybody*. So, I'm not interested at all that there will be some dancers who could do something of mine in the future. It wouldn't be right because I would have to do it myself.

Q: Have any of your ballets ever been lost because of this lack of notation?

BALANCHINE: Oh, yes. *Caracole* was one of my lost ballets. I redid it as *Divertimento No. 15*.

Q: Then you're really not concerned that a century from now your ballets will be extinct?

BALANCHINE: Absolutely not concerned. Besides, there will be different people then. The art of dancing will disappear—or maybe it will be done with acrobats. Who knows what they're going to do? But I don't want my ballets preserved as museum pieces for people to go and laugh at what used to be. *Absolutely not.*

Section Seven

RECENT REBELS

Q: The impact of the early modern dance had been violent—people either hated it or dedicated themselves to the cult of the revolution. But, as with all revolutions, the fervor was transitory; the excitement had to wear off as the artists got down to the business of consolidating their gains and exploring the ramifications of what had been accomplished. Unlike the ballet, in which few dancers wanted to do anything other than perform, the modern dance was geared to stimulate creativity; if choreography was a representation of personal experience, an expression of individual feeling, then each was entitled to depict his own.

From the companies of Graham and Humphrey-Weidman came young choreographers, most of them destined to develop the newly established tradition—though some were to break it.

Humphrey guided the first efforts of José Limón and remained his mentor throughout her life. His magnificent body brought special nobility to her movements; his own dances reflected her belief in the fundamental dignity of man. His first works drew on his Mexican heritage, but his themes grew in universality from the intimate tragedy of his four-character version of Othello, *The Moor's Pavane* (1949), to the baroque grandeur of *Missa Brevis* (1958). "I reach," he once wrote, "for demons, saints, martyrs, apostates, fools, and other impassioned visions." His models were the noble measures of Bach, the heroic figures of Michelangelo.

Also dramatic, but of tougher fibre than Limón, was Anna Sokolow, who had come from the Graham company. Rejecting narrative structures, she built dances on types of characters: the lonely and isolated who live in fantasy worlds, in *Rooms* (1955); the beatnik generation, in *Opus 65* (1965). Sokolow kept her stages bare, her costumes drab, so that attention was focused on telling forms of movement that derived from natural expressions of emotion. Differing from the Humphrey-Limón school of thought, she did not provide her works with optimistic endings; it was enough for her that they were provocative.

These were, in a sense, typical of the generation that followed the pioneers; but there were others—equally dissimilar—who worked deftly within the tradition which had no single style, only that consistent method of moving from the inside out.

Modern dance had broken with the established vocabulary of classical ballet, finding it inadequate to the expression of contemporary life, and had discovered other forms of movement better adapted to the portrayal of modern concerns. The change had been incited by dramatic needs, but in the process new languages had evolved, suggesting the possibility of movement provinces beyond those already explored. At mid-century the need for expressive motivation was questioned: wasn't the movement aspect of dance sufficiently interesting to make further dramatic content unnecessary? And wasn't the insistence on expressiveness limiting movement invention unnecessarily?

Leading the revolt was Merce Cunningham, who had danced with Graham. Denying himself the stimulation of plot or character portrayal, he looked for objective ways of combining and ordering movements, trying devices of chance or arbitrary systems. While musician John Cage worked independently, Cunningham arranged his dances without reference to accompanying sound patterns. The choreography was autonomous; free of drama, free of music. Nor was it bound by the conventional concept of structure. Cunningham's dances were open-ended: a number of sections were composed, but the toss of a coin could establish which sections were actually seen and in what order. Or indeterminacy was used: in *Field Dances* (1963) each participant had his own set of movements but in performance he did as few or as many as he wished and at any time that he wished. The result, Cunningham liked to say, was "beyond imagination"; he wanted to stretch the range of choreography further than the deliberate human mind could take it.

In addition to opening the field of movement and its manner of occupying time, Cunningham changed the dance's orientation in space. Asserting that any position in space was important, he upset the traditional soloist-ensemble dichotomy that had persisted from classical ballet through the days of early modern dance. With Cunningham the focus of the audience was no longer directed to the center of the stage; it was not directed at all but could wander to whatever group or individual seemed attractive at the moment. The meaning of the dance was left equally open. True, qualities seemed to emerge, and that was fine as long as the choreographer did not predetermine them. If a dance turned out to be sunny in feeling, it could be called *Summerspace* (1960); if it looked darkly ominous, it became *Winterbranch* (1965). But the choreographer's intention was simply to compose human movements in space and time.

While Cunningham made no attempt either to communicate feeling or to withhold it, Alwin Nikolais deliberately sought to wipe out vestiges of personal emotion. Believing that the dancer was limited by his pedestrian personality, Nikolais induced him to assume another identity by clothing him in fantastic garb or having him attached to a prop—a hoop, a pole, a cape—which seemed to become a part of his body. The equipment not only depersonalized the dancer but led to fresh movement ideas: How many ways can you move while holding a hoop? In dances like *Imago* (1963) and *Somniloquy* (1967), the movement of props, of fabrics, of lights, of colors, of slide projections, of electronic sounds, was an essential part of the choreography. The works were allowed to project their own kind of drama for, without explicit role playing, generic characters seemed to appear—proud, pathetic, coy, witty. Though the intention was to portray what Nikolais called the "primary qualities" of movement —feelings of heavy, light, thick, thin, fast, slow—the audience tended to make personal associations, to which Nikolais had no objection. The important thing was not to limit movement design by insisting that it represent emotions.

While both Cunningham and Nikolais used technically skilled dancers, other choreographers chose to eliminate this restriction as well. In the 1960's Ann Halprin arranged pieces that were structured by tasks: participants were assigned jobs to be done (carrying a load of objects or wading through mounds of wrapping paper), and the dance consisted of whatever movements were needed to accomplish the task. The group known as the Judson Dance Theatre resorted to nondancers in experiments that used ordinary movement, the kind any person in the street could do. But taking the movement out of its usual context gave it another look, focused attention on details or shape that would have gone unnoticed in its customary surroundings. Yvonne Rainer challenged herself to make movement as minimal as possible and discovered that, after a period of sparseness, an elbow wiggle looked positively virtuosic.

By using people who had no particular dance skills, these choreographers set up a new kind of relationship between the performer and his audience: they became peers. By erasing the distance between the skilled and unskilled, they led the audience to identify with the dancers, not as the kind of people they would like to be, but as the kind they really were.

Another limitation to be removed was the frame of the proscenium stage. Again Cunningham was the pioneer, taking his dances into art galleries to find new ways to defocus movements in space. Others tried city squares and parks, some of them devising pieces for such specific environments that they could be done nowhere else. Twyla Tharp did *Medley* (1969) on a college campus, where she used a tremendous expanse of lawn to make her audience see, now a few dancers at a great distance, then half a hundred dancers only a few feet away. Rudy Perez choreographed a ballet for automobiles (with drivers) performed in a parking lot, a modern counterpart of the horse ballets of the seventeenth century. James Cunningham's dancers finished a gymnasium presentation by running up to the bleachers and inviting the audience to join them in social dancing. It was considerably less formal than Beaujoyeulx' conclusion to the *Ballet Comique*, and everyone was wearing sneakers and jeans—but the ideas were similar.

Though many groups continued to be led by a single choreographer, some disdained this kind of dictatorship and chose a more democratic format. In some cases, individuals took turns composing; in others, they worked with improvisation, agreeing on certain rules to be observed by all but letting each player fill in the framework at will. Still others employed strict structures but worked as collaborative units that gave nearly equal authority to a core of creators. Some groups took names indicative of the cooperative nature of their venture—The House, The Collective, The Grand Union.

Then, just when it seemed that plots and skills and even the stage had been banished from contemporary choreography, they started creeping back; often one at a time, to be sure, and often in strange guises. One of the most conspicuous reversals was engineered by Paul Taylor, who had originally tested his audience's endurance by standing still and looking at them for what seemed interminable minutes. He gave in to skilled movement with *Aureole* (1962), which had an exultant wave of dancers filling the stage with swirling and leaping. Then, in *Big Bertha* (1970) he restored explicit content in a psychological study of the deterioration of a middle-class family mesmerized by a fairground automaton.

Meredith Monk's *Needle-brain Lloyd and the Systems Kid* (1970) was an outdoor pageant with multiple levels of imagery. The audience walked considerable distances to observe travelers—a couple in a boat, pioneers, horseback riders, motorcyclists—all involved in the journey of life. Kei Takei's *Diary of the Field* (1973) was a ritual of spring, a myth of creation, and a disclosure of the birth pains of making a dance.

Social consciousness, which had received little thought since the 1930's, became a significant factor, especially, though not exclusively, in the work of black choreographers. Earlier they had concentrated on theatricalizing ethnic forms. In the 1940's two dancers trained in anthropology put their research to practical use: Katherine Dunham translated ritual dances of the West Indies into presentations for both Broadway musicals and the concert stage; Pearl Primus drew on forms she had learned in Africa. A young member of Lester Horton's integrated Los Angeles company, Alvin Ailey, began his independent career along the lines of his mentor, using ritual and ethnic themes but adding to them elements from his own heritage, most notably in the suite based on traditional Negro folk music *Revelations* (1960). More recent choreographers have created ethnic works in more specifically contemporary veins, dealing with the violence and piteousness of life in the black ghettos of America, sometimes symbolically but more often with near literal realism. At the same time Arthur Mitchell, formerly a soloist with the New York City Ballet, formed the Dance Theatre of Harlem to perform works from the classical repertory as well as original choreography based on the balletic idiom.

In spite of the fact that Laban's efficient system of dance notation was not invented until after World War I and was not widely used until long after that, the ballet did have a sense of repertory. Works were passed down from one generation to the next by means of personal coaching, an older dancer teaching his role to a younger one who would teach it again when his turn came. Of course, changes were made along the way, but at least some identity persisted. Such a concept of continuity was alien to the nature of the original modern dance, where choreography was expected to represent a personal comment on contemporary life. As masterworks appeared, however, this attitude began to change; the public wanted to see not only the newest creations, but also the outstanding repertory of the past. While modern dance companies began to produce revivals, ballet companies got the idea of diversifying their repertories with works from modern choreographers. In the 1930's this would have been practically impossible; the techniques were so distinct that a dancer trained in one idiom would have had great difficulty adjusting to the demands of the other. But the modern dance had gradually broadened its base, assimilating more flowing and more virtuosic movement; meanwhile ballet choreographers were incorporating modern elements, especially those involving the use of the upper body, as dramatic situations seemed to warrant them.

In the late 1960's John Butler and Glen Tetley, both originally with Graham, received invitations to stage their works for ballet companies in Europe. Then the Royal Danish Ballet asked Paul Taylor for *Aureole* and the Royal Swedish Ballet took several pieces from José Limón. Soon after, American Ballet Theatre acquired *The Moor's Pavane*. The trend toward assimilation was climaxed (to date) when Robert Joffrey commissioned *Deuce Coupe* (1973) from Twyla Tharp. She made a witty, sophisticated commentary on styles, using the classical technique of the Joffrey company as well as the apparently casual (but highly calculated) jazz idiom of her own group, and producing the hit of the season.

Some observers have predicted an eventual merging of ballet and modern dance styles. Whether this will come about remains to be seen.

But the historical difference remains in the works of the past, and it is not so simple as just ballet versus modern. The Bournonville style distinguishes one kind of ballet; Balanchine another; Tudor still another. Graham choreography demands a particular kind of gut attack, where the Humphrey style requires a lyrical breath impulse and the Cunningham approach has a cool detachment. To reduce all of these (and more) to a mere dichotomy is to misrepresent an art that flourishes in its diversity. Our dance heritage has been enriched by numerous unique contributions. Preserving them while continuing to support innovative creativity is one of the great challenges of the present.

Merce Cunningham (1919–)
TWO QUESTIONS AND FIVE DANCES

Merce Cunningham studied tap dancing and ballet before encountering modern dance with Lester Horton and joining the company of Martha Graham. He began to choreograph in 1943, forming his own company nine years later. His sustained collaborations with John Cage, along with associations with other avant-garde composers and designers, produced theatre pieces that were, for many years, as widely condemned as they were praised. A series of European tours, beginning in 1958, spread the influence of his ideas.

As evidenced by the following statements, Cunningham's creative methods are precisely designed; the operations of chance and indeterminacy deliberately prepared. Previously each choreographer had determined exactly what and when his observers would see and hear. With Cunningham, the structure of dance has been opened, letting in a whole new range of possibilities.

How do you go about composing a particular dance?

In a direct way. I start with a step. Using the word "step" is a hangover from my adolescent vaudeville days. I "step" with my feet, legs, hands, body, head—that is what prompts me, and out of that other movements grow, and different elements (theatre) may be involved.

SOURCE: From *Dance Perspective, 34 (Summer, 1968).* © 1968 by Merce Cunningham.

This is not beginning with an idea that concerns character or story, a *fait accompli* around which the actions are grouped for reference purposes. I start with the movement, even something moving rather than someone (pillows in the air).* And I ordinarily start with myself; not always, it may be with one or two of the dancers. But then out of this the action begins to assume its own proportions, and other possibilities appear as the dance proceeds. New situations present themselves—between the dancers, the dancers and the space, the space and the time. It is not subject to a prearranged idea as to how it should go any more than a conversation you might have with a friend while out walking. It can take a momentum of its own, that is. That leaves open the possibility of surprise (chance), and that is essential.

Would you comment on the extraordinary intensity that is said to be the most marked characteristic of the dancers in your company?

The appearance of intensity may come from their devotion to what they are doing. It can give the look of being highly involved in the moment, that urgency that doing something precisely in the largest possible way can provoke. They also seem to me to sometimes have a sense of pleasure amongst each other, which isn't intensity, but has to do with individual relationships. My company has grown with the feeling that each dancer is a separate identity; that there is not a chorus along with which there are soloists, but rather that each in the company is a soloist, and in a given dance we may act sometimes separately and sometimes together. I would like to allow each dancer to appear in his way as a dancer, and that implies a good deal of trust between us—all of us.

I train them and then I give them the movements and actions to do in the dances, but I don't expect them to do those actions exactly in the way I do them. What I look for is a way to have the dancer move in the way he would move with the best amplification of that.

This relationship of good will (sometimes it is at stake) includes not only the dancers. It also includes the musicians, Mr. John Cage, Mr. David Tudor and Mr. Gordon Mumma, and the lighting designer, Miss Beverly Emmons, who work with us and act in their separate ways. It is an anarchic process of working, a number of people dealing in their separate ways with a common situation, and out of it can come a whole: an evening of dance; a museum event; a program of music; a lecture-demonstration with movement, sound and light; a seminar; a sudden change of program (given the immediate illness of a dancer) from three works to a dance event lasting two hours, a process where

*Andy Warhol's inflated silver ones—the source of *Rainforest* (ed.).

Photo, James Klosty

Merce Cunningham dances with his company in *Canfield* (1969). A performance of the complete work could occupy an entire evening, but segments of it could be presented independently, and the parts were interchangeable in their order. With all this freedom, however, the individual movements were strictly designed within a limited range, giving the dance its distinctive atmosphere.

the incapacity of one does not impoverish the whole, although his addition would have enriched it. Out of this comes a whole not dependent upon one thing; each person and the work he does is independent, and he acts with the others, not competitively, but complementarily. It is an interdependence that brings about what you speak of as intensity. Each person, observant of the others, is allowed to act freely.

The order of the dances discussed is as tossed for by Merce Cunningham, June 14,1968.

1960: The dance *Crises* (music, Conlon Nancarrow; costumes, Robert Rauschenberg), made in the summer at the Connecticut College School of Dance, was an adventure in partnering. I decided to allow for the dancers (there were five—four girls and one man) contacting each other, but not just through holding or being held, but through being attached by outside means. I used elastic bands around a wrist, an arm, a waist or a leg, and by one dancer inserting a hand under the band on another's wrist. They were attached but also, at the same instant, free.

But where these contacts came in the continuity or where they were broken was left to chance in the composition, and not to personal psychology or physical pressure.

The gamuts of movement were individualized to some degree for the five dancers, and I worked out the particular timing of each of them.

The music (Rhythm Studies #1, #2, #4, #5, #7 and #6 for Player Piano) was added after the dance was choreographed.

Facts like this—attaching people together by outward means, in this case elastic bands—always look as though they mean something. Well, they do. Or rather they are. Here two persons are held together, not only by the invisible bonds that can tie them, but visibly, and without being the instruments of the holding.

1951: It was in a dance called *16 Dances for Soloist and Company of Three* (music, John Cage; costumes and properties, Remy Charlip) that the first use of chance in my work appeared. This dance was a series of solos, duets, trios and quartets with an over-all rhythmic structure relating the small parts to the large in both the dance and the music. The form of the dances was not thematic (it never has been), but the objects in space relating in time; in this situation the relationship being pointed out by the dance joining with the music at structure points.

The entire dance dealt with the nine permanent emotions of the Indian classical theatre tradition. The sequence of the dances was arranged expressively, with a light emotion following a dark emotion (anger followed by mirth, the odious followed by wonder). But I could find no reason why a specific light should follow a specific dark, and threw a coin and let that decide. So the order became: anger, the humorous, sorrow, the heroic, the odious, the wondrous, fear, the erotic and finally tranquility. These were all solos with the exception of the erotic, which was a duet, and tranquility, which was a dance for the four of us. The solos were concerned with specific emotional qualities, but they were in image form and not personal—a yelling warrior for the odious, a man in a chair for the humorous, a bird-masked figure for the wondrous.

There were postludes to a number of the solos. Following fear was a quartet with a small gamut of movements, which was different for each dancer, and this was choreographed by chance means. That is, the individual sequences, and the length of time, and the directions in space of each were discovered by tossing coins. It was the first such experience for me and felt like "chaos has come again" when I worked on it.

1953: *Untitled Solo* (music, Christian Wolff, For Piano I) was the first in a trilogy of solos with music by Wolff, all concerned with the possibility of containment and explosion being instantaneous. A large gamut of movements was devised for this solo, movements for the arms, the legs, the head and the torso, which were separate and essentially tensile in character, and off the normal or tranquil body-balance. These separate movements were arranged in continuity by random means, allowing for the superimposition of one or more, each having its own rhythm and time-length.

The two solos that completed the trilogy (*Lavish Escapade*, 1956, and *Changeling*, 1958) also used chance procedures in the choreography, sometimes in the smallest of fragments and at others in large ways only. But all three succeeded in becoming continuous if I could wear them long enough, like a suit of clothes.

Learning how to wear one was another thing. *Untitled Solo* was first presented at Black Mountain College in the summer. I was trying to learn it on one of those hot, muggy days, rehearsing in the steamy dining-hall atmosphere with David Tudor at the piano, and I had stopped in fatigue and despair. He said: "This is clearly impossible, but we're going right ahead and do it anyway."

1953-59: Excerpt from lecture-demonstration: The dance *Suite for Five* (music, John Cage, Music for Piano 4-84; costumes, Robert Rauschenberg), which my company and I will present this evening, is a continuation of *Solo Suite in Space and Time*, a dance in five parts that I first presented in 1953.

The trio, the duet and the quintet were made in 1956, and the solo for Carolyn Brown was added in 1958.

The action of the seven dances that now comprise the suite is deliberate; that is, the movements are short or long, often surrounded by stillness and allowed to take place without strict regard for musical cues.

The movements may strike or not with the sounds, and although the dancers know the sequences of sound, the sounds do not necessarily happen in the same rhythm or time-lengths from performance to performance. The total length of a given dance, however, is identical each time.

The special plan for the dance, which was the beginning procedure, was found by numbering the imperfections on a piece of paper (one for each of the dances), and by random procedure finding the order of the numbers. The time-lengths were also found by numbering spots on paper; the movement by working it out and tossing coins.

Sometimes a simple movement came with a long stretch of time. So we could have stillness before it and/or after it.

The dances, despite the interval of years between the compositions, were all designed to be presented with the audience on four sides, and are so given when situations allow for this.

1963: *Story* (music, Toshi Ichiyanagi, Sapporo; costumes and décor, Robert Rauschenberg) was first presented in Royce Hall at the University of California, Los Angeles. It is a dance for x-number of people and had seven dancers in it at its first performance. Since that time it has been given nineteen times in the United States, with the number of performers ranging from five to eight. The structure is indeterminate, and the length is made to be varied. It has been as short as fifteen minutes and as long as forty.

We have presented it, among other places, on a huge stage in Augusta, Georgia—actually a double stage that was situated between two auditoriums. In this case both halls were open and visible to each other with all curtains lifted, and one hall being populated, the other empty. We have presented it on the thrust stage of the Tyrone Guthrie Theatre in Minneapolis, Minnesota, with exits through the tunnels under the seats; and on a miniscule stage in Duluth, Minnesota, where—to have more flexibility and space—we employed the floor of the auditorium in front of the stage, and the stairs and doors leading to it.

The dance was choreographed in a series of sections, and these were given names for reasons of identification—"Object," "Triangle," "Floor," "Tag," "Space," "Entrance" and others. "Object," for example, refers to an actual object constructed fresh for each performance, which is moved or carried around the stage by the dancers. "Floor" indicates a duet for two of the girls, Carolyn Brown and Viola Farber, which starts at any point in the space, on or off the stage. The two dancers move in a pronounced, slow tempo across the area, possibly separated, but more often together. There is a "Five-Part Trio," which is as it says, three people who have five phrases each to contend with, the movement in this section being swift. The entire number of possibilities consists of eighteen parts, all or any group of which may be done in a given performance.

The music by Mr. Ichiyanagi is a composition, in the composer's words, for "sustained sound(s), without attack and continuous." Into this atmosphere also may come sharp, vibrant sounds. The composer has left the players free as to choice of instruments.

My original idea for the costumes was that they be picked up or found in the particular playing situation we were in, and that the set, or the way the stage looked, would also be devised from the existing circumstances and environment at the time of the performance.

The variables in the structure, which are changed at each performance, are: the length of the whole, and the length of the separate sections, and the placement of the sections in the continuity. The relationship of the sound is constantly varied, as the only agreement between the dance and the music is the length decided upon for that performance. Although the dancers listen to the sounds and are sometimes engaged by them, this is not a support and certainly cannot be counted upon to happen again.

The title does not refer to any implicit or explicit narrative, but to the fact that each spectator may interpret the events in his own way.

Alwin Nikolais (1912–)
PLAN FOR A TELEVISION PRODUCTION OF "TENT"

First a musician and puppeteer, Nikolais worked with Hanya Holm, beginning to choreograph in 1939 and establishing his own company in 1948. A completely versatile man of the theatre, he experimented with new forms of lighting (he was the first dancer since Loïe Fuller to be so intrigued by it), with slide projections, and electronic scores. His productions featured movements, lights, colors, sounds—all by Nikolais.

Naturally, he has been fascinated by the medium of television, and his scientific mind is applied to it here. Tent was first choreographed for the stage in 1968; these notes, which have been edited by Marcia B. Siegel, were made for a Munich production the following year. Nikolais' exacting specifications amply demonstrate his difference from Cunningham: the master magician pulls all the strings himself, leaving not the minutest detail to chance—or anyone else for that matter. How the seventeenth century would have enjoyed these chrome-key transformations, which allow the choreographer to place his dancers (apparently) on sand or flowers or simply in mid-air, as a technical process blanks out their real, studio environment.

SOURCE: From *Dance Perspectives* 48 (Winter, 1971).

1. Entrance and Ground Ritual

The dancers enter in single file carrying the tent. They should appear to be coming from a timeless space and into an area suggesting a primitive ceremonial ground. Yet they (the dancers) are contemporary. They unfold the tent on the ground then proceed into a suggestion of a ritual dance. This continues first with a central solo figure then into duets, trios, etc. until one point of silence when all freeze. Silver balls descend. When the balls reach the floor the dancers suddenly break and fasten the tent ends to the balls. They then walk to a large hole in the middle of the tent, whereupon it begins to rise. At this moment the slide designs color the tent and it becomes an amorphous thing which engulfs or swallows the dancers. This tent shape remains but slide changes alter its color design. Then the outer ends of the tent lift—then the whole tent rises revealing the dancers underneath to commence scene II.

TECHNICAL SUGGESTIONS & POSSIBILITIES

A. A chrome-key blue floor and cyc might give the best flexibility here. Photo stills of desert or painted abstract landscape or small model could be inserted into the chrome-blue area. The chrome blue environment could also give possibility of keying out the dancers and allowing effective use of this device in later scenes.

B. Another possibility is to shoot the procession and ritual through a small model. This however poses the problem of control of the environmental look of the floor and cyc of the actual studio area in which the dancers perform. We do have strong slides for the stage but I'm not sure how effective these would be in the necessary illumination video-wise of the dancers themselves.

C. Without model and just the use of our projections we could try to create the environment. This depends upon how effective the slide projections register on camera. Perhaps the use of fog machine might make interesting designs in space as the projections hit fog areas.

D. About the silver balls: these should give the illusion of fantasy. Although 10 are practical in that they actually control the tent, the illusion would be preferably one of design rather than mechanical function. One suggestion is that numerous other silver balls of different sizes be suspended and manipulated in various movements of ascending as well as descending, and these be superimposed upon the actual scene. An illusion that would be very effective would be that of having faces or full figures reflected in these balls. I don't know how this could be done except by previous taping in which perhaps chrome-key device could accomplish the insertion of dancers' figures or faces in the balls and this taping in turn used as superimposition on the actual scene.

Photo, Dick Rowan

The marvels of technology shape and color and envelop the bodies of the dancers in Alwin Nikolais' *Tent*. By the time of this production (1968) the choreographer had made his point about dispensing with emotional motivation to concentrate on the "drama of motion," and he could even relent a bit as he allowed his dancers to react to the variously tender and threatening manifestations of the tent.

In any case, the actual mechanics of tent lifting should not seem to be too obviously related to the balls. As a matter of fact the tent could be suspended directly without the silver balls if this would make matters easier.

E. After the tent is spread the dancers stand on the tent and begin the ritual. There is a dominant central figure. The camera can come to close-up on him and also move to full scene—at the discretion of the director.

F. The fastening of the lines to the tent should not be made too important. The dancers do this nonchalantly. This should lead to somewhat of a visual shock as the tent rises and engulfs them.

INTERLUDE 1. The problem of the interlude is that on stage the dancers require this time to change costumes. Obviously this is not essential on T.V. However, the preferable implication is that something is happening under the tent. I believe this interlude, as well as the others, depends upon the visual interest we can get out of the projections.

II. Genesis (Primitive section under tent)

The tent raises slowly revealing the dancers who should now look nude. They are first menacingly still. They are like primitive creatures. They move in sharp gestures on hands & knees, occasionally spinning. They should look somewhat like an ant heap disturbed. They do wild actions then fling themselves upward toward the tent as if to strike off the overhead barrier. Finally they fall and jump up & dart forward & back as the tent descends—covering them.

It is difficult to describe the content of this scene except to say it should give the impression of the atavistic side of man in which he reflects primal behaviorism and generic or genetic suggestions. For a few brief moments at the end they reflect a curious tenderness only to be disturbed out of it and to fall back into the enclosure of the tent.

TECHNICAL SUGGESTIONS & POSSIBILITIES

A. If the chrome-key environment is used then we can use the same technical process as at first. The inserted scene should then be that of an abstract tall grass land. It could also occasionally suggest a stonehenge. It could interchange between the two. For example it could open with the grass-lands effect. The circle which follows could appear to happen on a high rock pinnacle. For the most part the dancers should look lilliputian —as if they were microbes. Of course occasional close-ups would be effective. Also in the double insect forms—alternate effects of lighted and shadow figures would prove effective. Strong color would also be acceptable. For example the hugging section could start in full pink then gradually change to deep red until the fall when it should go back to pink suddenly, then fade into the slide pattern.

B. As in the B suggestion of the previous scene this one too could be shot through a model.

C. Straight shooting here would in my mind be least effective and in the long run more difficult. I believe it would only be possible if we could fill the environment with strong projected design. Otherwise we will be left with an obvious studio or stage-like environment which would destroy the dimensional suggestion of the piece.

INTERLUDE 2. Although the tent shape is different in this interlude the problem here is still the same. My vision here for T.V. possibility is the superimposition of motion picture on the tent of live crawling things,—such as ants, beetles, snakes, etc.

III. The Cave (Eroticism)

This section is one of innocent eroticism and needs no further explanation. It opens with the tent suspended in such a way that the central hole becomes a cave. The hole is lit up and the arms and legs of a man seen rolling. At the same time 2 female figures roll out of the side periphery of the tent onto the tent itself and are caught only in the projected design. The central male figure comes out and away from the tent. Other figures fill the hole.

This is also the scene in which I would like to use the store dummies or mannikins painted black. They would be seen first as a group opposite the male soloist after he comes out of the cave.

The two separate female figures now join the male soloist—in front of the black mannikins—with the figures in the cave as a secondary vision. This trio should dominate.

This is followed by the group coming forward and dancing in and around the mannikins which are now painted the same flesh tones as the dancers. The male dancers now lift the females like dolls. They should also lift the mannikins. The illusion should be that one cannot distinguish the mannikins from the real. The mannikins are then left in a heap on the floor as all the dancers run into the cave. The tent is lifted and the dancers disappear.

TECHNICAL SUGGESTIONS & POSSIBILITIES

A possibility here would be inserting into the exposed chrome-blue areas photos or actual previously taken tape of real nude bodies in close-up & undulating slowly. It would appear then that the dancers coming forward of the tent would be dancing on the nude bodies.

IV. The Garden

The garden should be one of fantasy and prettiness. The dancers wear silver stripes that glitter in the projected light. Whereas the 1st scene is primitive—the second erotic—this third is one of beauty & prettiness. It is an indulgence in the orgy of color and glitter. It is impressionistic in design rather than specific as in the previous ones. It is man's joy of effulgent nature—and he identifies himself with it and becomes a part of its blossoming. He walks in the garden of light and color—he runs outside of it—falls in it and plays in it. He throws it and lets it engulf him. Finally it—as all other scenes—swallows him.

TECHNICAL SUGGESTIONS & POSSIBILITIES

A. Here again the chrome-key would be effective. Insertion of delicate flowers and occasional large outrageous ones. Also glass flowers—if they could be found. The scene would also be effective fragmented by prisms, glass rods, etc. One part might be effective as if seen in a crystal ball.

B. Without chrome-key this could be shot through miniature flower garden.

C. Straight shooting is also possible here because the scene does rely strongly upon the projections as does the previous scene.

Meredith Monk
"VESSEL": AN OPERA EPIC

Graduating in 1964 from Sarah Lawrence College, where she studied both dance and music, Meredith Monk began to present concerts of her own work in the same year. She calls her productions, not dances, but "composite theatre" or "nonverbal opera," blendings of movement, voice, costumes, lights, film, objects, and environment. Nevertheless, the basic concept is choreographic. The music is usually her own composition, and she directs the entire production, though individual contributions may be made by members of her company, The House.

In this interview with Brooks McNamara, Monk discusses the structure of Vessel. *Like the work of Nikolais, it is a multimedia theatre piece, but like that of Cunningham, it is concerned with manipulations of time and space. Unlike either, it is highly emotional. The drama is conveyed obliquely, by contrast and juxtaposition that gradually define the previously obscure images. This is a journey—but Prince Charming would never have found his way. Like the works of the early modern dance, its intention is not to entertain but to provoke.*

THE DRAMA REVIEW: First, let's talk about the loft on Great Jones Street, which you used for the first part of *Vessel*.

MONK: It's about 100 feet long and 25 feet wide. It has a very low ceiling.
. . .

It suggests a tunnel, or a long, narrow space in Renaissance perspective, with the floor boards going toward a vanishing point. . . .

TDR: Why did you decide to use your own house for the first part of *Vessel*?

MONK: Since the nature of my work has a lot to do with unconscious imagery and fantasy, I'm very interested in grounding it in what I call "reality space." Constructing a realistic set doesn't interest me; what

SOURCE: First published in *The Drama Review*, 16, No. 1, T-53 (March 1972). ©1972 by *The Drama Review*. Reprinted by permission. All rights reserved.

I'm interested in much more is using a reality situation and putting unusual images in that setting as counterpoint. The piece here in the loft is grounded in reality, but the images and the figures are strange. Because of that grounding in reality, the effect is surreal. When the performance moves later to the Performing Garage, it's almost totally in another world. Then, when we move to the parking lot for the third section, the performance goes back to reality set against fantasy.

TDR: When I saw the first part of *Vessel,* people were concentrated at one end of the room and there was a space which, at least during the first part of the performance, wasn't used, a space maybe 20 feet deep that created a kind of gulf between the actors and the audience at the other end.

MONK: Yes. Like a moat. The irony of the situation is that this section of the performance, which could be the most personal since it's my own house, was actually the most remote. Instead of becoming the most intimate part of the piece, it's the least intimate because I'm putting a bracket around my living situation by making it so that you are actually looking into a real room, but from a great distance away . . . what I was trying to do here, by lighting different areas at different times, was to see if I could continually transform the space and keep the audience from ever seeing what the whole space was like. When we got to the Garage, the attempt was just the opposite. There, the whole space was exposed, all at once. We saw everything at once. And all shifts of focus were done by the performers and their placement, but in the house, focus was shifted because we lit up a certain area of the room. That was a physiological shift of focus, whereas in the Garage the performers themselves shifted the focus of your eyes.

TDR: Can you give me an example of how you used lights in the first part?

MONK: Yes. There's a section where performers introduce themselves as they change into different costumes. We call that our flash forward section; what I wanted to do, since you go to the Garage later, was to present a glimpse, just a glimpse, of the characters that will appear there as if it were a coming attraction in a film. Then of course the audience goes to the Garage and actually sees them.

Each character—there are five of them sitting in the living room—is dressed in a very grotesque black costume. They're just sitting there; the image that we have, you know, is of people who have been in the loft for centuries, eons—as though they were in a castle waiting. And each person, one by one, leaves the room and goes into the kitchen and changes into a costume that has a much more specific character, a king, or a wizard—but they're very personal, very specific. And they come out and stand under a 200 watt bulb. They pull on the light cord, it's an overhead light, and they perform a scene. It's a small indication of what they're going to do in the Garage, a kind of introduction. Then they turn the light off and go back into the kitchen, change into their black clothes, and sit down again in the living room.

The house section was very much a black and white tapestry—not quite black and white because there was a bit of color, but it had a dull tone, almost the idea of black and white film. Then, when you get to the Garage, it's technicolor. For example, the madwoman who comes out and starts laughing in the loft had a greenish-grayish wig on, but then when she's in the Garage, she's got a bright red wig. The same image, except that it's color. And that's the way all of the images are.

TDR: How did you choose the properties? . . .

MONK: Well, actually I used objects in this piece which interested me a lot, and I used them like notes in a musical score. There's a repetition of certain objects that later serve different functions in different parts of *Vessel*. There's a woman with a rake in the loft; then when you go into the Garage the king's scepter is a rake, and when you go into the parking lot, the soldiers' weapons are rakes. It's like using the rake almost as you would use a note in a piece of music. Or it's like using it as an overlay, a transparency that gradually discloses levels of the object itself. . . . In the first section at the loft, objects are not of primary importance because I'm simply using objects already in my house. But later in the Garage there are many more things, more objects because the space is more abstract. For example, in the Garage, the madwoman, Lanny Harrison, has a kettle she puts herbs into. There is the cutting up of the vegetables; Monica Mosley doing calligraphy on a board; Danny Sverdlik mixing the blue mixture; Mark Monstermaker reading a book. Those are objects and activities. And all of them are almost like everyday activities, but there is a twist to them, a kind of irony. . . .

I always want to have a grounding in reality; I always need to have something that grounds because some images I use are so far away from reality, and I am trying to deal with simultaneous realities. So I try to make as much contrast as possible.

TDR: At the end of the first section, what happens?

MONK: The cast rented a bus and we get into the bus and go down to the Performing Garage, and the audience stays and has wine. Instead of keeping their distance, the audience can enter my house. Then the bus comes back for them and they go down to the Performing Garage. The bus is painted blue and has red and yellow stripes. Inside it has rugs all the way through, seats along the side, a few seats in the back of the bus, and a lot of space to sit on the floor. It's very warm and cosy. I was happy about it.

TDR: What were you trying to do with the bus in terms of the whole performance?

MONK: I called *Vessel* an epic because of the sense of journeying in the whole piece. Not only did I want the content of *Vessel* to be a journey, but the point of having the audience move from one place to another in one evening is that the audience is also on an epic, you know, they are literally going through the motions of traveling. . . .

TDR: How do you use sound in the first part at the loft?

MONK: Well, I am dealing with silence as a base and then working mostly in terms of contrasts—sometimes silence and then cutting to a very sharp sound; sometimes silence and then gradations of sound like somebody lighting a cigarette. In other words, you become more and more aware, but sometimes you become more aware by gradations or increments of sound, and sometimes the sound is just cut into very sharply. *Vessel* is structured like a piece of music; you *hear* how the piece is structured as much as you see it. That's the way I'm working now; not only am I working with music in terms of my own music, but in terms of everything I do in performance. There's lots of repetition of sound motifs like the three knockings, and the bell ringing. And all of the singing that I do with the organ has the same kind of texture even though there are different emotions and very different kinds of sound in it. But it all has the same texture, so it's like a repetition. And because of the stillness in the house all the incidental sounds become magnified. When someone's walking across the room, it's magnified; if you hear a floorboard squeak, you know, it's gigantic, because the basis is silence. If I don't teach people to hear in this piece, then I feel that I've failed, because I believe that hearing—the absolute expansion of auditory perception—is what this piece is about.

TDR: When you get to the Garage . . .

MONK: We connected the scaffolding and made an over-all Gestalt, a mountain of sorts, by hanging and draping white muslin. It's a mountain but it also looks like a clipper ship, a birthday cake. And it's very primitive. The second section of the piece is called Handmade Mountain, and we wanted very much that quality for the whole Garage, that's why we did it ourselves. I much prefer to show what I am doing. No one *designed* that mountain. We did it ourselves. In my group are weavers, and calligraphers, and people who dye fabrics—that is our group's sensibility. . . . I really like a certain kind of theatricality; I don't want to have people in blue jeans.

There's a kind of wryness to the whole Garage piece. It's not childish, it's child-like, and I think that's what we're trying for, not to lose those things. . . . A Sunday School play could use the things we do. But they wouldn't do it the same way, because they wouldn't be conscious

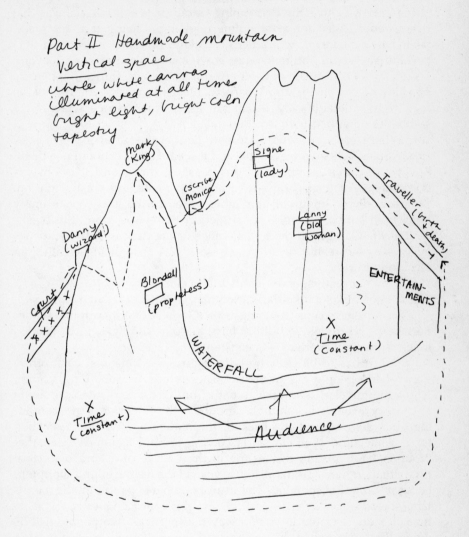

Vessel

Part II Handmade mountain
Vertical space
whole white canvas
illuminated at all times
bright light, bright coln
tapestry

mark
(King)

(scribe)
monica

Signe
(lady)

Traveller (birth + death)

Danny
(wizard)

Lanny
(old woman)

ENTERTAIN-
MENTS

Blondell
(prop/ess)

X
Time
(constant)

X
Time
(constant)

WATERFALL

Audience

The Drama Review

Meredith Monk's plan for Part II of *Vessel* shows the cubicles allotted to each performer and the path of the traveler. The room was covered with white muslin. From out of the whiteness, members of the audience let their eyes settle on whatever performing area they wanted to watch at the moment.

of what they were doing, and we're very conscious of what we're doing when we use paper bags or pieces of fabric with a hole cut in the middle for costumes.

The reason I chose the Performing Garage in the first place was that I had had an idea for a long time of doing a living tapestry piece, related to a medieval two-dimensional kind of visual perception. . . . In the first section, you're looking down a corridor at an event beyond a wall, beyond a moat; in the Performing Garage, things happen up and down; and in the third part, in the parking lot, you're looking from right to left. It's like a map, or like a cinemascope screen, or a scene photographed with a wide-angle lens.

TDR: What were you trying to do with light at the Garage?

MONK: Stage lights were available and it seemed that I should use them. But it is the most simple and direct use of them, and it is obvious that that's what it is. There's no attempt to create illusionistic lighting. Strangely, even though all the lights I used in the loft were ordinary household lamps, I would say the effect there was more illusionistic than at the Garage. In the loft, because of the darkness, the audience never sees the reality of the space, so it's as though I'm creating an illusion in a way.

TDR: Why not just use work lights in the Garage?

MONK: I don't like that kind of "scientific" look. I just wanted whiteness. . . . The tapestry keeps changing as the Gestalt of figures on that whiteness keeps changing, so I didn't have to do it with light; I just wanted to leave the light more or less constant.

I think it has to be clear how the figures work against each other. Each of the people has a cubicle. There's one person, Ping Chong, who's the traveler, who takes a path from one side of the scaffolding all the way through the mountain, around to the other side of the scaffolding, and then around the back of the audience. You don't see him for a while, and then he starts coming around again. We call that "rounds." So you get the feeling in the Garage of a kind of cyclical time situation, whereas in the house you get the feeling of time stopping, being absolutely suspended. There are a number of people on the mountain, spread out all over it, and they do different activities at the same time. It's orchestrated in such a way that perhaps two people will be doing the same activity in unison, and the others will be doing other activities; then everybody will be doing a different activity; and then, say, two more people will be doing the same activity. So that when you're in the audience, your eye keeps shifting. You are picking out what you want to see. Then other scenes are added, so that you might have two scenes simultaneously. But since the whole thing is vertical, you're seeing one on top of the other. One becomes figure, and the other becomes ground; then the first becomes ground, and the second becomes figure. It's like a tapestry that's continually changing.

During the first "round," for example, each character has five activities that he can choose from; and in the second "round" three more are added. I don't set it; I don't tell a certain person to wave at a certain point, for instance. So what you get are combinations like a slot machine. You'll have three people doing the same thing at the same time, and all of a sudden your eye starts lining things up. At other times you shift your focus, depending on which person draws your attention. It is similar with sound. Each of the performer's activities involves some kind of sound and your attention is drawn by it. So the madwoman is throwing herbs into a bowl, but she really has marbles in her hand, and you hear them clink.

TDR: Could you describe what happens when you go out of the Garage at the end of the second part?

MONK: You walk half a block away to a parking lot. The way we use the parking lot, it is a wide and not a deep space. It is probably a block wide and a third of a block deep. The audience sits on bleachers at one end. On one side, across the street, is the Canal Lumber Company and on the other side, across another street, is a church, St. Alphonsus, and you can see the tops of both buildings over the brick walls that enclose the parking lot. Straight ahead of the audience is a candy factory, an old building with a faded sign on it and a few straggly trees at its base. The ground is all asphalt, and there are eight trucks lined up facing the audience. . . . I was trying to find an outdoor space that had a specific New York ambience . . . one level of *Vessel* has to do with people opening up their eyes to New York. The park just doesn't have anything to do with the New York ambience, at least on our level. Our economic level, our life style, has most to do with complex interior spaces, and bleak outdoor spaces. This particular parking lot was the best of the large spaces I had seen. I knew I was going to be using many people and I wanted a pageant-like quality to the third part.

TDR: Can you explain how you use light in the third part?

MONK: I was trying to use every kind of light source that I could think of that was portable. So, there are five camp-fires, there's a lamp, there are two sun guns, which are power packed—in other words, these are power belts to which lighting instruments are attached so that people can carry them and run around with them. They are usually used for filming movies at night. There is a welder, and a red traffic flare. There is a kerosene torch, and lights from across the street in the church. And there are the lights from the micro-bus and motorcycles that are driven through the parking lot.

At the beginning of the piece there is cumulative lighting of different areas, so that finally you get all the realities simultaneously. For example, there is a light that represents the house from the first part—the room from the loft is now outdoors in the parking lot. That light is turned on, and goes out, and then five camp-fires are lit. Then the first sun gun is focused on a group of children, and the second sun gun is focused on people in a tree. So the effect is cumulative. That's one use of the lights. Then later there's a scene where everyone is moving at the same time. They're dancing and holding up corn cobs. My direction to the people with the sun guns was just to continue moving and lighting up different areas, because basically the whole canvas is in unison at that point. Each time a new light comes on it's lighting a different area, but the people are still performing the same activity, so it's like seeing another angle of the same thing each time.

TDR: What about the lights from the church across the street? . . .

MONK: It's like expanding the environment until you're aware of more and more and more in that parking lot. When you think you've got to the limits of the parking lot, the two brick walls, your eye moves across the street, expanding even more. I'm working like a filmmaker. I don't know why. That seems to be the way I think; the flash forward section of the first part is an example. I'm doing live movies.

SELECTIVE
BIBLIOGRAPHY

Only books and major monographs are listed here. The reader should be aware, however, that they form only a part of the historian's resources. The serious researcher also works with more ephemeral material—playbills, librettos, reviews in newspapers and periodicals, unpublished letters and diaries, records in theatre and local archives, along with vast amounts of general background information on the social and cultural history of the period he is investigating. Some of the works cited here contain extensive listings of such materials.

Citations are limited to the best books in any given area—when a choice was available. English translations of foreign language books are given wherever they exist. Paperback editions are identified with an asterisk; "R" indicates a reprint. When several reprints are available, preference is given to paperbacks and/or American publishers.

The following abbreviations are used:

Publishers:

DH: Dance Horizons, Brooklyn, N. Y.
UM: University Microfilms, Ltd., High Wycombe, Buckinghamshire (England)
WUP: Wesleyan University Press, Middletown, Conn.

Monograph Series:

DI: *Dance Index*, 1942–1948 (R: New York, Arno Press, 1971)
DP: *Dance Perspectives* (New York, Dance Perspectives Foundation, 1959–)

Introduction: The Evolution of Theatre Dance

For bibliographies: an outdated but still useful list of holdings in the British Museum is contained in Cyril W. Beaumont's *A Bibliography of Dancing* (London, 1929; R: New York, Blom) and a list of holdings in several major libraries to date in Paul Magriel's *A Bibliography of Dancing* (New York, 1936; R: London, Dance Books). The *Dictionary Catalog of the Dance Collection* of The New York Public Library (Boston, G.K. Hall, 1974) is indispensable. The only reference work in the field, a meagre one volume and not completely accurate, is *The Dance Encyclopedia* by Anatole Chujoy and P. W. Manchester (New York, Simon and Schuster, 1967). Briefer but more dependable is the third edition of

G. B. L. Wilson's *Dictionary of Ballet* (New York, Theatre Arts Books, 1974). More useful are the nine volumes with supplements of the broader *Enciclopedia dello Spettacolo* (Florence and Rome, Casa Editrice le Maschere, 1954–62). Peter Brinson's *Backgrounds to European Ballet* (Leyden, A. W. Sijthoff, 1966*) cites fascinating source materials in European libraries.

Of the historical surveys the best is still Lincoln Kirstein's erudite *Dance: A Short History of Classical Theatrical Dancing* (New York, 1935; R: DH*); his *Movement and Metaphor* (New York, Praeger, 1970) discusses selected ballets in a broad cultural context with lavish illustrations. *The Dancer's Heritage* by Ivor Guest (London, The Dancing Times, 1973*) is an excellent brief history of ballet. *Images of the Dance* by Lillian Moore (New York, The New York Public Library, 1966) covers the period 1581–1861, has a short but informative text, and a wealth of pictures. Also containing lavish displays of pictures and with a dependable commentary that brings the story up to date is *Ballet: An Illustrated History* by Mary Clarke and Clement Crisp (New York, Universe Books, 1973). History as revealed through technical manuals from the fourteenth century through the 19th is the subject of Ferdinando Reyna's provocative *Des Origines du ballet* (Paris, A. Tallone, 1955). Alan Story analyzes choreographic theories from Noverre to Tudor in *Arabesques* (London, Newman, Wolsey, Ltd., 1948).

More specialized works that span our chronological divisions are Cyril Beaumont's volumes devoted to the backgrounds and plots of the classical repertory: *Complete Book of Ballets* (Garden City, N.Y., Garden City Publishing Co., 1941), *Supplement to Complete Book of Ballets* (London, Putnam, 1942), *Ballets of Today* (London, Putnam, 1954), *Ballets Past and Present* (London, Putnam, 1955). *Balanchine's New Complete Stories of the Great Ballets* (Garden City, New York, Doubleday, 1968) gives more attention to choreographic design. Lillian Moore's *Artists of the Dance* (New York, 1938; R: DH*) provides brief but accurate biographies of artists from Camargo to Jooss.

Two books deal, though just adequately, with ideas about music and the dance: Paul Nettl's *The Story of Dance Music* (New York, Philosophical Library, 1947) and Humphrey Searle's *Ballet Music* (London, Cassell, 1958). More illuminating are Minna Lederman's symposium on "Stravinsky in the Theatre" (DI, Oct.–Dec., 1947) and the statements prepared by writers of commissioned scores for "Composer/Choreographer" (DP 16 1963*). Ballet design is well represented by *Art in Modern Ballet* by George Amberg (New York, Pantheon, 1946), *Ballet Design, Past and Present* by Beaumont (London, The Studio, 1946), *Modern Ballet Design* by Richard Buckle (New York, Macmillan, 1955), and *Ballet Design and Illustrations* by Brian Reade (London, Her Majesty's Stationery Office, 1967). All, naturally, are beautifully illustrated. *Dance Index* produced some notable monographs on important artists: "Pavel Tchelitchew" by Donald Windham (Jan., Feb., 1944); "Marc Chagall" (Nov., 1945); "The Stage and Ballet Designs of Eugene Berman" by Allison Delarue (Jan., 1946); and "Picasso and the Ballet" by William S. Lieberman (Nov., Dec., 1946).

Section One: The Court Ballet

Several excellent studies have been made of the court ballet. Henry Prunières, *Le Ballet de cour en France* (Paris, 1914; R: New York, Johnson Reprint Corp.) and

Margaret M. MacGowan, *L'Art du Ballet de cour* (Paris, E.C.N.R.S., 1936) trace the history from Beaujoyeulx to the mid-seventeenth century. The later decades are covered by Marie-Françoise Christout, *Le Balet de cour de Louis XIV* (Paris, A. et J. Picard, 1967) and Charles Silin, *Benserade and His Ballets de Cour* (Baltimore, Johns Hopkins Press, 1940). The *Ballet Comique de la Royne* of Balthasar de Beaujoyeulx (Paris, 1582; R: UM*) is available in the original French, while Paul Lacroix collected six volumes of librettos in *Ballets et mascarades de cour* (Geneva, J. Gayet, 1868–70). The English scene is covered by Enid Welsford in her definitive work *The Court Masque* (London, 1927; R: New York, Russell & Russell*). The splendors of Sweden's royal entertainments are depicted in "Ballet under the Three Crowns" by Mary Skeaping (DP 32, 1968*); Portugal's noble diversions are in "Feasts and Folias" by José Sasportes (DP 42, 1970*)—both unique.

Technical materials for this period include: *A Jewish Dancing Master of the Renaissance: Guglielmo Ebreo* by Otto Kinkeldey (New York, 1929; R: DH*); Fabritio Caroso's *Il Ballarino* (Venice, 1581) and *Nobilità di Dame* (Venice, 1600; both R: UM*); Cesare Negri's *Le Gratie d'Amore* (Milan, 1602; R: New York, Broude); Thoinot Arbeau, *Orchésographie* (Paris, 1589), tr. Mary Stewart Evans (New York, 1948; R: New York, Dover*); F. de Lauze, *Apologie de la danse* (1623), tr. Joan Wildeblood (London, Frederick Muller, 1952).

An interesting theoretical discussion is Guillaume Dumanoir's *Le Marriage de la musique avec la danse* (Paris, 1664; R: New York, Burt Franklin). *Des Ballets anciens et modernes* of Claude Ménestrier (Paris, 1682; R: UM*) provides a systematic and detailed analysis of contemporary choreography.

Section Two: Dance for the Eye and the Heart: The Eighteenth Century

The only publication to cover the period in England is *Famed for Dance: Essays on the Theory and Practice of Theatrical Dance in England, 1660–1740* by Ifan Kyrle Fletcher, Selma Jeanne Cohen, and Roger Lonsdale (New York: The New York Public Library, 1960*). Several of John Weaver's most important works, originally published in London, are available, among them *An Essay Towards an History of Dancing* (1712), and *Anatomical and Mechanical Lectures upon Dancing* (1721; both R: UM*). Jean Georges Noverre's *Lettres sur la danse et les ballets* (Stuttgart, 1760) may be had in the Beaumont translation (London, 1930; R: DH*), and there is Deryck Lynham's fine biography *The Chevalier Noverre* (London, 1950; R: London, Dance Books*), though Arthur Michel has demonstrated that the acknowledged master was only one, and not the first of a line of defenders of dramatic dance: "The Ballet d'Action before Noverre" (DI, March, 1947). The theory of dramatic ballet also gets brilliant support from Louis de Cahusac in *La Danse ancienne et moderne* (Paris, 1754), while an excellent later version of the theory may be found in August Baron's *Lettres à Sophie sur la danse* (Paris, 1825; R: UM*).

Marie Sallé is the only ballerina of the period to have merited an extensive, though not thorough, biography, Émile Dacier's *Une Danseuse de l' Opéra* (Paris, 1909; R: Geneva, Minkoff). There is a better one of the Vestris family, Gaston Capon's *Les Vestris* (Paris, Société du Mercure de France, 1908). Lillian Moore's pioneering study of little known performers "The Duport Mystery" (DP 7, 1960*) reveals a wealth of dance activity in the eighteenth-century United States.

Feuillet's *Chorégraphie* (Paris, 1701; R: UM*) is the key to the dance technique of the eighteenth century. Gregorio Lambranzi's *New and Curious School of Theatrical Dancing* (Nuremburg, 1716) is available in Derra de Moroda's translation (London, 1928; R: DH*), giving instructions for various character and comedy dances. For the minuet, *Le Maître à danser* of P. Rameau (Paris, 1725) is the standard text, tr. Cyril W. Beaumont (London, 1931; R: DH*). Gottfried Taubert's *Der Rechtschaffener Tantzmeister* (Leipzig, 1717), not yet translated, represents the German version, and Kellom Tomlison's *The Art of Dancing* (London, 1735; R: UM*) tells the story from England. Giovanni Gallini published two works that reflect contemporary trends in technique and theory: *A Treatise on the Art of Dancing* (London, 1762) and *Critical Observations on the Art of Dancing* (London, 1770; both R: UM*). Ballet terminology, eighteenth-century style, may be found in Charles Compan's *Dictionnaire de danse* (Paris, 1787; R: UM*). To close the era, there is Ivor Guest's first-rate edition of essays on the history of *La Fille Mal Gardée* (London, The Dancing Times, 1960*).

Section Three: The Invasion of the Air: The Romantic Era

To see why the romantic period has fascinated historians more than any other in dance history, start with Cyril W.Beaumont and Sacheverell Sitwell, *The Romantic Ballet in Lithographs of the Time* (London, Faber and Faber, 1938). Then get the facts, fully and accurately, from Ivor Guest: *The Romantic Ballet in England* (WUP, 1972); and *The Romantic Ballet in Paris* (Ibid., 1966). The prints have also been subjected to scholarly cataloging and discussion by George Chaffee for *Dance Index*: "American Lithographs of the Romantic Ballet" (Feb., 1942), "American Music Prints of the Romantic Ballet" (Dec., 1942), "The Romantic Ballet in London" (Nov., Dec., 1943), "Three or Four Graces" (Sept.–Nov., 1944). Lillian Moore performed a similar service for Currier and Ives in "Prints on Pushcarts" (DP 15, 1962*), while Edwin Binney 3rd has finished off the major collections with "A Century of German Dance Prints, 1790–1890" (DP 47, 1971*) and "Sixty Years of Italian Dance Prints, 1815–1875" (DP 53, 1973*). A tantalizing sampling of contemporary reviews is contained in Cyril W. Beaumont's *The Romantic Ballet as Seen by Théophile Gautier* (London, 1932 R: DH*). The history of Gautier's most famous libretto has been told by Beaumont in *The Ballet Called Giselle* (London, 1948; R: DH*), and all the librettos have been thoroughly examined by Edwin Binney 3rd in *Les Ballets de Théophile Gautier* (Paris, Nizet, 1966).

Naturally the ballerinas have reaped their tributes. Beaumont has translated André Levinson's biography *Taglioni* (London, Beaumont, 1930) and Doris Langley Moore has done Serge Lifar's *Carlotta Grisi* (London, Lehman, 1947). Most comprehensive are two by Guest: *Fanny Cerrito* (London, Phoenix House, 1956) and *Fanny Elssler* (WUP, 1970). Two male dancers have rated excellent biographies: "Jules Perrot," by the Soviet historian Yury Slonimsky is translated by Anatole Chujoy (DI, Dec., 1945) while Charles Didelot has received his due in Mary Grace Swift's *A Loftier Flight* (WUP, 1974). Wesleyan will also publish August Bournonville's monumental autobiography, *Mit Theaterliv* (Copenhagen, 1848), which has been translated by Patricia McAndrew. The Danish master is also the subject of a fine collection of scholarly essays, *Theatre Research Studies II* (Copenhagen, University of Copenhagen, 1972*). *Dance Index* published exemplary research on several American dancers: "John Durang" (Aug., Sept., 1942),

"Mary Ann Lee" (May, 1943), and "George Washington Smith" (Aug., 1945), all by Lillian Moore, as well as "Augusta Maywood" (Jan., Feb., 1943) by Marian Hannah Winter.

Standard and accessible on technique is Carlo Blasis' *Theory and Practice of the Art of Dancing* (London, 1820; R: New York, Dover*), but his *Code of Terpsichore* (London, 1830) contains much additional historical and theoretical material. G. Léopold Adice comments on technique and other matters in *Théorie de la Gymnastique de la danse théâtrale* (Paris, Chaix, 1859). *Bournonville and Ballet Technique* by Erik Bruhn and Lillian Moore (London, 1961; R: London, Dance Books) is a brilliant analysis of the values of the Danish school of training.

The era draws to its sad close: Ivor Guest, *The Ballet of the Second Empire* (London, A. and C. Black, 1953), "The Alhambra Ballet" (DP 4, 1959*), and *The Empire Ballet* (London, Society for Theatre Research, 1962)

Section Four: New Life from Russia

Natalia Roslavleva, *Era of the Russian Ballet* (New York, Dutton, 1966) is a comprehensive survey of the scene from the eighteenth century to the present. Two of the great ballets of Imperial Russia have been studied in scholarly detail: *The Ballet Called Swan Lake* by Cyril Beaumont (London, Beaumont, 1952) and "Marius Petipa and The Sleeping Beauty" by Vera Krasovskaya (DP 49, 1972*). The story of the Diaghilev Ballet has been told by two of the men who were associated with it: Alexandre Benois in *Reminiscences of the Russian Ballet* (London, Putnam, 1947) and Serge Grigoriev in *The Diaghilev Ballet* (London, Constable, 1953; R:DH). John Percival's *The World of Diaghilev* (New York, Dutton, 1971*) presents a readable survey of the period. Lillian Moore edited the rather bland memoirs of Marius Petipa, *Russian Ballet Master* (London, 1958; R: London, Dance Books), while Yury Slonimsky's comprehensive biography was translated by Anatole Chujoy, "Marius Petipa" (DI, May, June, 1947). Other valuable autobiographies are: Tamara Karsavina, *Theatre Street* (New York, 1931; R: DH*); Michel Fokine, *Fokine: Memoirs of a Ballet Master* (Boston, Little, Brown, 1961); Lydia Sokolova, *Dancing for Diaghilev* (New York, Macmillan, 1960); Massine, *My Life in Ballet* (New York, St. Martin's Press, 1968). Fokine's memoirs should be supplemented by Beaumont's *Michel Fokine and His Ballets* (London, Beaumont, 1935), which contains translations of Fokine's important statements about the rationale of his ballet reforms. *Diaghilev* by Arnold L. Haskell and Walter Nouvel (New York, Simon and Schuster, 1935) is not definitive, but it is the best biography we have. A better portrait of the complex personality comes from Richard Buckle's *Nijinsky* (New York, Simon and Schuster, 1972). Romola Nijinsky's life of her husband *Nijinsky* (New York, Simon and Schuster, 1935) should also be read. Two pleasant books of essays concern the era's most famous ballerina: Paul Magriel's *Pavlova* (New York, Henry Holt, 1947) and Arthur Franks' *Pavlova* (New York, Macmillan, 1956).

The reviews of two contemporary critics are outstanding: André Levinson, *La Danse d'aujourd'hui* (Paris, Editions Duchartre, 1929) and Valerian Svetloff, *Le Ballet contemporain* (Paris, R. Golick and A. Willborg, 1912).

The teaching methods of Enrico Cecchetti have been documented by Cyril Beaumont with Stanislas Idzikowski in *A Manual of the Theory and Practice of Classical Theatrical Dancing* (London, Beaumont, 1947) and with Margaret Craske in *The Theory and Practice of Allegro in Classical Ballet* (London, Beaumont, 1946). Miss Craske collaborated with Derra de Moroda on *The Theory and Practice of Advanced Allegro in Classical Ballet* (London, Beaumont, 1956).

Section Five: The Modern Dance: Moving from the Inside Out

John Martin has written the definitive books on the theory of the contemporary expressive dance: *The Modern Dance* (New York, 1933; R: DH*) and, the most comprehensive statement, *Introduction to the Dance* (New York, 1939; R: DH*). Margaret Lloyd made the only survey of the period, *The Borzoi Book of Modern Dance* (New York, 1949; R: DH*). A number of choreographers spoke for themselves in Frederick R. Rogers' collection of essays *Dance: A Basic Educational Technique* (New York, Macmillan, 1941).

Since the modern dance was so much a product of individual creativities, there are many books about single choreographers. Maud Allan wrote her own story in *My Life and Dancing* (London, Everett, 1908) and so did Loïe Fuller in *Fifteen Years of a Dancer's Life* (London, Herbert Jenkins, 1913), though the latter lady receives more objective treatment in "Loïe Fuller: The Fairy of Light" by Clare de Morinni (DI, March, 1942). Isadora Duncan's *My Life* (New York, 1927; R: New York, Liveright*) is factually untrustworthy but revealing nevertheless. More important are the ideas expressed in her *The Art of the Dance* (New York, 1928; R: New York, Theatre Arts Books). Of the many books about Duncan, the best are Irma Duncan's *Duncan Dancer* (WUP, 1966) and Victor Seroff's *The Real Isadora* (New York, Dial, 1971). Ruth St. Denis told *An Unfinished Life* (New York, 1939; R: DH*), while Christena Schlundt has meticulously chronicled the career of Denishawn in *The Professional Appearances of Ruth St. Denis and Ted Shawn* (New York, The New York Public Library, 1962*). Mrs. Schlundt has also covered *The Professional Appearances of Ted Shawn & His Men Dancers* (Ibid., 1967*), discussed the Denishawn phenomenon in the light of American values in "Into the Mystic with Miss Ruth" (DP 46, 1971*), and provided another valuable documentary in *Tamiris: A Chronicle of Her Dance Career* (New York, The New York Public Library, 1972*). The early career of a great innovator has been documented in essays collected by Merle Armitage, *Martha Graham* (New York, 1937; R: DH*) and in the telling photographs of Barbara Morgan, *Martha Graham* (New York, Duell, Sloan and Pearce, 1941). *The Notebooks of Martha Graham* (New York, Harcourt, Brace, Jovanovitch, 1973) provide remarkable insights into the workings of an extraordinary mind in the process of dance creation. Don McDonagh's *Martha Graham* (New York, Praeger, 1973) adds many facts but little insight. A choreographer's unfinished autobiography and her personal letters are the basis of Selma Jeanne Cohen's *Doris Humphrey: An Artist First* (WUP, 1972). Colleagues of an interesting California choreographer assess his contribution in "The Dance Theater of Lester Horton" (DP 31, 1967*). Rudolf von Laban's autobiography *Ein Leben für dem Tanz* (Dresden, Carl Reissner, 1935) remains the only work on this master inventor, but fortunately we have Walter Sorell's translation of Mary Wigman's illuminating discussions of her own choreography, *The Language of Dance* (WUP, 1966). A. V. Coton's *The New Ballet* (London, Dobson, 1946) is an excellent analysis of the work of Kurt Jooss. And there is Walter Sorell's rather sanguine biography *Hanya Holm* (WUP, 1969).

Lacking the established vocabulary of ballet, the modern damcers have published little on their craft. Irma Duncan has described her teacher's method in *The Technique of Isadora Duncan* (New York, Kamin, n.d.), while Gertrude Shurr and Rachael Yocum have analyzed their version of the Graham system in *Modern Dance: Techniques and Teaching* (New York, Barnes, 1949). The modern approach to choreography is, however, another matter. Louis Horst summarized the contents of his famous composition classes in *Pre-Classic Dance Forms* (New York, 1950; R: DH*) and, with Carroll Russell, in *Modern Dance Forms* (San Francisco, 1961; R: DH*). Doris Humphrey's systematic approach is lucidly analyzed in her *The Art of Making Dances* (Philadelphia, 1959; R: New York, Grove Press, 1962*).

Section Six: The Extension of the Classical Tradition

Mary Grace Swift's *The Art of the Dance in the USSR* (University of Notre Dame [Indiana] Press, 1968) covers contemporary Russia with detailed documentation; Yuri Slonimsky describes it from another point of view in *The Bolshoi Ballet* (Moscow, Foreign Languages Publishing House [1960]). Natalia Roslavleva has discussed the Russian contribution to ballet dramaturgy in "Stanislavsky and the Ballet" (DP 23, 1965). Albert E. Kahn has contributed his own marvelous photographs as well as a perceptive text to *Days with Ulanova* (New York, Simon and Schuster, 1962). The British situation is reviewed by Fernau Hall in *Modern English Ballet* (London, Melrose, 1950) and by John Percival, who also includes the American picture, in *Modern Ballet* (New York, Dutton, 1970). George Amberg's *Ballet in America* (New York, Duell, Sloan and Pearce, 1949) covers the United States briefly but perceptively. The New York Public Library, however, has collected the thoroughly researched articles of Lillian Moore in "Studies in American Dance History" which can be consulted in the Dance Collection.

The English have taken justifiable pride in their companies. Mary Clarke has traced the history of two of them: *The Sadler's Wells Ballet* (later the Royal) (London, A. and C. Black, 1955) and Ballet Rambert, *Dancers of Mercury* (Ibid., 1962). Each director has told her own story as well: de Valois in *Come Dance with Me* (London, H. Hamilton, 1957) and Rambert in *Quicksilver* (London, Macmillan, 1972). Of the several books on Britain's prima ballerina, James Monahan's *Fonteyn* (London, A. & C. Black, 1957) is the best. The development of contemporary ballet in America is traced from its beginnings in Lincoln Kirstein's "Entries from an Early Diary" (DP 54, 1973*) and followed through to its brilliant fulfillment in Anatole Chujoy's *The New York City Ballet* (New York, Knopf, 1953) and Kirstein's production with the same title (New York, Knopf, 1973). Selma Jeanne Cohen and A. J. Pischl have chronicled twenty years of performances in "The American Ballet Theatre, 1940–1960" (DP 6, 1960*). Bernard Taper's biography *Balanchine* (New York, Harper & Row, 1963) is an excellent account of the choreographer's life though it does little toward defining his artistic contribution. There are also Agnes de Mille's fine autobiographies: *Dance to the Piper* (Boston, Little, Brown, 1952), *And Promenade Home* (Ibid., 1958), and *Speak to Me, Dance with Me* (Ibid. 1972).

Contemporary technique is succinctly outlined in Agrippina Vaganova's *Basic Principles of Classical Ballet*, translated by Anatole Chujoy (New York, 1946; R: Dover*). Muriel Stuart describes the training in the school that prepares the dancers of the New York City Ballet in *The Classical Ballet* (New York, Knopf,

1952). Tamara Karsavina brings her heritage of technical knowledge to bear on *Ballet Technique* (New York, Theatre Arts Books, 1969). The extent of the present vocabulary is seen in Gail Grant's *The Technical Manual and Dictionary of Classical Ballet* (New York, 1950; R: Dover*), which distinguishes divergent usages in the various systems of teaching. The work remaining after the vocabulary has been mastered, the art of interpretation, is sensitively analyzed by one of the greatest contemporary performers: Erik Bruhn: "Beyond Technique" (DP 36, 1968*).

Two fine Englishmen have applied their perceptive minds to the theory of modern ballet: Adrian Stokes in *Tonight the Ballet* (London, Faber and Faber, 1934) and Rayner Heppenstall in *Apology for Dancing* (Ibid., 1936). Edwin Denby, America's most sensitive ballet critic, has published two volumes of essays and reviews: *Looking at Dance* (New York, 1949) and *Dancers, Buildings and People in the Streets* (New York, 1965; both R: Curtis Books*).

Section Seven: Recent Rebels

The contemporary rebels are not yet well represented in book form. The generation of consolidators define their own approaches in Selma Jeanne Cohen's collection *The Modern Dance: Seven Statements of Belief* (WUP, 1966*). The next generation is sympathetically but superficially portrayed in Don McDonagh's *The Rise and Fall and Rise of Modern Dance* (New York, 1970; R: Curtis Books*). Marcia B. Siegel examines the avant-garde in perceptive reviews in *At the Vanishing Point: A Critic Looks at Dance* (New York, Saturday Review Press, 1972*). Merce Cunningham has done his own book in characteristically experimental format: *Changes: Notes on Choreography* (New York, Something Else Press, 1968), while his colleague Carolyn Brown and others discuss his work in "Time to Walk in Space" (DP 34, 1968*). Letters and journals of Alwin Nikolais form the basis of Marcia B. Siegel's "Nik: A Documentary" (DP 48, 1971*).

One facet of black performers is well surveyed in Marshall and Jean Stearns' *Jazz Dance* (New York, Macmillan, 1968) and the full range of their activities is included in Lynne Emery's especially well-researched *Black Dance in the United States from 1619 to 1970* (Palo Alto, National Press Books, 1972).

For a solution to the problems of the preservation of choreography, see Ann Hutchinson, *Labanotation*, 2nd edition, (New York, Theatre Arts Books, 1970*). Some of the best dance on film is perceptively analyzed by Arlene Croce in *The Fred Astaire & Ginger Rogers Book* (New York, Outerbridge and Lazard, 1972), while experiments involving the film-maker as co-choreographer are provocatively considered in "Cine-Dance" (DP 30, 1967*).

88 89 90 20 19 18 17 16 15 14 13 12